LINC⊕LNSHIRE COUNTY
EDUCATION and CU~~~~~ ~eturned on ~~ ~~~ ~ ~ ⌐ 3
T~ ~ book should ~~ ~~ow
I 7 MAR 1989

KENNETH CAMERON

This book is a guide to the major names of the
whole county of Lincolnshire.
Professor Cameron's work makes available the fruit of
thirty-five years' research into Lincolnshire place-names,
and combines detailed and authoritative commentary
on the names with a unique knowledge of the setting,
languages and history which gave rise to them.

This book will provide absorbing reading
and will prove an important resource
for anyone interested in the past of the county
and the origins of it names.

Cover illustration: R. Morden, *Map of Lincolnshire*, London 1695.

A Dictionary of Lincolnshire Place-Names, by Kenneth Cameron
Published by The English Place-Name Society, 1998
ISBN 0 904 889 58 0

3

AD 02912696

ENGLISH PLACE-NAME SOCIETY
POPULAR SERIES
VOLUME 1

GENERAL EDITOR

VICTOR WATTS

A DICTIONARY OF LINCOLNSHIRE PLACE-NAMES

A DICTIONARY OF LINCOLNSHIRE PLACE-NAMES

BY

KENNETH CAMERON

WITH CONTRIBUTIONS BY

JOHN INSLEY

NOTTINGHAM
ENGLISH PLACE-NAME SOCIETY
1998

Published by the English Place-Name Society
School of English Studies,
University of Nottingham,
Nottingham NG7 2RD
Tel. 0115 951 5919
Fax. 0115 951 5924
Registered Charity No. 257891

© English Place-Name Society 1998

All rights reserved.
No part of this publication may be reproduced,
stored in a retrieval system or transmitted
in any form or by any means, without prior permission of the
English Place-Name Society.

ISBN 0 904889 58 0

Distributed by Paul Watkins Publishing,
18 Adelaide Street,
Stamford, Lincolnshire PE9 2EN

LINCOLNSHIRE
COUNTY COUNCIL

L.929.4

Typeset by Paul Cavill & Printed in Great Britain
by Woolnough Bookbinding, Irthlingborough, Northants.

To Jean
for all her help and support

PREFACE

For some thirty-five years I have been engaged in the collection of material for the place- and field-names of Lincolnshire. This is housed in the Library of the English Place-Name Survey in the School of English in the University of Nottingham. So far, five volumes have been published by the English Place-Name Society dealing with the County of the City of Lincoln and the whole of the North Riding of Lindsey. The collection itself covers the whole of the county and from this the present volume has been written.

I owe my very grateful thanks to a number of people. Over the years my friend Mr Arthur Owen has made suggestions of etymology, but more importantly he has verbally and in learned articles drawn attention to the wider relationship between place-names and topography. Numerous of his suggestions have been silently incorporated in my text and only he will know which were originally his.

My former research student and friend, Dr John Insley, has as usual made a considerable number of suggestions of etymology, so that it is right and fitting that his name should appear on the title page. He is an outstanding Germanic scholar and an expert on personal names. Again I have accepted silently his numerous suggestions, and I owe him a very great debt of gratitude.

I also have to thank Dr Paul Cavill and Mrs Janet Rudkin for all their help in the preparation of the disk from which this volume has been printed. Their kindness and patience has been considerable. Nothing has been too much trouble.

My debt is greatest to Mrs Jean Russell-Gebbett, to whom this volume is dedicated. We have spent many enjoyable "practical place-name trips" around the county checking the topography of individual places. To her must go the prize of having spotted the meaning of **Bag** in **Bag Enderby**. I owe her more than I can say.

Kenneth Cameron

INTRODUCTION

The earliest identifiable names in Lincolnshire are those of the rivers **Ancholme, Humber, Welland** and **Witham**, together with **Swallow** which was originally the name of a stream. These are, in all probability, Pre-Celtic names and belong to an archaic phase of undifferentiated Old European, since they cannot be derived from known or suspected roots in Celtic (Primitive Welsh) or Old English. Frequently one can, at best, only ascribe a general meaning to such names.

There are, however, several river-names which are of Celtic origin — **Glen, Lymn, Nene, Trent** and probably **Cocker** (see **Cockerington**), as well as **Lincoln** and **Lindsey**, the first el. of which is PrW *linn 'a pool', and **Kesteven**, the first part of which is PrW **ceto-** 'a wood'. In addition, **Horncastle** in which the first element OE **horn** 'a horn-shaped piece of land' is a "translation" of PrW **banno-** 'a spur of land', the first el. of *Bannovalum*, the Celtic name of Horncastle. The similarity in the meaning of **banno-** and **horn** can hardly be coincidental, and **Horncastle** could only have been given by people who knew the meaning of both words.

The certain Celtic names in Lincolnshire are river-names and three place-names referring to 'a pool', 'a wood' and 'a spur of land' respectively, all names of topographical features, none containing a word for a habitation or settlement. Though the number in Lincolnshire is small, this is a feature of Celtic names in general. It seems that the Britons defined their settlements by giving them the name of nearby topographical features.

Tealby is a further name the etymology of which points to a very early date. This name in all probability contains the East Germanic tribal-name *Taifali* (which would give *Tāflas, Tǣflas* in Old English), detachments of which are recorded in Britain by the beginning of the 5th century. It is very likely that they retained their separate identity for some time in post-Roman Britain. **Tealby** would then originally have been the simplex form of the tribal-name, *Tāflas, Tǣflas*. Old Norse **bȳ** must have been added to this when the Danes occupied the area.

A further name belonging to a very early phase of Anglo-Saxon settlement in Lincolnshire is **Ingham**. The etymology of the **Inghams** in Norfolk and Suffolk has been reexamined and it seems highly likely that they are ancient cult names meaning 'the homestead, estate of the devotees of Ing'. The Lincolnshire **Ingham** seems to have a similar etymology and if so it must have been given before the end of the 5th century at latest.

A group of place-names, those reflecting features of Anglo-Saxon paganism, must also have been given in an earlier rather than later period of Anglo-Saxon name-giving here. Apart from the reference to *Ing* in **Ingham** there are no names denoting the cult-centres of individual pagan gods, like **Wensley** in Derbyshire, 'the glade dedicated to Woden'. However, there are two commemorating the sites of pagan shrines — **Wyham** 'at the pagan shrines' and **Wyeville** (earlier **Wyewell**) 'the spring by the heathen shrine'. It is worth noting that **Wyham** is the most northerly example in the whole country of this group of names.

There is evidence in Lincolnshire for the continued presence of Welshmen among the local English population, for there are three **Walcot(t)s** and a **Walton** 'the cottage' and 'the farmstead, village of the Welshmen'. These names clearly demonstrate that there were still isolated groups of Welshmen in the county, recognisable as such, perhaps as late as the end of the 7th century.

The colonisation of Lincolnshire by the Anglo-Saxons in the period post mid 5th century is testified by the large number of Old English place-names derived from elements like **burh, cot, hām, tūn, wīc** and **worth** (for the meanings, see **Place-Name Elements** below), all terms for places where people lived. One cannot suggest a stratification for such names, though occasionally it can be shown that a particular type is early, like the **Wykehams**, derived from Old English **wīchām**. These settlements have a direct connection with Romano-British sites.

It was believed that such names as **Healing** 'the family, the dependents of Hægel' (in origin a group-name, which later became the name of a place) and **Alvingham** 'the homestead, the estate of the Ælfingas (the family, the dependents of Ælf(a))' were the earliest identifiable habitative names, belonging to the earliest phase of Anglo-Saxon settlement in England. This was in part because they denote a social structure associated with the migration period of the Germanic peoples. However, it has been shown that, for various reasons, they belong to a secondary stage of settlement here, to a colonising phase as it has been called. It seems highly likely that such names were given in the period AD 450–650.

A similar group of names, those reflecting Anglo-Saxon paganism, must also belong to an earlier rather than a later phase of name-giving here. In Lincolnshire there are two such names, **Wyham** and **Wyeville** (earlier **Wyewell**), see above. It has been shown that Old English had a large vocabulary of topographical terms in which there were few synonyms. Most of the words for physical features denoted different shapes of hills and valleys, different types of marsh, different aspects of streams. Such words as **brōc, burna, cumb, dūn, ēa, ēg, feld, ford, halh, hop** and **lēah** (for the meanings see **Place-Name Elements** below) are all found in Lincolnshire place-names. As a result of research over the past twenty-five years or so, it is now believed that place-names of this type are the first to be given by settlers in a new land. Further, it seems clear that many of these terms had a quasi-habitative function, describing the position of a settlement in relation to a topographical feature, as in e.g. **Alford** and **Swinhope**. In this they are comparable to names of Celtic origin.

In 877 a third division of the Danish army, which had ravaged England from 865, partitioned Mercia and made settlements in the Danelaw in the area which became known as the Kingdom of the Five Boroughs, Derby, Leicester, Nottingham, Stamford and Lincoln. For long it was believed that these settlements were made by the retired vikings of the Great Army, numbering several thousand men, and that this would account for the great number of Danish place-names found here. A contrary view, however, argued that the army consisted of only two to three hundred men and that the place-names were rather the result of later expansion of settlements. A third contribution to the argument restored the concept of a large army and this is my own interpretation of the evidence. However, as has been said elsewhere, once the question of numbers had been raised, it was apparent that the Danish place-names here are far too numerous to be solely the result of retired vikings who had been members of armies of any conceivable size. After all there are over 200 names derived from **bȳ** and nearly 70 from **thorp** recorded in Domesday Book from Lincolnshire alone. Further, amongst these names are **Firsby** (twice) and **Friesthorpe, Irby** (twice), **Normanby** (four times) and **Normanton**. These denoted isolated groups of Frisians, Irish vikings and Norwegians who accompanied the Danes in the settlement of Lincolnshire.

A number of names like **Appleby** and **Riby**, both Anglo-Danish formations, suggest that they may well be partial Scandinavianisations of English names, in which Old Norse **bȳ** has replaced Old English **tūn**.

Partial Scandinavianisation has also taken place in the so-called Toton-hybrids, names like **Barkston, Branston, Croxton, Foston, Gelston** and **Swaton,** in which the first element is a Danish personal name, the second Old English **tūn**. It seems as certain as can be that as a group these hybrid names represent earlier villages taken over and partially re-named by the vikings. They must belong to an early phase of Danish settlement here. It should be noted that there are only ten or so such names recorded in Domesday Book in Lincolnshire as compared with about 50 in the rest of the Kingdom of the Five Boroughs. There is only a single example in the heavily Danish settled North Riding of Lindsey, where names in -by are very common.

The evidence of place-names points clearly to Danish settlers for the most part taking over land not occupied at the time, frequently on less attractive sites. When we compare the sites and situations of Danish place-names in -by, for instance, with neighbouring English-named villages we can demonstrate that the latter had preferable situations for agricultural exploitation. Some existing villages were occupied without a change of name; some names were partially changed. We can call this colonisation in the strict sense.

It would appear that besides veterans from the victorious army settling here there must have been others, immigrant farmers from the homeland who came to eastern England for several generations after the initial settlements. They took over vacant plots between existing villages in marginal areas; they were responsible for the fragmentation of existing estates and also for the reclamation of land once occupied but then deserted. That farmers were involved in this settlement is indicated by the striking variety of Danish words for different pieces of land and of terms for different types of fields. Such field-names are found in places with English names too. Widely scattered among the minor names and field-names of the county are names in **beck** 'a stream', **carr** 'a marsh overgrown with brushwood', **dale** 'a share of land (in the common field)', **garth** 'an enclosure', **gate** 'a way, a path; a right of passage', **holme** 'higher ground in marsh', **ing** 'meadow, pasture', **intake** 'a piece of land taken in', **kirk** 'a church', **lathe** 'a barn', **rigg** 'a ridge, a cultivated strip of ground', **roe** and **wroe** 'a corner of land', **stang** and **stong** 'a pole, a measure of land' and **wang** and **wong** 'a garden, an in-field', all words of Danish origin. Even distinctively Scandinavian grammatical features are found in the forms of field-names. All this is impressive evidence of the influence of the Danish settlers, influence which can only be the result of settlement on a very considerable scale. Clearly there must have been settlers who were farmers, entering the county by way of the Humber estuary, the Wash and the ports on the Lincolnshire coast.

The extent and density of Danish settlement is emphasised, for example, by the fact that the shire is divided into **wapentakes**, not **hundreds** as in most parts of England, and that Lindsey is divided into **ridings**, both words of Danish origin; that the same personal name (presumably the same man) occurs both in the name of a wapentake and of a village in that wapentake, **Aswardhurn** and **Aswarby**, **Haverstoe** and **Hawerby**, **Walshcroft** and **Walesby** and **Wraggoe** and **Wragby**, a feature not found elsewhere in the East Midlands; that the only Scandinavian pagan place-name surviving in the Midland Danelaw is likely to be **Thoresway** 'the shrine dedicated to Thor'. There is a unique group of place-names in Lincolnshire, for example **Braceby, Calceby, Goulceby, Haceby, Laceby, Rauceby, Ulceby** (twice) and **Winceby**, the forms of which show that they must have been given by Danish speakers. The first element of each is a Danish personal name in the genitive singular and each has the distinctive Scandinavian form which survives today pronounced [s] in contrast to English [z]. This group of names is not concentrated in one area, being found in each division of Lincolnshire except Holland.

Holland has, comparatively, many fewer Scandinavian place-names than the rest of the county. Even there, most of the elements quoted above are found frequently in the field-names of the district, surprisingly more so than the evidence of major place-names would suggest. If Danish names are scarce, Danish influence is considerable. Such influence is found in the forms of English names which have been modified by distinctively Danish sounds. *K-* has replaced *Ch-* in **Casewick, Kelstern, Kirkstead** and **Kirton** and *-sk-* occurs instead of *-sh-* in **Fiskerton**; **geit** has replaced **gāt** in **Gayton** and **methal** similarly has replaced **middel** in **Melton Ross**.

Lincolnshire is first recorded in the annal for 1016 in *The Anglo-Saxon Chronicle* and is no doubt an English creation after the reconquest of the Danelaw in the earlier 10th century. It must have included at least the areas under the control of the Danish armies of Lincoln and Stamford. The creation of the shire is the direct result of the Danish settlements which began in 877.

The French element in Lincolnshire place-names is very slight, for the Norman Conquest was not followed by a peasant migration. It consists of three names, (Temple) **Brewer**, **Kirmond** (le Mire) and **Vaudey** (Abbey), and the use of the French diminutive suffix -**el** in the early forms of **Little Bytham**.

There are no early place-names in -**ville** in England and **Eastville**, **Midville**, **Westville** and **Frithville** are all 19th century formations, based on names recorded much earlier. The change of **Wywell** to **Wyville** is similarly late.

The pseudo-French spelling **Eau** in some Lincolnshire stream-names is not historical. It is spelt *ea*, *eay*, *ei*, *ee*, etc. in early forms, being derived from OE *ēa* 'a river, a stream'. It may be noted that the modern local pronunciation of *eau* rhymes with *sea*.

In the discussion of individual place-names some early spellings are noted as being due to "Anglo-Norman influence", see **Holland**. This is a feature of French influence which has given rise elsewhere, for example, to a modern form **Nottingham** instead of **Snottingham**. Such changes have been traditionally explained as being due to the difficulties of French speakers pronouncing names of Anglo-Saxon origin. Recently, it has been shown that this interpretation is too simplistic and it is clear that much research is needed before we are able to explain them. There does not appear, however, to be a place-name in Lincolnshire in which the modern form has been radically changed.

ARRANGEMENT

With only one or two exceptions, all the place-names in this **Dictionary** are recorded on the 1:50,000 O.S. Map. They comprise all the names of parishes and joint-parishes and also those of less important places recorded from the 12th to 15th centuries. Few names, first found in post-1500 sources, have been included since they are either self-explanatory or of uncertain meaning. "Lost" village names are included where the site and the name are recorded on the O.S. Map.

Each place-name is printed in bold type, followed in brackets by the Division of Lincolnshire in which it is situated. Where the place-name is not itself a Civil Parish, the name of the relevant parish is included in the bracket. The head-forms are followed by a series of early spellings printed in italics, then the date of the document in which each is found and the source of those forms, abbreviated. These abbreviations are listed in a section entitled **Abbreviations**. The spellings or forms of the place-names themselves are taken from a large collection housed in the English Place-Name Society Library in the University of Nottingham. For the most part they are pre early 13th century.

Unpublished sources are indicated by printing the abbreviation for the source in italics. The abbreviation for a published source is printed in roman type. Where two dates are given for an early spelling, e.g. 1190 (1330) Ch, Hy2 (1409) Gilb, the first is the date at which the document purports to have been composed and the second that of the copy which has come down to us. In many cases the latter is a *Cartulary*, ecclesiastic or lay. Some sources which cannot be fixed to a particular date are dated by centuries 12th, 13th etc., often more specifically e13th, m13th, l13th etc., early, mid and late 13th century respectively. Others are identified by regnal date, e.g. Hy2, Hy3, Edl, or by a range of years, e.g 1133–47, 1155–62 etc. Where c is followed by a date it indicates the approximate date of the document (i.e. c1115 is "about 1115").

In the list of spellings of individual place-names no attempt has been made to differentiate between those which refer to the name of a place and those which are found as a person's name, not primarily as a reference to a place.

The forms of the individual place-name are followed by the meaning of the name wherever it is possible. Where this is not so, the meaning is clearly noted as "obscure", "unknown" or the like. The word(s) from which the place-name is derived are given in bold type. Personal names which form the first part of a p.n. are printed in italics. The term element, abbreviated to el., denotes a word found as first or second part of a compound place-name, whilst simplex refers to a place-name comprising a single element. A list of elements is given in the section entitled **Place-Name Elements in Lincolnshire Place-Names**.

PRONUNCIATION OF
OLD ENGLISH AND OLD NORSE SPELLINGS

The equivalents, below, are from Standard English except where stated and are purely approximate. In some cases they are of necessity simplified. They are intended as a guide to the pronunciation of the OE and ON words quoted in the text.

Vowels

It should be noted that the ON letters probably had nearly the same value as those of OE, but one or two letters used only in ON are added below. The sign above the vowel, as ā, indicates a long vowel in OE and that above the vowel, as á, a long vowel in ON.

a	German M*a*nn	ī	*see*
ā	f*a*ther	o	h*o*t
æ, Æ	h*a*t	ō	French b*eau*
ǣ	f*a*re	u	f*u*ll
e	s*e*t	ū	f*oo*l
ē	German S*ee*	y	French t*u*
i	s*i*t	ȳ	French p*u*r
ON			
ǫ	h*o*t		

Diphthongs

The OE diphthong was pronounced as a single glide, but each of the vowels from which it was formed was heard. It will be sufficient for the purpose to assume that the pronunciation of each part was the same as that of the vowel itself. The ON diphthongs, found in words quoted in the text, can be represented as follows:

au = ǫ+u   **ei** = e+i   **ey** = e+y

Consonants

All the OE consonants were pronounced, so that **ng**=n+g, **hl**=h+l
(compare Welsh ll), **wr**=w+r. They were pronounced like their modern
equivalents in Standard English with these (simplified) exceptions:

c	before *e* and *i*, and after *i*, as in *c*hild; elsewhere as in *c*old
cg	as in *ju*dge
g	before *e* and *i*, and after *æ*, *e* and *i*, as in *y*et, elsewhere as in *g*o
h	initially as in *h*at; elsewhere as in Scots lo*ch*
sc	as in *sh*all
f	usually as in *f*ill; between vowels as in o*v*en
s	usually as in *s*it; between vowels as in *z*est
th	between vowels as in fa*th*er; elsewhere as in *th*in. Note that **th** does not occur in OE manuscripts, the two sounds being represented by the symbols þ and ð (called *thorn* and *eth* respectively). These are, however, written indiscriminately to represent the two sounds in fa*th*er and *th*in noted above.

Two additional Old Norse (ON) symbols should be noted:

j ON	as in *y*oung
v ON	as in *w*ill

ABBREVIATIONS

a	ante
adj.	adjective
AASR	*Reports and Papers read at the Meetings of the Architectural Societies of Lincoln* etc., 1–52, 1850–1930
Abbr	*Placitorum Abbrevatio* (RC), London 1811
AC	*Ancient Charters* (PR Soc 10), 1888
AD	*Catalogue of Ancient Deeds* (PRO), London 1890
AD	Unpublished Ancient Deeds in PRO
AddCh	Additional Charters in BrMus
AddR	Additional Rolls in BrMus
adj.	adjective
Admin	*Calendars of Administrations in the Consistory Court of Lincoln AD 1540–1659*, ed. C.W. Foster (LRS 16) 1921
Ætheweard	*The Chronicle of Æthelweard*, ed. A. Campbell, London 1962
Allt	Alltyrodyn Deeds in the National Library of Wales (penes the late O.K. Schram)
Alv	The Cartulary of Alvingham Priory, Bodleian MS Laud 642 (13th)
AN	Anglo-Norman
Anc	Ancaster Muniments in LAO
And	Documents in the Anderson Collection in LAO
AntIt	*Itinerarium Provinciarum Antonini Augusti*, in O. Cuntz, *Itineraria Romana*, i, Leipzig 1929. A.L.F. Rivet, 'The British Section of the Antonine Itinerary', with an appendix on the Place-Names by Kenneth Jackson, *Britannia*, i, 1970
AOMB	Augmentation Office Miscellaneous Books in PRO
ASC	*The Anglo-Saxon Chronicle*, ed. B. Thorpe, 2 vols (RS) 1861; *Two of the Saxon Chronicles Parallel*, ed. C. Plummer, 2 vols, Oxford 1892–99
AScand	Anglo-Scandinavian
ASCharters	*Anglo-Saxon Charters*, ed. A.J. Robertson, 2nd ed., Cambridge 1956
Ass	*The Earliest Lincolnshire Assize Rolls AD 1202–1209*, ed. Doris M. Stenton (LRS 22) 1926; *A Lincolnshire Assize Roll for 1298*, ed. W.S. Thompson (LRS 36) 1944; *Sessions of the Peace . . . 1351–54*, ed. Elisabeth G. Kimball (LRS 65); *Rolls of the Justices in Eyre . . . 1218–19*, ed. Doris M. Stenton (Selden Soc. 53), 1934; *Some Extracts from Lincoln Assize Rolls*, LNQ viii–ix 1904–7

Ass	Unpublished Assize Rolls in PRO
ASWills	*Anglo-Saxon Wills*, ed. Dorothy Whitelock, Cambridge 1930
Banco	*Placita de Banco 1327-8* (PRO Lists and Indexes no. 32), London 1909
Bard	The Cartulary of Bardney Abbey, BrMus MS Cotton Vespasian E 20 (p1269)
Barl	The Cartulary of Barlings Abbey, BrMus MS Cotton Faust. B. i (l13th with additions)
BCS	*Cartularium Saxonicum*, ed. W. de G. Birch, 3 vols, London 1885–93
Bede	*Historia Ecclesiastica* in *Venerabilis Baedae Opera Historica*, ed. C. Plummer, Oxford 1896
Bly	*Blyborough Charters*, ed. Kathleen Major, in *A Medieval Miscellany for Doris Mary Stenton* (PR Soc 36), 1962
Blyth	R.T. Timson, *The Cartulary of Blyth Priory* (HMC), 1972 (l13th with continuations)
BMFacs	*Facsimiles of Royal and other Charters in the British Museum*, London 1903
Bodl	*Calendar of Charters and Rolls preserved in the Bodleian Library*, Oxford 1878
BostCC	Registrum et Calendarium Fraternitatis Corp. Chris. de Boston, BrMus MS Harley 4795 (l15th)
BostHistS	*History of Boston Series*, in progress
Brid	*Chartulary of the Priory of Bridlington*. ed. W.T. Lancaster, Leeds 1912 (various dates)
BS	*Sir Christopher Hatton's Book of Seals*, ed. L.C.Loyd, Doris M. Stenton, Oxford 1950
BT	Bishop's Transcripts in LAO
BuryF	*Feudal Documents from the Abbey of Bury St Edmunds*, ed. D.C. Douglas, London 1932
c	circa
Camden	W. Camden, *Britannia*, 1587, 1607
CampbCh	Campbell Charters in BrMus
CartAnt	*The Cartae Antiquae Rolls 1–20* (PRSoc NS 17, 33), 1939, 1960
Castleacre	The Cartulary of Castleacre Priory, BrMus MS Harley 2110 (13th)
Cf., cf.	Compare
Ch	*Calendar of Charter Rolls* (PRO), 6 vols, 1903–27
ChancR	Variant readings from the Chancellor's copy of the Pipe Rolls, as noted in PRSoc vols, and the Chancellors Roll for 1196 (PRSoc NS 7)
ChantCertC.	W. Foster and A. Hamilton Thompson, *The Chantry Certificates for Lincoln and Lincolnshire* (AASR 36–37), 1921–22, 1923–25
ChorCart	The Choristers' Cartulary, D&C A/1/4/3 (14th)
ChR	*Rotuli Chartarum* (RC), London 1837

ChronLP	*Chronicon Abbatie de Parco Lude* (LRS 1) 1891
ChronPetro	*Chronicon Petroburgense* (Camden Soc 47), 1849
Cl	*Calendar of Close Rolls* (PRO), in progress
Clerk	*Cartulary of St Mary Clerkenwell* (Camden Soc, Third Series lxxi), 1959
ClR	*Rotuli Litterarum Clausarum* (RC), London 1833–44
CM	Crowle Manor Documents in LAO
CollTop	J.G. Nichols, *Collectanea Topographica et Genealogica*, London 1834–43
Cor	Unpublished Coroners' Rolls in PRO
CrowEst	Frances M. Page, *The Estates of Crowland Abbey*, Cambridge 1934
CrowR	Register of Crowland Abbey, All Souls College, Oxford, MS 32 (15th)
CrowReg	Register of Crowland Abbey, BrMus MS Add. 25302 (15th-16th)
Cur	*Curia Regis Rolls* (PRO), in progress
CurP	*A Roll of the King's Court* (PRSoc 24), 1900; *Three Rolls of the King's Court* (PRSoc 14), 1891
Cust	E. and L. Cust, *Records of the Cust Family*, London 1898–1927
Dane	*Documents illustrative of the Social and Economic History of the Danelaw*, ed. F.M. Stenton, London 1920
dat.	dative
DB	*The Lincolnshire Domesday and the Lindsey Survey*, ed. C.W. Foster and T. Longley with an introduction by F.M. Stenton (LRS 19), 1924
DC	Charters of the Dean and Chapter of the Cathedral Church of Lincoln in LAO
DCAcct	Dean and Chapter Accounts and Rentals in LAO
DCLB	Dean and Chapter Lease Books in LAO
Deep	Cartulary of Deeping Priory, BrMus MS Harley 3658 (1332)
DIn	*The Domesday of Inclosures*, ed. I.S. Leadham, 2 vols, London 1897
Dods	Dodsworth MSS 75, 95, 135,144 in Bodleian Library
Drax	The Cartulary of Drax Priory, Bodleian Library Top Yorks c.72 (m14th)
DuDCCh	Durham Dean and Chapter Charters
Dugd	W. Dugdale, *Monasticon Anglicanum*, 6 vols, London 1817–30
DuLa	Calendar of Royal Charter; Duchy of Lancaster, etc. (Deputy Keeper's Reports 31, 35, 36), London 1870–75
DuLaCh	Duchy of Lancaster Charters in PRO
e	early
EECE	C.R. Hart, *The Early Charters of Eastern England*, Leicester 1966
el.	Place-name element

ExchKR	Exchequer King's Remembrancer, Miscellaneous Book 43 in PRO
Extent	Ancient Extents in PRO
Eyns	*The Cartulary of the Abbey of Eynsham*, ed. H.E. Salter (Oxford Historical Society 49, 51), 1907–8
FA	*Feudal Aids* (PRO), 6 vols, London 1899–1920
Fane	Documents in the Fane Collection in LAO
Fees	*The Book of Fees* (PRO), 3 vols, London 1920–31
fem.	feminine
FenNQ	*Fenland Notes and Queries*, 7 vols, 1889–1909
FF	*Feet of Fines* (PRSoc 17, 20, 23, 24), 1894, 1896, 1898, 1900. *Final Concords of the County of Lincoln*, vol. 2, ed. C.W. Foster (LRS 17), 1920. *Abstracts of Final Concords*, vol. 1, ed. W.O. Massingberd, London 1898. *Feet of Fines for the County of Lincoln for the reign of King John 1199–1216* (PRSoc NS 29), 1953
FF	Unpublished Feet of Fines in PRO
Fine	*Calendar of Fine Rolls* (PRO) in progress
FineR	*Excerpta e rotulis finium* (RC), London 1836
Fleet	*A Terrier of Fleet Lincolnshire*, ed. N. Neilson, London 1920
Foster	Documents in the Foster Library in LAO
FountainsC	W.T. Lancaster, *Chartulary of Fountains Abbey*, 2 vols, Leeds 1915 (15th)
France	*Calendar of Documents preserved in France* (PRO), 1899
GCB	Great Coucher Book of the Duchy of Lancaster, PRO Misc. Books 2 (Hy4)
Gilb	*Transcripts of Charters relating to Gilbertine Houses*, ed. F.M. Stenton (LRS 18), 1922
Goke	F.P. Lowe, *On Some Charters relating to the Nunnery of Gokewell in Lincolnshire*, AASR iii, 1884–85
Gough	*Facsimile of the Ancient Map of Great Britain in the Bodleian Library, Oxford*, O.S. 1966
Gox	The Goxhill Leiger, Peterborough D&C MS 23 (l14th)
GrimsCB	Grimsby Court Books i–xvi in North-East Lincolnshire Archives
Guis	*Cartularium Prioratus de Gyseburne* (Surtees Soc 86, 91), 1889, 1894
HarlCh	Harley Charters in BrMus
Harm	Documents in the G. Harmsworth Collection in LAO
Harrison	W. Harrison, *Description of Britain* (in Hollinshed's *Chronicles*), London 1877
HC	*The Chronicle of Hugh Candidus*, ed. W.T. Mellors, Oxford 1949
HC	Huntingfield Cartulary in LAO
HDMan	Manorial Documents in the Holland Deposit in LAO
Holl	The Holland Division of Lincolnshire

Holles	*Lincolnshire Church Notes made by Gervase Holles 1634 to 1642*, ed. R.E.G. Cole (LRS 1), 1911
Holywell	Documents in the Holywell Deposit in LAO
ib, *ib*	ibidem
IBC.	W. Foster, *Institutions to Benefices in the Diocese of Lincoln*, AASR xxxix 1928–29
IBL	A. Hamilton Thompson, *Lambeth Institutions to Benefices*, AASR xi 1930–1
IMBW.	Dugdale, *The History of Imbanking and Draining of Divers Fens and Marshes*, London 1662
IngCt	Court Rolls of the Manor of Ingoldmells, ed. W.O. Massingberd, London 1902
Inqaqd	*Calendarium Inquisitionum ad quod damnum* (RC), London 1803; *Inquisitions ad quod damnum* (PRO, Lists and Indexes 17, 22), London 1904, 1906
InstBen	C.W. Foster, Institutions to Benefices in the Diocese of Lincoln in the Sixteenth Century, LNQ v–vi 1898–1901
Inv	Inventories in LAO
Ipm	*Calendar of Inquisitiones post mortem* (PRO) in progress; W.O. Massingberd, *Early Lincolnshire Inquisitions post mortem*, AASR xxv 1899–1900
IpmR	*Calendarium Inquisitionum post mortem* (RC), London 1802–28
JEPNS	*Journal of the English Place-Name Society*, in progress
KCD	J.M. Kemble, *Codex Diplomaticus Aevi Saxonici*, 6 vols, London 1839–48
Kest	The Kesteven Division of Lincolnshire
Kirkst	The Kirkstead Abbey Cartulary, BrMus Cotton Vespasian E xviii (p1259)
KirkstInv i	Inventory of Kirkstead Abbey, BrMus Harley Roll G 21 (mainly 12th)
KirkstInv ii	Inventory of Kirkstead Abbey, BrMus Harley Roll O 5 (e13th)
KirkstPsalt	B. Webb, *An early Map and Description of the Inquest on Wildmore Fen in the Twelfth Century*, LAAS ii 1928–40
l	late
LAAS	*Lincolnshire Architectural and Archaeological Society Reports and Papers*, 1–10 1936–64
LAHW	A. Gibbons, *Liber Antiquus de Ordinationibus Vicariorum tempore Hugonis Welles, Lincolniensis Episcopi, 1209–1235*, Lincoln 1888
LAO	Lincolnshire Archives Office
LCCA	Lincoln Cathedral Chapter Acts in LAO
LDRH	*List of the Lands of Dissolved Religious Houses*, PRO Lists and Indexes, Supplementary Series No 111, vol. 2, 1964
Leland	*The Itinerary of John Leland*, ed. L. Toulmin Smith, 5 vols, London 1906

Lib   *Calendar of Liberate Rolls* (PRO) in progress
LibEl   *Liber Eliensis*, ed. E.O. Blake (Camden Society Third Series xcii), 1962
LMR   Lindsey Manorial Rolls in LAO
LN   *Liber Niger Scaccarii*, ed. T. Hearne, 2 vols, 1888–1936
LNQ   *Lincolnshire Notes and Queries*, 14 vols 1888–1936
LNR   The North Riding of Lindsey
LOC   Liber de Ordinationibus Cantariarum, D&C A/1/8 in LAO (14th)
LP   *Letters and Papers, Foreign and Domestic of the reign of Henry VIII* (PRO), London 1864–1932
LRMB   Land Revenue Miscellaneous Books in PRO
LRS   Publications of the Lincoln Record Society
LS   see DB
LSR   The South Riding of Lindsey
LWR   The West Riding of Lindsey
m   mid
Mad   Documents in the Maddison Deposit in LAO
Map   Maps and Plans in the PRO
Margary   I.D. Margary, *Roman Roads in Britain*, revised in one volume, London 1967
MC   Marsh Chapel Parish Documents in LAO
ME   Middle English
MiD   Documents in the Middleton Collection in the University of Nottingham Archives
MinAcct   Ministers' Accounts in PRO
Misc   *Calendar of Miscellaneous Inquisitions* (PRO) in progress
MiscDon   Miscellaneous Donations in LAO
MLM   *The Medieval Lindsey Marsh Select Documents*, ed. A.E.B. Owen (LRS 85), 1996
Monson   Documents in the Monson Collection at South Carlton
MM   Documents in the Massinberd Mundy Collection in LAO
Ncot   The Cartulary of Nun Coatham Priory, Bodleian MS Top. Lincs d. 1 (e13th)
neut.   neuter
Newh   The Cartulary of Newhouse or Newsham Priory, the Earl of Yarbrough MS (e13th)
NI   *Nonarum inquisitiones* (RC), 1807
nom.   nominative
Nostell   The Cartulary of Nostell Priory, BrMus MS Cotton Vespasian E xix (p1263 with additions)
NthCh   *Facsimiles of Early Charters from Northamptonshire Collections*, ed. F.M. Stenton (Northamptonshire Record Society iv), 1930
O   *Ordnance Survey Map*, first ed., 1824
OblR   *Rotuli de Oblatis et Finibus* (RC), London 1835

ODan	Old Danish
OE	Old English
OE Bede	*The Old English Version of Bede's Ecclesiastical History* (Early English Text Society 95–96), London 1890–98
OFr	Old French
OGerm	Old German
ON	Old Norse
Ord	*The Ecclesiastical History of Orderic Vitalis*, ed. Marjorie Chibnall, Oxford in progress
Orig	*Abbrevatio Rotulorum Originalium* (RC), London 1805–10
Ormsby	W.O. Massingberd, *History of the Parish of Ormsby-cum-Ketsby*, Lincoln n.d.
p	post
P	*Pipe Rolls* (Pipe Roll Soc) in progress
Pap	*Calendar of Papal Registers* (PRO), in progress
ParlSur	Parliamentary Surveys, E 317/1–4, in PRO
Pat	*Calendar of Patent Rolls* (PRO), in progress
PatR	*Rotuli Litterarum Patentium* (RC), London 1835
Peace	*Some Sessions of the Peace in Lincolnshire 1361–1396*, ed. Elisabeth G. Kimball, 2 vols (LRS 49, 56), 1955, 1962; *Some Sessions of the Peace in Lincolnshire 1360–1375*, ed. Rosalind Sillem (LRS 30), 1937; *Sessions of the Peace . . . 1351–1354*, ed. Elisabeth G. Kimball (LRS 65), 1971
Ped	The Cartulary of the Pedwardine Family, BrMus MS Additional 323101 (l14th)
PetLN	Liber Niger of Peterborough Monastery, Soc of Antiquaries MS 60 (12th, with additions to 14th)
PetLM	Register of Peterborough Abbey, Soc of Antiquaries MS 38 (m14th)
P&H	Nicholaus Pevsner and John Harris, revised by Nicholas Antram, *The Buildings of England, Lincolnshire*, London 1989
PipeS	The Cartulary of Pipewell Abbey, BrMus MS Stowe 937 (m13th)
pl.	plural
PRO	(Records preserved in or published by) the Public Record Office
PrW	Primitive Welsh
Ptolemy	*Claudii Ptolemaei Geographia*, ed. G. Parthey and M. Pinder, Berlin 1860, ed. C. Muller, Paris 1883
Queen's	Rentals, Surveys, etc. relating to the lands of the Bishop of Lincoln, Queen's College, Oxford, MS 366 (14th)
QW	*Placita de Quo Warranto* (RC), London 1818
RA	*Registrum Antiquissimum* (LRS), 10 vols, 1931–73
Rams	*Cartularium Monasterii de Ramesia* (Rolls Series), London 1884–93
RamsChron	*Chronicon Abbatiæ Rameseiensis* (Rolls Series), London 1886

Ravenna	I. A. Richmond and O.G.S. Crawford, 'The British Section of the Ravenna *Cosmography*', *Archaeologia* xciii, 1949
RC	Publications of the Record Commission, London
Rental	Rentals in the PRO
Revesby	'Some Revesby Charters in the Soke of Bolingbroke', ed. Dorothy M. Owen, in *Early Medieval Miscellany for Doris M. Stenton*, PRSoc 36, 1962
RevesbyInv	Inventory of charters of Revesby Abbey, BrMus MS Egerton 3058 (12th)
RH	*Rotuli Hundredorum* (RC), London 1812–18
RotDom	*Rotuli de Dominabus et Pueris et Puellis* (Pipe Roll Soc 35), 1913
RPD	*Feodarium Prioratus Dunelmensis* (Surtees Soc 58), 1872
r.n.	river-name
RRAN	*Regesta Regum Anglo-Normanorum*, ed. H.W.C. Davis etc., 3 vols, Oxford 1913–68
RRep	*The Register of Bishop Philip Repingdon 1404–1419*, ed. Margaret Archer (LRS 57, 58, 74), 1963, 1982
RRG	*Rotuli Roberti Grosseteste*, ed. F.N. Davis (LRS 20), 1914
RRGr	*Rotuli Ricardi Gravesend*, ed. F.N. Davis, C.W. Foster and A. Hamilton Thompson (LRS 20), 1925
RS	Rolls Series
RSu	*The Rolls and Register of Bishop Oliver Sutton 1280–1299*, ed. Rosalind M.T. Hill (LRS 39, 43, 48, 52, 60), 1948–65
S	P.H. Sawyer, *Anglo-Saxon Charters*, London 1968, followed by a number
s.a.	*sub anno*
Saints	*Die Heiligen Englands*, ed. F. Liebermann, Hanover 1889
Samson	*The Kalendar of Abbot Samson of Bury St Edmonds and Related Documents*, ed. R.H.C. Davis (Camden Soc Third Series lxxxiv), 1954
Saxton	C. Saxton, *Map of Lincolnshire*, 1576
SC	*The State of the Church*, ed. C.W. Foster (LRS 23), 1926
Scand.	Scandinavian
SDL	*Speculum Dioeceseos Lincolniensis*, ed. R.E.G. Cole (LRS 4), 1913
Selby	*The Coucher Book of Selby*, ed. J.T. Fowler (Yorkshire Archaeological Association x, xiii), 1891–93 (13th-14th)
SelectPleas	*Select Pleas* (Selden Soc 1, 2), 1888–89
Semp	*Charters relating to the Priory of Sempringham* (Genealogist NS 15–16), 1899–1900; C.W. Foster, *Grants to Sempringham Priory by members of the Langton Family* (AASR xxxvii), 1923–25
Sewer	*The Records of the Commissioners of Sewers in the Parts of Holland 1547–1603*, ed. A. Mary Kirkus (LRS 54), 1959; vols 2–3, ed. A.E.B. Owen (LRS 63, 71), 1968, 1977
Sewer	Unpublished Sewer Records in LAO
sg.	singular

Spald i	The Cartulary of Spalding Priory, BrMus MS Additional 35206 (c1331)
Spald ii	The Cartulary of Spalding Priory, BrMus MS Harley 742 (c1331)
SR	Unpublished Subsidy Rolls in PRO
Stix	The Cartulary of Stixwould Priory, BrMus MS Additional 46701 (l13th)
StJ	Unpublished documents in the possession of St John's College, Cambridge
StM	A Cartulary of St Mary's Abbey, York, Bodleian Library MS Dodsworth 76 (l13th)
Stubbs	Documents in the Stubbs Deposit in LAO
Stukeley	W. Stukeley, *Itinerarium Curiosum*, London 1724
Sub	*A Subsidy collected in the Diocese of Lincoln in 1526*, ed. H. Salter (Oxford Historical Soc. lxiii), 1909
TA	Tithe Awards in LAO and PRO
Tax	*Taxatio Ecclesiastica Angliæ et Walliæ* (RC), 1802
Templar	*Records of the Templars in England in the Twelfth Century*, ed. Beatrice E. Lees, London 1935
Terrier	Unpublished Terriers in LAO
Thompson	P. Thompson, *The History and Antiquities of Boston*, London 1856
Thorpe	B. Thorpe, *Diplomatarium anglicum aevi Saxonici*, London 1865
Thurg	The Cartulary of Thurgarton Priory, Southwell Minster MS 3 (c1340)
TP	Documents in the Tweed and Peacock Deposit in LAO
TYR	Documents in the Tyrwhitt-Drake Deposit in LAO
ValNor	*The Valuation of Norwich*, ed. W.E. Lunt, Oxford 1926
VC	The Cartulary of the Vicars Choral, Lincoln, LI RO VC 2/1 in LAO (14th)
VE	*Valor Ecclesiasticus* (RC), 6 vols, 1810–34
Walth	The Cartulary of Waltham Abbey, Essex, BrMus MS Cotton Tiberius c ix (Hy3)
Welb	The Cartulary of Welbeck Abbey, BrMus MS Harley 3640 (14th)
Welbourne	The Chantries of John de Welburne and Henry, Duke of Lancaster, D&C A/1/10 in LAO (c1380)
Welles	*Rotuli Hugonis de Welles*, 3 vols (LRS 3, 6, 9), 1912–14
WellesLA	*Liber Antiquus de Ordinationibus Vicariorum Tempore Hugonis Wells, Lincolniensis Episcopi 1209–1235*, ed. Alfred Gibbons, privately printed 1858
WellesW	*Will of Bishop Hugh of Wells* (in *Giraldi Cambrensis Opera*), vol. vii, App. G., pp. 223–31 (RS), 1877
Werb	*The Chartulary or Register of the Abbey of St Werburgh, Chester* (Cheetham Soc 79, 82), 1902–3 (c1310)

Westm	The Westminster Abbey 'Domesday', Muniment Book II (14th)
Wheeler	W.H. Wheeler, *A History of the Fens of South Lincolnshire*, 2nd ed., Boston 1894
Whit, Whitby	*Cartularium Abbathiæ de Whiteby* (Surtees Soc 69, 72), 1879, 1881
White	W. White, *History, Gazetteer, and Directory of Lincolnshire*, Sheffield 1826, 1842
Wills	*Lincoln Wills*, ed. C.W. Foster, 3 vols (LRS 5, 10, 24), 1914, 1918, 1930
WillsPCC	C.W. Foster, *Abstracts of Lincolnshire Wills proved in the Prerogative Court of Canterbury*, LNQ xvii–xxiii 1922–24, AASR xli 1932
Works	*Public Works in Medieval Law* (Selden Soc 32, 40), 1915–23
Ych	*Early Yorkshire Charters*, ed. W. Farrer, C.T. Clay, 12 vols, Edinburgh and Yorkshire Archaeological Society Record Series 1914–65
YD	*Yorkshire Deeds* (Yorkshire Archaeological Soc.) in progress
YearBk	*Year Books of Edward II, Edward IV and Henry VI* (Selden Year Book Series) in progress

LINCOLNSHIRE PLACE-NAMES

A

Aby (LSR), *Abi* 1086 DB, c1115 LS, c1150, eHy2, c1175 Dane, *Aby* 1212 Fees, 'the farmstead, village on the stream', from ON **á** and ODan **bȳ**. It is situated beside Great Eau.

Ackthorpe (South Elkington, LSR), *Achetorp* Hy2 (1314) Ch, *Achathorp* Hy2 (1409) Gilb, *Haketorp* 1190 P, *Acketorp* 1212 Fees, 'Āki's secondary settlement (in relation to **South Elkington**)' from the ODan pers.n. *Āki* and ODan **thorp**. This is an extinct village, now represented by **Ackthorpe Hall**.

Addlethorpe (LSR), *Arduluetorp* 1086 DB, *Hardelstorp, Hardelisthorp* Hy2 (c1331) *Spald i*, *Hardeltorp* 1199 (1330) Ch, *Addeltorp* 1202 Ass, *Ardeltorp* 1212 Fees, a hybrid p.n. 'Eardwulf's secondary settlement (perhaps in relation to **Ingoldmells**)' from the OE pers.n. *Eardwulf* and ODan **thorp**. Identical with **Addlethorpe** in the West Riding of Yorkshire.

Ailby (Rigsby with Ailby, LSR), *Halebi* 1086 DB, Hy2 Dane, *Alebi* 1086 DB, Hy2, l12th Dane, *Alesbi* Hy2 ib, 'Ali's farmstead, village' from the ODan pers.n. *Āli* and ODan **bȳ**. The same pers.n. occurs in **Althorpe** and **Aylesby**.

Aisby (Corrringham, LWR), *Asebi, -by* 1086, c1128 (12th) ChronPetro, c1200 RA iv, *-bia* c1145 Dane, *Acebi* 1195, 1197 P. **Aisby** (Heydour, Kest), *Asebi* 1086 DB, 1188, 1194 P, 1202 Ass, 1203 Abbr. Both mean 'Ási's farmstead, village' from the ON pers.n. *Ási* and ODan **bȳ**.

Aisthorpe (LWR), *Æstorp* 1086 DB, *Estorp* 1086 ib, 1200 Cur, *Esttorp* c1115 LS, *Astorp* Hy2 (1409) Gilb, lHy2 Dane, probably 'the secondary settlement to the east (perhaps of **Sturton by Stow**)' from OE **ēast** and ODan **thorp**.

1

Alford (LSR), *Alforde* 1086 DB, *-worda* (sic) c1115 LS, *-ford* eHy2, c1190 Dane, *Auford* p1169 ib, 1195 FF, probably 'the old ford' from OE (Anglian) **ald** and OE **ford**. Forms in *Au-* are due to the vocalisation of *-l-*. It has recently been pointed out that finds of Romano-British coins and pottery have been made here and that the road carried by the ford has every appearance of Roman origin.

Algarkirk (Hol), *Alfgare* (sic, 2x) 1086 DB, *Algarescherche* 1194 P, *Algerchierch'* 1200 ib, *Algarcherch'* 1201 ib, *Algareschierche* 1219 Ass, *Algarkierc* 1200 P, *Algarekirke* 1212 Fees, *Algerekirk'* 1202 Ass, cf. *Algarhundredo* 1200 Cur, *Algerhundr'* 1206 Ass. It is presumably to be assumed that the DB form, which is recorded twice, is a pers.n., OE *Ælfgār* (or perhaps ODan *Alger*) to which was added OE **cirice** 'a church'. This was later replaced by the cognate ON **kirkja** (for a similar development see **Gosberton**). Hence the name means '*Ælfgār*'s or *Alger*'s church'. It will be noted that *Alger* is also the first el. of the name of a hundred, a local division of land, thought to be part of Algarkirk.

Alkborough (LWR), *Alchebarge* 1086 DB, *-barua* c1115 LS, *-barue* c1128 (12th) ChronPetro, *Alkebarwe* m12th (c1331) *Spald i*, 1219 Ass, *-barwa* 1190 (1301) Dugd vi, 'Al(u)ca's grove' from the OE pers.n. *Al(u)ca* and OE **bearu**. There are numerous 13th century spellings in *Altebarge, Haltebarge, Hautebarge*, due initially to the confusion of *-c-* and *-t-* and then to popular etymology associating the name with French *haut* 'high'.

Allington (Kest), *Adelinctune, Adelingetone* 1086 DB, *Alintuna* 1106–23 (1333) Ch, *-tune* 1185 Templar, *Alinton'* 1191 P, *Athelinton'* 1202 Ass, 1202 FF, *Athelynton'* 1351 Cor, 'the village of the princes, noblemen' from the gen.pl. **æthelinga** of OE **ætheling** 'a prince, a nobleman' and OE **tūn**.

Althorpe (Keadby with Althorpe, LWR), *Aletorp* 1067–69 (c.1150) *HC*, 1086 DB, 1179 P, 1185 Templar, 1199 P, *-thorp* 1185 Templar, 'Áli's secondary settlement (presumably of **Keadby**)', from the ODan pers.n. *Áli* and ODan **thorp**. The same pers.n. occurs in **Ailby** and **Aylesby**.

Alvingham (LSR), *Alvingeham* 1086 DB, 1199 ChR, c1221 Welles, *Aluingeham* 1202 FF, 1218 Ass, *Alvingham* 1086 DB, *Alvingheheim* c1115 LS, 'the homestead, the estate of the Ælfingas (the followers, the dependents of Ælf(a))' from the gen.pl. *Ælfinga* of the OE group-name *Ælfingas* and OE **hām**. The form in *-heim* is from ON **heim** cognate with OE **hām**.

Amber Hill (Hol), *Amber Hyll* 1575 Sewer iii, - *Hill* 1824 O, the first el. perhaps being an OE bird-name OE **amer** 'a bunting'. This was a plot of land of 30 acres allotted under the Holland Fen Enclosure Award to provide materials for repairing the roads of several parishes having rights of common in Holland Fen. The parish was formed in 1880 by uniting the Fen Allotments of **Algarkirk** and **Sutterton** and the extra-parochial place **Amber Hill**.

Amcotts (LWR), *Amecotes* 1086 DB, 1099–1123, 1154, 1155–62 (e14th) Selby, c1184 (15th) Templar, *Ammecotes* 1155 (c1200) CartAnt, 'Amma's cottages, huts' from the OE pers.n. *Amma* and OE **cot** in the pl.

Ancaster (Kest), *de Anacastro* c1150 Anc, *Anecastre* Hy2 Dane, 1185 Templar, *-castr'* 1197 P, 1200 Cur. 'Ana's Roman station' from the OE pers.n. *Ana* and OE **cæster**.

Ancholme, R. (LWR), *thare ea the is genemnod Oncel* c1000 Saints, *Ancolnam* 1150–60 Dane, *Ancolna* 1150–60 ib, *Ancolnie* Hy2 ib, *Ancolnia* Hy2 (13th) Stix, *Ancolne* Hy2 (e14th) Selby, 1160–66 Dane. This is a pre-English r.n. the etymology of which is uncertain.

Anderby (LSR), *Andreby* 1123–47 RA i, Hy2 Dane, e13th *HarlCh*, *Anderby* 1145–53 (e14th) YCh ii, *-bi* c1200 RA vi. The first el. is uncertain; the second is ODan **bȳ** 'a farmstead, a village'.

Anwick (Kest), *Amuinc* (sic), *Haniwic* (*-ni-* = *-m-*) 1086 DB, *Amewich* 1175 (1333) Ch, *-wic* 1185 Templar, *-wyc* 1182 Gilb, *-wyk* 1184 (1407) ib, *Ammewic'* 1208 FF, 'Amma's farm, dairy farm' from the OE pers.n. *Amma* (also found in **Amcotts**) and OE **wīc**. Sporadic forms in *-n-* occur early, e.g. *Anewic* c1221 Welles but such spellings do not become common until the 16th century.

Apley (LSR), *Apelei* 1086 DB, *Apeleia* 1086 ib, c1115 LS, *Appelay* eHy2 (m13th) NCot, *-leye* 1219 Cur, 'the apple wood' from OE **æppel** and OE **lēah**.

Appleby (LWR), *Aplebi* 1086 DB, c1115 LS, 1130 P, *-beia* 1088 (l13th) Blyth, *Apelbi* c1128 (l12th) ChronPetro, *Appelbiea* 1086–8 (l13th) Blyth, *-by* 1154–55 RBE, *-bi* c1160 Semp, 'the farmstead, village where apples grow' from OE **æppel** and ON **bȳ**. It may well be that **bȳ** has replaced OE **tūn** here.

Asen Dyke (Hol), *Esendic* s.a. 656 (1121) ASC E, *fossam quæ Asendic dicitur* c1125 Ord, *-dich* 1227 Ch, *Assendike, -dyke* 1281 QW; it is referred to as *the Greate Dreyne called Assendike alias Gallylode* 1650 *ParlSurv.* The second el. is clearly OE **dīc** 'a trench, a drainage channel', and for the first see **Aswick Grange**. **Asen Dyke** runs from Aswick Grange to the R. Welland at Cloot Ho.

Asgarby (LSR), *Asgerebi* 1086 DB, 1163 RA i, *Asgerbi* 1100–15, 1127–30, 1162 ib, *Asgreby* c1150 RA ii, *Ansgerby* 1135–47, 1140–44 RA i. **Asgarby** (Asgarby and Howell, Kest), *Asgerb'* 1185 Templar, 1200 RA vii, *-by* l12th Semp, 1200 RA vii, *-bi* 1207 Cur, *Asgerebi* e13th RA vii. Both mean 'Ásgeirr's farmstead, village' from the ON pers.n. *Ásgeirr* and ODan **bȳ**. This pers.n. occurs several times in L in DB. Forms with initial *Ans-* are due to Norman influence.

Ashby (Ashby cum Fenby, LNR), *Aschebi* 1086 DB, c1115 LS, *-by* 1275 RH, *Askebi* 1196 ChancR, *-by* 1202 FF, 1205 Cur. **Ashby** (now in Scunthorpe, LWR), *Aschebi* 1086 DB, c1115 LS, *Esebi* c1090 (1402) Pat, *Askebi* 1178 P, 1194 CurP, *-by* Hy2 (e14th) Selby. **Ashby, West** (LSR), *Aschebi* 1086 DB, c1115 LS, *Ascbi* c1115 ib, *Askebi* lHy2 (13th) *Kirkst*, 1196–99 RA ii, *-by* l12th RA vi, *Askeby iuxta Hornecastre* 1212–15 RA vi, *West Asby* 1528 Wills ii. **Ashby by Partney** (LSR), *Aschebi* 1086 DB, c1115 LS, *Askebi* lHy2 Dane, *-by* 1203 Cur, 1212 Fees, *Estaskebi* John Abbr, 1208 Cur, *Askeby iuxta Partenaye* 1282 *FF.* **Ashby de la Launde** (Kest), *Aschebi* 1086 DB, p1160, a1167 Dane, *Asckebi* 1185 Templar, *Askebi* 1199 CurR, 1202 Ass, *Ashebye alias Asheby Dallalande* (sic) 1580 *Fane.* **Ashby Puerorum** (LSR), *Aschebi* 1086 DB, 1164–75 (13th) YCh iii, *-by* 1154 (14th) Selby, *Ascbi* c1115 LS, *Askebi* c1172 LAAS v, *-by* 1198 (1328) Ch, *Parva Askebi* 1269 RRGr, *Askeby puerorum* 1351 *CampbCh*, *Askeby Puerorum* 1390 Cl. Probably from the ODan pers.n. *Aski*, found in independent sources in L, and ODan **bȳ** 'a farmstead, a village'. Alternatively the meaning might be 'the farmstead, village where ash-trees grow', the first el. then being ON **askr** 'an ash-tree'. **West Ashby** is distinguished first as "near Horncastle", then in the 16th century as **West**; **Ashby by Parteney** is earlier **East**; the affix in **Ashby de la Launde** is from the family who held a manor here, note William *de La Laund'* 1327 *SR.* **Ashby Puerorum** is earlier called **Little**, then later **Puerorum**, the gen.pl. of Latin **puer**, "of the boys", i.e. the choir boys of Lincoln Cathedral, the manor of Ashby having been appropriated to the use of the choir boys, see RSu 1, p.29.

Aslackby (Aslackby and Laughton, Kest), *Aslachebi* 1086 DB, p1147 Dugd v, 1167 P, *Aslakeby* a1160 Semp, 1195 P, *Aselakesbi* 1161 ib, 'Áslák's farmstead, village' from the ON pers.n. *Áslákr* and ODan **bȳ**. The same pers.n. occurs also in **Aslacoe Wapentake**.

Aslacoe Wapentake (LWR), *Aslacheshou* 1086 DB, 1175 P, *Aslocahou* c1115 LS, *Aslachou* 1130 P, *Aslakesho* 1177 ChancR, *Aselakesho* 1184 P. The forms are preceded or followed by some form of Latin *wapentacium*. 'Áslák's mound, hill' from the ON pers.n. *Áslákr* and ON **haugr**, but the site of the meeting-place of the wapentake (ON **vápnatak**, late OE **wæpengetæc** 'a subdivision of a shire') is not known.

Asperton (Wigtoft, Hol), *Osfyryhtunæ* 1060 (Inspeximus) Thorpe, *Asferton'* 1200 Cur, 1316 Ch, *Aspreton* 1356 *HC*, 'Ōsfrith's farmstead' from the OE pers.n. *Ōsfrith* and OE **tūn**, with *Ōs-* later replaced by ON *Ás-*.

Asserby (Bilsby, LSR), *Asfortby* eHy2 (1409) Gilb, *Hasfordebi* 1198 Cur, *Asforhebi* l12th Dane, *Asforthebi* c1200 ib, *Asfordeb'* e13th RA vi, -*bi* 1201 Cur, 'Asforth's farmstead, village' from the pers.n. *Asforth*, recorded in DB in L and Nottinghamshire as *Asfort*, -*ford* and derived from ON *Ásfrothr*, and ODan **bȳ**.

Asterby (LSR), *Estrebi* 1086 DB, 1130 P, *Eisterby* 1135–54 (l13th) *Stix*, *Esterby* eHy2 (l13th) *ib*, -*bi* 1160–70 RA vi, 1185 Templar, *Aistrebi* 1175–78 *Anc*, 'the more easterly farmstead, village' from ON **eystri** 'more easterly' and ODan **bȳ**, probably in relation to **Goulceby**.

Aswarby (Aswarby & Swarby, Kest), *Wardeby* (sic), *Aswardebi* 1086 DB, 1125 (p1269) *Bard*, 1197 P, 1201 Cur, 1206 FF, 1213 Cur, 'Aswarth's farmstead, village' from the ODan pers.n. *Aswarth* and ODan **bȳ**, identical with **Aswardby**. The pers.n. *Aswarth* is the first el. of both the settlement name and the district name, **Aswardhurn**, and presumably refers to the same man.

Aswardby (LSR), *Aswardebi* 1195 P, 1196 FF, 1202 P, 1212 Fees, *Assewartheby* 1219 Welles, 'Aswarth's farmstead. village' from the ODan pers.n. *Aswarth* and ODan **bȳ**.

Aswardhurn Wapentake (Kest), *Asuuardetierne* 1086 DB, *Haswertherne* 1130 P, *Oswardtirne* 1168 ib, *Aswardehirne* 1175 ib, *Aswardeschirne* 1176 ib, *Aswardeskirne* 1178 ib, -*kerne* 1182, 1192 ib, *Asewardethirn'* 1201 Ass, -*thirne*

1212 Fees; the forms are preceded or followed by some form of Latin *wapentacium*. 'Aswarth's thorn-bush' from the ODan pers.n. *Aswarth* and ON **thyrnir**. The first el. of **Aswarby** in this wapentake is also *Aswarth* and presumably refers to the same man. The site of the meeting-place of the wapentake (ON **vápnatak**, late OE **wæpengetæc** 'a subdivision of a shire') is not known, but may well have been at a prominent thorn-bush near **Aswarby**.

Aswick Grange (Whaplode, Hol), *Asewic* 1232, 1256 (c1331) *Spald ii*, 1259 CrowEst, 1284 (c1331) *Spald ii*, cf. *Asenwictoft* c1155, 1194 (c1200) CartAnt, *Asewictoft* 1232 *Spald ii*, *Asewyktoft* 1280 *FF*, now lost but shown on 1824 O as *Aswicktoft*, where **Aswick Grange** is marked today. **Aswick** must be taken with **Asen Dyke**, since the early forms of both names clearly suggest that each has the same first el. However, the etymology of *Asen-* is quite obscure. The second el. of Aswick appears to be OE **wīc** in one of its senses, 'a dwelling, a trading centre, a dairy farm'. ODan **toft** 'a messuage, a curtilage' has been added to **Aswick** in **Aswicktoft**.

Atterby (Bishop Norton, LWR), *Adredeb'* 1185 Templar, *-by* 1210 P, *Atheradeby* 1202 Ass, *Atheredeby* c1230 (14th) *VC*, *Athereby* c1225 (14th) Queen's, 'Ēadrēd's farmstead, village', a hybrid Anglo-Danish p.n. from the OE pers.n. *Ēadrēd* and ODan **bȳ**. There are no traces of the OE gen.sg. *-es* in the forms for Atterby and we have frequent *-th-* indicating Scand. influence. It is, therefore, likely that the name was given by Scand. settlers. See further **Autby**.

Aubourn (Aubourn, Haddington & South Hykeham, Kest), *Aburne* 1086 DB, *-burn'* 1194, 1198 P, *-burna iuxta Lincoln'* l12th BS, *Alburne* 1160–76 ib, *Auburn* 1212 Fees, c1221 Welles, perhaps 'the stream where alders grow' from OE **alor** and OE **burna**. Forms in *Au-* are the result of the vocalisation of *-l-*.

Audleby (Caistor, LNR), *Aldulvebi* 1086 DB, *Aldolbi* c1115 LS, *Adolfbie* c1150 *TYR*, *-by* 1299 *FF*, an Anglo-Danish hybrid 'Aldwulf's farmstead, village' from the OE pers.n. *Aldwulf* and ODan **bȳ**. There are no traces of the OE gen.sg. *-es* in the forms for **Audleby** and it is likely that the name was given by Scand. settlers here. See further **Autby**.

Aunby (Careby, Kest), *Onnebi* (*-nn-* = *-un-*) 1203 Abbr, *Ounesbi* 1206, 1219 Ass, *Ounebi* 1219 ib, *-by* 1223 Cur, 1228 Pat, *Aunebi* 1219 Ass, probably 'Aun's farmstead, village' from the ON pers.n. *Au(n)n*, a shortened form of

Authu(n), and ODan **bȳ**, cf. **Owmby by Spital**.

Aunsby (Aunsby & Dembleby, Kest), *Ounesbi* 1086 DB, 1202 FF, 1219 Ass, *-by* 1238 FF, *Ouneby* 1243 RRG, 1271 FF, *Oudneby* 1242–43 Fees, *Outhenby* 1281 Ch, identical with **Owmby**, this is 'Outhen's farmstead, village' from the Anglo-Scand. pers.n. *Outhen*, corresponding to ON *Authun(n)*, and ODan **bȳ**.

Austendike (Moulton, Hol), *Alstandike* 1248 FF, *Alstondik* 1248, lHy3 (c1331) *Spald i*, *Alstonedyke* 1308 *MM*, probably an Anglo-Danish p.n. from the ME pers.n. *Alstan* (from OE *Ælfstān* or *Aldstān*) and **dík** 'a ditch'.

Austen Fen (Grainthorpe, LSR), *Hadestanefene* Hy2 (1409) Gilb, *Adestanefen* l12th RA v, *Astanfen* c1300 *Monson*, 1308 *MM*, probably 'Ēadstān's fen, marshland' from the OE pers.n. *Ēadstān* and OE **fenn**.

Austerby, The (Bourne, Kest), *Austrebi* 1167 P, *Oustreby* 1206 Ass, 1327 Ch, *Oustirby* 1354 *AddCh*, 'the more easterly farmstead (presumably in relation to **Bourne**)' from ON **austarr** and ODan **bȳ**.

Autby (North Thoresby, LNR), *Aduluesbi, Aldulvebi* 1086 DB, *Alwoldesbi* 1086 ib, *Alwoldebi* 1086 ib, *Aluoldebi* c1115 LS, *-b'* 1238–41 Fees, *Alwaldebi* 1196 ChancR, *Alewardebi* 1202 *HarlCh*. This is a very difficult name because of the number of variant spellings no doubt induced by the early ME tendency for middle syllables to be reduced. On balance, however, it may be suggested that the first el. is the OE pers.n. *Æthelwald* with the second ODan **bȳ** 'a farmstead, a village', a hybrid name. Spellings in *-es-* are very rare, the gen.sg. being represented by *-e-*, which seems to represent Scand. *-a-* < *-ar-*, suggesting that the name had been given by Scandinavians.

Authorpe (LSR), *Agetorp* 1086 DB, eHy2, 1187 Dane, *Haghetorp* c1115 LS, *Aggetorp* Hy2, l12th Dane, *Aghtorpa* a1219 Welles. **Authorpe** (Mumby, LSR), *Aghetorp* c1115 LS, *Aggetorp* e13th RA vi, *Agthorp* 1230–39, a1232 ib, *Aggethorp'* 1272 *Ass*, 1282 FF, now represented by **Authorpe Row**. Both these names mean 'Aghi's secondary settlement', derived from the ODan pers.n. *Aghi* and ODan **thorp**.

Aveland Wapentake (Kest), *Avelunt* 1086 DB, *-lund* 1167 P, 1199–1216 Abbr, *Auelun* 1130, 1162 P, *Auelund* 1163, 1176, 1181 ib, 'Afi's grove' from the OE pers.n. *Afi* and ON **lundr**. The forms are preceded or followed by some form of Latin *wapentacium*. The wapentake (ON **vápnatak**, late OE

wæpengetæc 'a subdivision of a shire') traditionally met at a moated enclosure called **The Aveland** about one mile west of Aslackby. The pers.n. *Afi* is also the first el. of the lost **Avethorpe** in Aslackby parish, presumably the same man giving his name both to the settlement and the district.

Axholme, Isle of (LWR), *Haxeholm* c1115 LS, 1200 CurR, *Axiholm* 1135–54 *HarlCh*, 1159, 1181 P, l12th *HarlCh*, 'the raised ground in marsh belonging to Haxey' from the village-name **Haxey** and ON **holmr**.

Aylesby (LNR), *Alesbi* 1086 DB, c1115 LS, 1130 P, 1185 Templar, -*by* 1221 Welles, 1225 Cur, probably 'Āli's farmstead, village' from the ODan pers.n. *Āli* and ODan **bȳ**. *Āli* is also the first el. of **Ailby** and **Althorpe** for which gen.sg. spellings in -*es*- are not found. In **Aylesby**, -*es*- presumably represents a secondary ME gen.sg. form.

B

Bain, R. (LSR), *Bayna* 1135–54 (p1269) *Bard*, *ueterem Beinam* 1140–50 Dane, Hy2 (p1259) *Kirkst*, *Beinam* 1150–60 Dane, *Beyne* 1147 (p1269) *Bard*, *Beine* eHy2 (1411) Gilb, lHy2 (m13th) *NCot*, *Baine* Hy2 Dane. This is a Scand. r.n. derived from the ON adj. **beinn** 'straight, direct; helpful', later 'convenient'. The **Bain** is certainly not straight, but a meaning 'helpful' might be considered.

Banthorpe (Braceborough, Kest), *Barnetorpi* (sic), *Barnetorp* 1086 DB, *Barutorp* (*-u-* = *-n-*) 1242–43 Fees, *Barnethorp'* 1287 *Ass*, 'Barni's secondary settlement (of **Braceborough**)' from the ON pers.n. *Barni* and ODan **thorp**. The name survives in **Banthorpe Lodge**.

Bardney (LSR), *on Bearddan igge* s.a. 716 (c900) ASC A, *on Beardanege* s.a. 716 (c1000) ib B, *monasterium nobile in prouincia Lindissi nomine Beardaneu* 731 Bede, *in thæm mynstre in Beardan ea* c890 (10th) OEBede, *of Beardan igge* s.a. 906 (c1050) ASC D, s.a. 909 (c1050) ASC C, *on tham mynstre the is genemnod Bardan ege* c1000 Saints, *Bardenai* 1086 DB, *-ey* 1100–14 (p1269) *Bard*, *Bardanai* c1115 LS, 'B(e)arda's island of land' from the OE pers.n. *B(e)arda* and OE **ēg**. Bede's form in *-eu* is typically Northumbrian. Cf. **Partney**.

Barholm (Barholm & Stowe), *Bercaham*, *Bercheham*, *Bercham* 1086 DB, *Bercham* c1128 (12th) ChronPetro, 1202 Ass, *Berham* 1138 NthCh, 1189 (1332) Ch, *Bergham* 1242–43 ib, *Barhome* 1494 Pat, 'the homestead, estate on the hill' from OE **beorg** and OE **hām**. The change of *-ham* to *-holm(e)* is common in L. The place is on a slight rise.

Barkston (Kest), *Barchestune*, *-tone* 1086 DB, *Barkestun* 1159 (l13th) *Stix*, *-ton'* 1174, 1188 P, 1185 Templar, 1195 P, 'Bark's farmstead, village' from the characteristically West Scandinavian pers.n. *Bǫrkr* and OE **tūn**. The vowel *-a-* in the above forms is from the Scand. gen.sg. *Barkar* > *Barka*. **Barkston** probably represents an earlier Anglo-Saxon settlement taken over and partially renamed by the Danes.

Barkwith, East & West (LSR), *Barcuurde*, *-uorde* 1086 DB, *-worda* c1115 LS, *-word* c1150 (1409) Gilb, *Barkewrth* eHy2 (m13th) *NCot*, *Barchewrda* 1155–60 Dane, *-worthe* Hy2 ib, *Barkwortha* l12th ib, *Est Barkeword* 1165 ib,

Westbarkeworth' 1202 Ass; **West Barkwith** is probably to be identified with *Parva Barcwrth'* 1224 Welles, *parva Barkeworth* 1291 Tax. The first el. is obscure; the second is OE **worth** 'an enclosure', which was changed to **with**, apparently in the 17th century, note *East -, West Barkwith* 1653 *ParlSurv.*

Barlings (LWR), *Berlinge* 1086 DB, *Berlinga* c1115 LS, *Berlinges* 1123, 1126 France, 1195 P, lHy2 Dane, *Barlinges* Hy2 (1291) Ch, *Barlinge* l12th Dane, 'the family, the dependents, the people of Bǣrla', from the OE pers.n. *Bǣrla* and the OE pl. suffix **-ingas** 'the family, the dependents, the people'. **Barlings** is in origin a group-name, denoting a body of people bound by kinship or lordship, *Bǣrla* being the name of the leader. It became a p.n. when the *Bǣrlingas* settled in what is today **Barlings**. An abbey was founded here at a place called *Oxeneye* Hy2 (Ed1) *Barl*, *Oxeneia* 1202 Ass, *insulam que dicitur Oxen'* l12th (Ed1) *Barl*, *Oxenay* 1202 Ass, from **oxa** (gen.pl. **oxna**) 'an ox' and OE **ēg** 'an island, etc.'.

Barnetby le Wold (LNR), *Bernodebi, Bernedebi* 1086 DB, *Bernetebi* 1086 ib, c1115 LS, c1160 Dane, 1191 P, *Bernetteby* 1190 (1301) Dugd vi. This is a difficult name but is probably 'Beornede's farmstead, village' from an unrecorded, but perfectly regular OE pers.n. **Beornede* and ODan **bȳ**. The affix **le Wold** is self-explanatory and has not been noted before *Barnetby le Wold* 1824 O.

Barnoldby le Beck (LNR), *Bernulfbi* 1086 DB, 1196 ChancR, *-by* 1230 Cl, *Bernoluebi* 1178 P, *Bernoleby* 1231 Ch, *Bernolbi* 1204 P, 'Bernulf's farmstead, village' from the pers.n. *Bernulf* (ON *Biǫrnúlfr* or OE *Beornwulf,* with the former more likely here) and ODan **bȳ**. The earliest reference to the **Beck** (ON **bekkr** 'a stream') is *Barnoldby upon Becke* 1662 *Terrier.*

Barrow upon Humber (LNR), *in loco qui dicitur Adbaruae* 731 Bede, *Bearuwe* 737–40 (11th) BCS 165 (S 599), *æt Bearuwe* 971 (12th) *PetLN*, 973 (15th) BCS 1297 (S 792), *in thære stowe the is nemned Æt Bearwe* c890 (10th) OEBede, *to Baruwe* 971 (12th) *PetLN, Beruwe in Lindesige* 973 (15th) BCS 1297 (S 792). It is *Barewe* "upon" *Humbre* 1371 Pat. 'At the grove', from the dat.sg. **b(e)arwe** of OE **b(e)aru** 'a grove', all the forms of the name retaining the -*w*- of the oblique case.

Barrowby (Kest), *Bergebi* 1086 DB, 1123–25 (1396) Dugd iii, 1135–54 (13th) ib, Hy2 (1316) Ch, 1199 P, *Bergheby* 1156–62 (1396) Ch, 'the farmstead, village on the hills' from ON **berg** and ODan **bȳ**.

Barton Street (LNR/LSR), *stratam de Barton'* e13th (p1259) *Kirk*, *Bartunestrete* c1240 *HarlCh*, *regia via que vocatur Barton Strete* 1375 Works, - *Gate* 1424 *AddCh*, - *streate* 1580 *Terrier*. This is a presumed pre-Roman track leading from Louth to Barton upon Humber. It is also called **Louth Street**, *Luthestret* c1150 (Ed1) *Newb*, c1150 Dane, l12th (Ed1) *Newb*, *Ludhestrete* 1199–1216 *HarlCh*, *regie strata versus Ludam* c1260 RA iv, *the high way or streete called Lowth streete* 1601 *Terrier*.

Barton upon Humber (LNR), *Bertune* 1086 DB, *-tuna* c1115 LS, *Bartuna* c1115 ib, eHy2, l12 Dane, *-ton'* 1115 (14th) *Bard*, - *iuxta Humbriam* l12 (1269) *ib*, 'the barley farm, the outlying grange' from OE **bær-tūn**, no doubt so-named in relation to **Barrow upon Humber**.

Bassingham (Kest), *Basingeham* 1086 DB, c1150 Dane, 1176, 1177, 1230 P, *Basingham* 1174–84 BS, l12th Dane, 'the homestead, the estate of the Basingas' from the gen.pl. *Basinga* of the OE group-name *Basingas* 'the family, the followers of Basa' and OE **hām**.

Bassingthorpe (Bitchfield, Kest), *Torp* 1086, c1135, 1143–47, 1172 all (l13th) *Stix*, *Torpe* a1160 RA vii, *Thorp'* c1221 Welles, *Bassuintorp* lHy2 (l13th) *Stix*, *Basewinttorp* 1201 Ass. This was originally a simplex p.n. 'the secondary settlement (of **Westby** or **Bitchfield**)' from ODan **thorp**. To this was prefixed the surn. *Basewin*, note *Rogerus basuin de torp* 1135–54 (l13th) *Stix*. *Basuin* occurs as the name of a man who held land at Creeton, Bitchfield and Westby in 1086. The name belongs to Continental Germanic *Baswin*.

Baston (Kest), *Bacstune, Bastune* 1086 DB, *-ton'* 1188, 1194, 1199 P, 1202 Ass, 'Bak's farmstead, village' from the ON byname *Bak* and OE **tūn**. This is an Anglo-Danish pers.n. hybrid and probably represents an earlier Anglo-Saxon settlement taken over and partially renamed by the Danes.

Baumber (LSR), *Badeburg* 1086 DB, *Baburc* c1115 LS, *Baunburg'* 1115 (14th) *Bard, Baenburg'* 1125 (p1269) *ib, -burc* 1158, 1193 P, *Baemburg'* c1145 (p1269) *Bard, Bamburg* 1147–56 (15th) *ib*, 1198 CurP, *Baumburgh* 1156 (p1269) *Bard*. The forms are varied and difficult, but it is likely that the first el. is the OE pers.n. *Badda*; the second el. is OE **burh** 'a fortified place'.

Baythorpe (Swineshead, Hol), *Barthorp* 1307 Pap, 1358 *FF*, (*de Swynesed'*) 1366 Cor, 1370 Ipm, *-thorpe de Swynesheued* 1375 Peace; the first el. is uncertain, the second being ODan **thorp** 'a secondary settlement'. It was the site of a chapel, certainly from the 14th to 16th centuries. The 1358 and

1375 references make it clear that **Baythorpe** was an outlying settlement of **Swineshead**.

Beasthorpe (Thornton le Moor, LNR), *Besthorp(')* 1318 *FF*, 1331 Ch, 1384 *FF*, *Beesthorp'* 1336 *ib*, probably a hybrid name from OE **bēos** 'bent grass' and ODan **thorp** 'a secondary settlement', presumably of **Thornton le Moor**. It lies in the carrs.

Beckering (Holton cum Beckering, LSR), *Bechelinge* 1086 DB, *Becheringa* c1115 LS, *-ing* Hy2 Dane, *Bekeringa* 1165 ib, 1190 P, l12th Dane, *-ing'* 1170, 1188 P, *-inge* Hy2 (1409) Gilb, c1190 Dane, 1199 FF, 1202 Cur. This is from OE **Beclingas* 'the family, the people of Bec(c)el', an **-ingas** formation from an OE pers.n. **Bec(c)el*, which itself corresponds to Old High German *Pecchilo* (sic) (from **Bakilo*). The change of *-l-* to *-r-* is paralleled in other p.ns. For this formation see **Healing**.

Beckingham (Kest), *Bekingham* c1145, 1156 (p1269) *Bard*, l12th Templar, l12th Dane, *Bekingeham* 1177, 1194 P, 1209 FF, 'the homestead, the estate of the Beccingas' from the gen.pl. *Beccinga* of the OE group-name *Beccingas* 'the family, the followers of *Becca*' and OE **hām**.

Beelsby (LNR), *Belesbi* 1086 DB, c1115 LS, 1130 P, 1200 Cur, *-by* 1202 Ass, *Belebi* 1198 Cur, 1202 Ass, perhaps 'Beli's farmstead, village' from the rare ON pers.n. *Beli* and ODan **bȳ**.

Beesby (Hawerby cum Beesby, LNR), *Basebi* (sic) 1086 DB, *Besebi* 1086 DB, 1180 P, Hy2 Dane, 1202 *HarlCh*, *Beisebi* 1161 P. **Beesby in the Marsh** (LSR), *Besebi*, *Bizebi* 1086 DB, *Beseby* c1155, 1182 (1409) Gilb, l12th Dane. Both are derived from the ON pers.n. *Besi* and ODan **bȳ** 'a farmstead, a village'. *Besi* is recorded independently in L in DB. The affix **in the Marsh** is self-explanatory.

Belchford (LSR), *Beldeforda* 1075 (a1331) *Spald i*, *Beldforda* c1155 Dane, *Beltesford* 1086 DB, *-forda* c1155 Dane, *-ford'* 1185 RotDom, *Beltisford* l11th, 1123–29 (c1331) *Spald i*, probably 'Belt's ford' from the OE pers.n. **Belt* (found also in **Beltisloe Wapentake**) and OE **ford**. The ford carries the Roman road, Margary 27.

Belleau (LSR), *Elgelo* 1086 DB, *Helgeloue* eHy2 Dane, 1202 Ass, *Helegelo* 1191 P, *Helgelo* l12th Dane, *-loe* e13th *HarlCh*, 'Helgi's meadow, glade' from the ON pers.n. *Helgi* and ON **ló**, the only p.n. in L derived from ON **ló**.

The change to Belleau has not been noted before *Bellowe* 1536 LNQ xv and the reason is not evident.

Belnie (Gosberton, Hol), *Graungie . . . voc' Bellnes* 1535–46 *MinAcct*, *Belnies* 1552 Sewer i, *Belnes* 1562 ib, no doubt named from the family of *Racelin de Belnes* Hy2 (1269) Ch, well-recorded in **Gosberton** from the 12th to 14th centuries.

Beltisloe Wapentake (Kest), *Belteslau, -lawe* 1086 DB, *-lawe* 1168, 1187 P, *-lawa* 1169, 1184 ib, *-law'* 1181 ib, 'Belt's mound, hill' from the OE pers.n. *Belt* and OE **hlāw**, a rare el. in L. The same pers.n. occurs also in **Belchford**. The early forms are preceded or followed by some form of Latin *wapentacium*. The site of the meeting-place of the Wapentake (ON **vápnatak**, late OE **wæpengetac** 'a subdivision of a shire') is unknown.

Beltoft (Belton, LWR), *Beltot* (sic) 1086 DB, 1179 P, *-toft* c1184 (15th) Templar, c1200 Dane, 1202 Ass; for the first el. see **Belton**, the second el. being ODan **toft** 'a curtilage, a messuage'.

Belton (Belton & Manthorpe, Kest), *Beltone* 1086 DB, l12th Semp, *-tuna* 1146 RA i, *-tona* 1163 ib, *-ton'* 1185 Templar. **Belton** (LWR), *Beltone* 1086 DB, *-tona* m12th Dugd vi, m12th (13th) *Nostell*, l12th *AD*, *-ton'* e13th *AddCh*. Both are probably from OE **bel* 'a piece of dry ground in fen' and OE **tūn** 'a farmstead, a village'.

Belwood (Belton, LWR), *Belwod'* c1184 (15th) Templar, *-wud* l12th *AD*, *-wod* 1275 RH, *Belewod* 1284 Pat; for the first el. see **Belton**, the second being OE **wudu** 'a wood'.

Benington (Hol), *Benington* 1166, 1180 P, 1206 Ass, *Beninton'* 1181 ChancR, 1206 Ass, *Benigton'* 1181 P, *Benitun* lHy2 Dane. **Bennington, Long** (Kest), *Beninctun, -ingtone* 1086 DB, *-ington* 1150–53 France, 1180 P, 1196 ChancR, *Bennington* c1163, 1174 France, *Longebeniton* 1274 Cl. Both mean 'the farmstead, village associated with or called after Be(o)nna' from the OE pers.n. *Be(o)nna*, with the OE connective particle **-ing-** and OE **tūn**. The affix in the second denotes a long straggling village. For the same pers.n. cf. **Benniworth**.

Benniworth (LSR), *Beningurde* 1086 DB, *Beningeorde* c1135 Dane, *-wurtha* 1171, 1185 P, *-worth'* 1200 Cur, *Benigworda* c1115 LS, *-wrda* 1163 Dane, *-worth* 1189–99 *HarlCh*, 'the enclosure of the Be(o)nningas' from

Be(o)nninga, the gen.pl. of the OE group-name *Be(o)nningas* 'the family, the dependents of *Be(o)nna*' and OE **worth**. For the same pers.n., cf. **Benington**.

Bicker (Hol), *Bichere* 1086 DB, 1212 Cur, *Bicra* c1180 (13th) *Castelacre*, *Bicre* 1200 Cur, *Bikere* 1176 P, *Biker*' 1202 FF. Identical with Bicker is probably a field-name in **Stallingborough** (LNR), recorded as *Biker* eHy3 (13th-14th) Selby, 1352 AASR xxiii surviving as *Bicar* 1842 *TA*. **Bicker** is probably an elliptical name from the OE preposition **bī** 'by, beside' and ON **kjarr** 'a marsh', hence '(the place) near or by the marsh'.

Bigby (LNR), *Bechebi* 1086 DB, c1115 LS, *Bekebi* 1191 P, 1212 Fees, *-by* 1219 ib, *Bigby* 1526 Sub, probably 'Bekki's farmstead, village' from the ON pers.n. *Bekki* and ODan **bȳ**. The 16th century development of *-k-* to *-g-* is paralleled in other p.ns.

Billingborough (Kest), *Bolinburg* (sic), *Bellingeburg* 1086 DB, *Bilinge-*, *Billingeburg* 1086 ib, 1185 P, *-burc* 1167 ib, 1200 Cur, *Billincheburc* c1180 *AddCh*, *Billingburc* 1150–60 Semp, 'the fortified place of the Billingas' from the gen.pl. *Billinga* of the OE group-name *Billingas* 'the family, the followers of *Billa*' and OE **burh**. The same group probably gave its name also to **Horbling** and to **Billinghay**.

Billinghay (Kest), *Belingei* 1086 DB, *Belyngeia* 12th (1407) Dugd vi, *Bilingeia* eHy2 Dane, *Billingeie* Hy2 ib, 1200 FF, *Billingeeia* 1186 P, *Billingeia* 1188 ib, *Bilingheia* 1185 Templar, probably 'the island of land of the Billingas (the people of, the followers of Bill(a))' from the gen.pl. *Billinga* of the OE group-name *Billingas* and OE **ēg**.

Bilsby (LSR), *Billesbi* 1086 DB, 1193 FF, e13th RA vi, *Bilesbi* 1150–60 Dane, lHy2 RA vi, l12th Dane, probably 'Billi's farmstead, village' from the ON pers.n. *Billi* and ODan **bȳ**.

Binbrook (LNR), *Binnibroc* 1086 DB, c1115 LS, *Binibroch*' 1179 P, *Bynibroke* Hy3 (1409) Gilb, *Biningbroc* 1237 (13th) *LOC*, *Binne broke* 1088–93 (14th) YCh i, *Binnebroke* 1156–57 (Ed2) ib, *Bynnebroc* 1099 RA i, *Binebroc*' c1189 LAAS v, 'Bynna's brook' from the OE pers.n. *Bynna* and **brōc**. The early forms *Binnibroc* etc., together with the later *Biningbroc*, suggest that there was a variant form to OE **Bynnanbrōc* with OE medial **-ing-**, hence **Bynningbrōc*, meaning 'the brook associated with or named after Bynna'.

Birkwood Hall (Mareham le Fen, LSR), *Birchewda* (sic) Hy2 RPD, *-wud'* John ib, *Birkewude* 1210 FF, *-wde* 1225 (p1259) *Kirkst*, 'the wood where birch trees grow' from OE **birce** and OE **wudu**. OE **birce** has been replaced by the cognate ON **birki**.

Birthorpe (Billingborough, Kest), *Berchetorp* 1086 DB, *Birchetorp* Hy2, c1180 *AddCh*, *Birkethorp* 1189 (1341) Semp, 1195–1200 RA ii, l12th Semp, 'the secondary settlement where birch-trees grow' from ON **birki** and ODan **thorp**. Alternatively, the first el. may be OE **birce** 'a birch-tree', replaced later by ON **birki**. Presumably it was dependent on **Billingborough**.

Biscathorpe (LSR), *Biscopetorp* 1086 DB, c1115 LS, *Biscopatorp* 1150–60 Dane, *Biscoptorp* 1162 ib, Hy2 (13th) *Kirkst*, *Bisshopesthorp* 1195 (1335) Ch, 'the bishop's secondary settlement' from ON **biskup** and ODan **thorp**. The manor was held by the Bishop of Durham in 1086.

Bishopbridge (Glentham, LWR), *Biscopbrigg* Hy3 (1291) Ch, "Bishop's Bridge" 1290, 1312 Pat, *Bishoppbrigg* 1331 ib, self-explanatory from OE **biscop** and OE **brycg**; in the early forms **brycg** has been Scandinavianised. Presumably the reference is to the Bishop of Lincoln.

Bitchfield (Bitchfield & Bassingthorpe, Kest), *Billefelt* 1086 DB, *Billesfelt* 1086 ib, *-feld* a1160 RA vii, 1172 Dane, l12th *AD*, l12th Semp, 'Bill's open country' from the OE pers.n. *Bill* and OE **feld**. The development to **Bitch-** is late, note *Bychefeld* 1554 Pat.

Blankney (Kest), *Blachene* (sic) 1086 DB, *Blanchenia* 1140 (p1259) *Kirkst*, *-eye* l12th (1409) Gilb, *Blankenai* 1135–54 (p1259) *Kirkst*, *Blankeney* Hy2 (1409) Gilb, *Blanckenneia* 1185 Templar. 'Blanca's island of land' from the OE pers.n. **Blanca* and OE **ēg**.

Bleasby (Legsby, LSR), *Blasebi* (sic), *Blesebi* 1086 DB, c1115 LS, lHy2 Dane, 1195 P, l12th RA v, *-by* c1150 Hy2 (1409) Gilb, 'Blesi's farmstead, village', from the ON byname *Blesi* and ODan **bȳ**.

Bloxholm (Ashby de la Launde, Kest), *Blochesham* 1086 DB, 1175 (1337), Hy2 (1316) Ch, *Bloxeham* 1130 P, *Blocchesham* 1185 RotDom, 'Blocc's homestead, estate' from the OE pers.n. *Blocc* and OE **hām**. The replacement of **hām** by ON **holmr** first appears in *Bloxholm'* 1281 QW, and is the result of weakening of the final syllable.

Blyborough (LWR), *Bliburg* 1086 DB, 1181 (l13th) Bly, *-burc* c1115 LS, 1148 (l13th) Bly, *Blieburc* 1181 P, *Blitheburc'* l12th *DuDCCh, -burgh'* 1286 *FF, Blithbury* 1203 Abbr. On topographical grounds it is unlikely that the first el. is the OE r.n. *Blīthe*; perhaps it is an unrecorded OE nickname **Blītha*, cf. the early forms for **Blyton**. The second el. is OE **burh** 'a fortified place'. Most of the forms show loss of medial *-th-* due to Anglo-Norman influence.

Blyton (LWR), *Blitone* 1086 DB, *-tuna* c1115 LS, *-tun'* Hy2 BS, *-tona* 1139 RA i, *-ton'* 1185 Templar, *Blittone* 1086 DB, *-ton'* 1211 P; the first el. is uncertain, but may be an unrecorded OE nickname **Blītha*, as in **Blyborough**; the second is OE **tūn** 'a farmstead, a village'.

Bolingbroke (LSR), *Bolincbrok'* 1075 (c1331) *Spald i, Bolinbroc* 1086 DB, c1135 Dane, *Bolingbrok'* l11th (c1331) *Spald i, Bulingbroch* 1142–53 Dane, 1148–51 RA vi, c1193 Dane, *Bulinbroc* 1151–53 ib, 1185 Templar, 'the brook associated with or called after Bula' from the OE pers.n. *Bula* and OE **brōc**, with the OE connective particle **-ing-** and OE **tūn**.

Bolingbroke Wapentake (LSR), *Bolinbroc* 1086 DB, c1115 LS, *Bolingbroc, Bulincbroc* 1123–47 RA i, *Bulinbroc* 1140–47 ib, *Bulingbroc* 1158 P. The early forms are usually preceded or followed by some form of Latin *wapentacium*. The wapentake (ON **vápnatak**, late OE **wæpengetæc** 'a subdivision of a shire') is named from **Bolingbroke** presumably the site of its meeting-place.

Bonby (LNY), *Bundebi* 1086 DB, 1212 Fees, *Bondebi* c1115 LS, l12th Dane, *-by* 1200 CartAnt, 1208 FF. This is either 'Bōndi's farmstead, village' from the ODan pers.n. *Bondi, Bundi* and ODan **bȳ** or from the appellative **bondi, bunde** 'a peasant proprietor', the source of the pers.n., and **bȳ**. No certainty is possible since both compounds would have given the same early forms.

Bonthorpe (Willoughby with Sloothby, LSR), *Brunetorp* 1086 DB, *Bruntorp* l12th Dane, 1212, 1242–43 Fees, 1251 Ch, *Burnetorp* (sic) c1115 LS, 'Brúni's secondary settlement (presumably of **Willoughby**)', from the ON pers.n. *Brúni* and ODan **thorp**. The loss of *-r-* does not take place till the late 15th century.

Boothby (Welton le Marsh, LSR), *Bodebi* 1086 DB, *Bothebi* 1170, 1171 P, 1212 Fees, *Boebi* c1115 LS, 1212 Fees. **Boothby Graffoe** (Kest), *Bodebi* 1086 DB, 1135–54, 1162 (p1259) *Kirkst, -beia* 1094 France, *Bothebi* 1202 Ass, *Bobi* 1202 ib. **Boothby Pagnell** (Kest), *Bodebi* 1086 DB, *-by* 1150–60 (1409) Gilb,

Boebi 1138 NthCh, 1147–66 (1409) Gilb, 1185 Templar, *Botheby* Hy2 (l13th) *Stix*. Each means literally 'the farmstead, village of the booths', from the gen.pl. of ODan **bōth** and ODan **bȳ**. The loss of medial *-th-* is due to Norman influence. The first survives as **Boothby Hall**. The affix in **Boothby Graffoe** is the name of the wapentake in which **Boothby** is situated. **Boothby Pagnell** was held by the *Paynel* family, note John *Paynel* 1346 FA.

Boothby Graffoe Wapentake (Kest), originally two separate wapentakes. **Boothby Wapentake**, *Bobi* 1168, 1169, 1178, 1200 P, 1212 Fees, *Boby* 1219 ib, *Botheby* 1284–85 FA. Forms with loss of medial *-th-* are due to Norman influence. All spellings are preceded or followed by some form of Latin *wapentacium*. The wapentake (ON **vápnatak**, late OE **wæpengetæc** 'a subdivision of a shire') presumably met at **Boothby Graffoe** from which it was named. **Boothby Wapentake** was later joined with **Graffoe Wapentake** to become **Boothby Graffoe Wapentake**. **Graffoe Wapentake** is *Grafho* 1166, 1177, 1185, 1200 P, *-hou* 1167 ChancR, *-how'* 1202 Ass. The spellings are preceded or followed by some form of Latin *wapentacium*. **Graffoe** probably means 'the grove on a heel, a spur of land' from OE **grāf** and OE **hōh**, the site of which is unknown.

Boston (Hol), *Botelvestan* (with *-ol-* read as *-el-*) p1114 Dugd iv, *Botuluestan* 1130 P, *Botoluestan* m12th (l14th) *Ped*, *Botulfstan* 1281 QW, *Botelstane* 1323 Cl, from the OE pers.n. *Bōtwulf* (probably St Botulf) and OE **stān** 'a stone'. The vast majority of medieval forms for Boston are of the type *villa Sancti Botulfi* 1093–1136 RA vii, where clearly the name has been associated with the Saint and the second el. erroneously with OE **tūn** 'a farmstead, a village'. **Boston** has been identified with *Icanho* s.a. 654 (c1121) ASC (E), where St Botulf founded a monastery, but this is **Iken** in Suffolk.

Bottesford (LWR), *Budlesforde*, *Bulesforde* (sic) 1086 DB, *Botlesforda* c1115 LS, *-ford'* 1196 ChancR, 1202 Ass, *Botelesforde* c1128 (12th) ChronPetro, *-ford'* 1220 Cur, *Botenesford'* 1189 (e14th) Selby, 'the ford by the house' from OE **bōtl** and OE **ford**.

Boughton (Asgarby, Kest), *Backeton'* 1185 Templar, 1202 Ass, *Bakton'* 1324 *Extent*, *Baghton* 1348–49 *Queen's*, 1375 Peace. The early forms suggest that this is 'Bacca's farmstead, village' from the OE pers.n. *Bacca* and OE **tūn**. The later development of the name to **Boughton** does not seem to have parallels elsewhere.

Boultham (Kest), *Buletham* 1086 DB, 1147 (p1269) *Bard*, 12th RA ii, *Bultham* 1178 (p1269) *Bard*, *Bulteham* 1201 Ass. The only suggestion which can be made is 'the homestead, estate where ragged robin grows', from OE **bulut** and OE **hām**.

Bourne (Kest), *Brune* 1086 DB, 1147–66 (1409) Gilb, *Bruna* p1176 NthCh, *Brunna* 1138 ib, c1150 *Anc*, c1160 RA ii, 1167 P, lHy2 *Anc*, *Brunne* 1139–54 Dane, 1166 RBE, 1180 P, *Brunum* 1150–60 (1409) Gilb, 1201 (1343) Ch, probably from the dat.pl. **brunnum** of ON **brunnr** 'a spring, a stream'. There is a "copious spring to the south-east of the church . . . now known as St. Peter's Pool . . . the supply of water being so large as to . . . form a stream . . . called the Bourne Eau", see AASR xx, p.2 and **Bourne Eau**.

Bourne Eau (Kest), *aqua que uocatur Brunne* 1240 (c1331) *Spald ii, ripam que uocatur Brunnee* lHy3 (c1331) *ib*, *Brunne Ee* 1295 *Ass*, *Brune Hee* 1329 (p1336) *HC*, *le Brunne Hee* 1349 Works, *Brunehee* 1365 ib, named from **Bourne** and OE **ēa** 'a river, a stream'.

Braceborough (Braceborough & Wilsthorpe, Kest), *Braseborg, Breseburg' -burc* 1086 DB, *Bresseburc* 1180 P, *-burg'* 1189 Dugd v, 1202 FF, *Bresenburc* 1191 P, *Brasingeburc* 1195 (m14th) *PetML*, *Bressingburg'* 1212 Fees, *Brassingburg'* 1221 Welles; the first el. is obscure, the second is OE **burh** 'a fortified place'.

Bracebridge (Kest), *Brachebrige* 1086 DB, *Bracebrig(e)* 1147 (p1269) *Bard*, 1156–62 RA i, 1185 Templar, *Brascebricg'* Hy2 (1406) Pat. The first el. is uncertain; the second is OE **brycg** 'a bridge'.

Braceby (Braceby & Sapperton, Kest), *Breizbi, Brezbi* 1086 DB, *Brescebi* 1174, 1186 P, 1202 Ass, *Breicebi* 1216 Cur, 'Breith's farmstead, village' from the ON pers.n. *Breithr* and ODan **bȳ**. The gen.sg., pronounced [s] in all spellings, is Scand. in contrast to English [z], indicating that the name had been given by Danes.

Bracken (Woodhall, LSR), *Brakene* Hy2 (13th) *Stix*, 1202 FF, 1252 Ch, *Braken* 1196–98 Dane, 1202 FF, 'the place where bracken grows' from ON **brakni**. The name survives in **Bracken Wood**; it was a wood belonging to the Abbot of Kirkstead in 1259. Cf. **Bracon**.

Brackenborough (LNR), *Brachenberg* 1086 DB, *Brakenberga* 1150–60 Dane, *-berge* 1202 Ass, *Brackenberg* 112 Dane, *-borough* 1495 Pat, 'the bracken-covered hill', a Scand. compound from ON **brakni** and ON **berg** 'a hill'. Subsequent confusion with OE **burh** 'a fortified place' has taken place, hence the present-day spelling.

Bracon (Belton, LWR), *Brakene* 1179 P, 1546 WillsStow, from ON **brakni** 'bracken, fern', denoting a place where bracken grows, cf. **Bracken**.

Bradley (LNR), *Bredelou* (sic) 1086 DB, *-lai* c1115 LS, *-lay* 1177 P, *-le* a1183 Dane, *-leya* 1201 ChR, *Braidelai* l12 RA ix, *Bradleie* 1196 Cur, from OE **brād** 'broad, wide' and **lēah** 'a wood, a clearing in a wood'; the form in *Braide-* is due to Scand. influence. A fairly extensive wood still survives in the parish.

Bradley Wapentake (LNR), *Bradelai* 1086 DB, 1177 P, *-le* 1191 ib, 1197 ChancR, *Bradle* lHy3 *NCot*, *Bradeleye* 1287 Ipm. The forms are preceded or followed by some form of Latin *wapentacium*. The wapentake (ON **vápnatak**, late OE **wæpengetæc**, 'a sub-division of a shire') takes its name from **Bradley**, where presumably the meeting-place was situated. It was subsequently joined with **Haverstoe** to become known as **Bradley Haverstoe Wapentake**, note *Bradley Haverstow* 1653 *ParlSurv*.

Brampton (LWR), *Branthon* 1054–57 (12th) Eyns, *-tune* 1075–92 (12th) ib, 1086 DB, *-tonam* 1091 (12th) Eyns, *-tona* 1155–58 (1329) Ch, *Bramton'* 1206 Cur, 'the farmstead, village where broom grows' from OE **brōm** and OE **tūn**. The universal spellings in *Bram-* are due to the early shortening of *-ō-* and since many dialects had only short *-a-* before a nasal consonant *brom* became *bram*.

Brandon (Hough on the Hill, Kest), *Brandune* 1086 DB, *-done* 1166 RBE, *-don'* 1188, 1190 P, 1199 CurR, perhaps 'the hill overlooking the R. Brant' from the r.n. and OE **dūn**.

Bransby (Sturton by Stow, LWR), *Branzbi* 1086 DB, c1115 LS, *Brancebi* 1163 RA i, 1204–5 ib iv, *Branzceb'* 1212 Fees, 'Brand's farmstead, village' from the ON pers.n. *Brandr* and ODan **bȳ**; for the same pers.n. see **Branston**.

Branston (Branston & Mere, Kest), *Branztun(e)* 1086 DB, 1169 (13th) *Kirkst*, *Branceton* 1185 Templar, 1208 FF, *Brandeston* 1234, 1292 ib, 'Brand's farmstead, village' a hybrid p.n. from the ON pers.n. *Brandr* and OE **tūn**, probably an Anglo-Saxon settlement taken over and partially renamed by

the Danes. The original Scand. gen.sg. -s survives in the present-day
pronunciation. For the same pers.n. see **Bransby**.

Brant, R. (Kest), *Brante* Hy3 (1301), 1295 Ipm, *Brant* lHy3 (14th) *Barl*, 1288
Ipm, c1296 *Welbourne*, probably from OE **brant** 'high, steep' probably also
'deep', which would be appropriate for the **R. Brant** in winter.

Bratoft (LSR), *Bretoft, Breietoft* 1086 DB, *Breitoft* c1115 LS, 1200 FF,
Braitoft 1156 (p1269) *Bard*, 1166 RBE, *Braidtoft* 1178 (p1269) *Bard*, 'the
broad, spacious curtilage or messuage' from ON **breithr** and ODan **toft**,
with an early loss of medial *-th-*.

Brattleby (LWR), *Brotulbi* 1086 DB, *Brotulebi* c1115 LS, *Brotelbi* lHy2
Dane, *Brotlebi* l12th ib, *-by* 1202 Ass, 'Brot-Ulf's farmstead, village' from the
unrecorded ON pers.n. **Brot-Ulfr* and ODan **bȳ**.

Brauncewell (Kest), *Branzewelle* 1086 DB, *Brauncewell* 1150–60 Semp, *-wella*
Hy2 (1407) Gilb, *Brancewelle* 1166 RBE, 1185 Templar. Probably a hybrid
p.n. 'Brand's spring' from the ON pers.n. *Brandr* and OE **wella**. Forms in
-au- are due to Norman influence. The original Scand. gen.sg. -s- survives in
the modern pronunciation as [s], indicating that the name had been given
by Danes.

Brayford (Lincoln), *Braidemere* 1228–31 RA x, *Bradeford'* 1267–73 (l14th)
Gox, Braydeford' a1189 (14th) *Welb*. The earliest reference means 'the broad
pool' from ON **breithr** 'broad' and OE **mere** 'a pool'; the subsequent ones
are from OE **brād** 'broad', and **ford** 'a ford', **brād** being replaced by ON
breithr.

Brewer, Temple (Kest), *de Brueria* 1163 Dane, 1187 P, *In templo Bruerie*
1185 Templar, *la Bruiera* 1201 Cur, *Bruer'* 1201 ib, 'the heath, heathland'
from OFr **bruiere**. It is **Temple** from the Preceptory of the Knight
Templars founded here at the beginning of the reign of Henry II.

Bridge End (Horbling, Kest). The bridge itself is first recorded as *de Ponti
Aslaci videlicet Hoilondbrige* 1199 ChR, - *uidelicet Hoilandebrig'* 1199
CartAnt, *Pons Aslaci* "or" *Hoylandebrig* 1227 Ch, *Pons Aslaci* 1331 Pat,
'Áslák' bridge' from the ON pers.n. *Áslákr* and OE **brycg**; then, *Pontis
Hoylandie* (gen.) 1255 Pat, *Holand Brigge* 1335 ib, and alternative forms
above, with references to the 18th century, 'the bridge leading to Holland'
from **Holland** and OE **brycg**. References to **Bridge End** have been noted

from *attebrighend* 1327 *Barl*, *Brigende* 1328 Banco, *Briggesende* 1396 Cl from OE **brycg** and OE **ende**, many referring to the Priory of St Saviour there, sometimes *Villa Sancti Salvatoris* as in 1305 Pat; from the 16th century it is further called *Brygdyke Ende* 1515 LP ii, compare *Brigdyk* 1388 Pat, *Brigdyke* 1389 Cl and *pro reparaciona ponti de Brygdyk* 1411 RRep, from OE **brycg** and ON **dík**. In each case OE **brycg** is in a Scandinavianised form. **Bridge End Causeway** is referred to as "the bridge and causey of" *Hoiland* 1301 Pat, *pontem calceti holand* 1313 *Spald ii*, *calcetum de Holandbrigg* 1333 Dugd vi.

Brigg (LNR), see **Glanford Brigg**.

Brigsley (LNR), *Brigeslai* 1086 DB, *-lea* 1196 ChancR, *Brigesla*, *Brighesla* c1115 LS, *Briggesle* 1202 FF, *Brigelai* 1086 DB, *Brighelai* c1115 LS; forms in *-e-* and *-es-* occur side by side representing spellings without and with the gen.sg., suggesting that **Brigsley** means 'the wood, the glade of the bridge' side by side with 'the wood, the glade by the bridge' from OE **brycg** and **lēah**. The form has been Scandinavianised through the influence of ON **bryggja**.

Brocklesby (LNR), *Brochelesbi* 1086 DB, *Broclesbi* c1115 LS, *Broclousebi* 1143–47, a1150 Dane, *Broclousbi*, *Broclausbi* c1150 ib, 'Bróklauss' farmstead, village' from the ON pers.n. *Bróklauss* and ODan **bý**. The first el. is a nickname meaning 'breechless', recorded independently in DB in Middle Rasen.

Brotherhouse Bar (Crowland, Hol), *Brotherhus* 1278 *FF*, 1308 Ch, *le brotherhous* 1278 (c1331) *Spald ii*, *Brotherhouses in Croilaund* 1329 *Ass*, the house of the brothers of Crowland Abbey from OE **brōthor** and OE **hūs**.

Brothertoft (Hol), *Brothertoft* 1531 Wills iii, *Brodertoft* 1535 VE iv, *Brotherthofte* 1538 *AOMB*. The forms are late but this may be derived from the ODan pers.n. *Brōthir* and ON **toft** 'a messuage, a curtilage'.

Broughton (LWR), *Bertone* 1086 DB, 1100–8 France, *-tona* 1090–1100 (1402) YCh vi, *-tuna* c1115 LS, *Berchtun* c1128 (12th) ChronPetro, 1185 Templar, *Berton'* 1185 RotDom, *Bergtun* 1212 Fees, 'the farmstead, village on the hill' from OE **beorg** and OE **tūn**.

Broughton, Brant (Brant Broughton & Sragglethorpe, Kest), *Burtune* 1086 DB, *Bructun* 1185 Templar, *-ton'* 1193 P, *Brocton'* 1207 Cur, *-tone* 1210–12

RBE, *Bruchton* 1225 Pat, *Brent Broughton* 1245 Ipm, *Brendebrocton* 1250 FF, 'the farmstead, village by or belonging to a fortified place' from OE **burh** and OE **tūn**. OE *Burh-* became *Bruh-* by metathesis of the *-r-*. The affix **Brant** is the ME past participle **brende** 'burnt'; the village must have been burnt down perhaps in the early 13th century. The modern form **Brant** has no doubt been influenced by that of the **R. Brant** on which **Broughton** stands, but which has a different etymology.

Broxholme (LWR), *Broxholme* 1086 DB, c1115 LS, *Brocsholm* 1210 RA ix, *Brokesholme* 1219 Welles, *-holm* 1248 FF, from the gen.sg. of ODan **brōk** 'a marsh' and ON **holmr** 'raised land amidst marsh' which would be topographically appropriate here. The gen.sg. pronounced [s] is Scand. in contrast to English [z], indicating that the name had been given by Danes.

Brumby (LWR), *Brunebi* 1086 DB, a1175 Goke, 1196 ChancR, *Brunneby* 1271 Ch, 1272 FF, 'Brúni's farmstead, village' from the ON pers.n. *Brúni* and ODan **bȳ**.

Buckland (Woodhall, LSR), *Bochelanda* c1115 LS, *Boclande* 1154 *HarlCh*, *-land'* Hy2 (l13th) *Stix*, 1196 ChancR, 1198 P, 'land granted by charter' from OE **bōcland**. This was land in which certain rights and privileges were granted by charter, free from certain services, freehold land. This is the most northerly example of a name which is common in the south of the country. **Bōcland** contrasts with OE **folcland** 'folk-land', land held according to folk-right and denoted land from which the king drew food-rents and customary services.

Bucknall (LSR), *Buchehale* 1086 DB, *-hal'* 1166, 1167 P, *Bukenhale* m12th (l13th) *Stix*, 1194 Abbr, *Buchenhal'* 1194 CurR, 'Bucca's nook of land' from the OE pers.n. *Bucca* and OE **halh** (dat.sg. **hale**). The old village is situated on a slight eminence above the flatlands down to the **R. Witham**.

Bulby (Irnham, Kest), *Bolebi* 1086 Db, c1170 Semp, 1176, 1190 P, *-by* 1150–60 Semp, 1200 FF, 'Boli's farmstead, village' from the ON byname *Boli* and ODan **bȳ**. This pers.n. is recorded in DB in L.

Bullington (LSR), *Bolintone* 1086 DB, lHy2 Dane, *-tona* Hy2, l12th ib, *Bulingtuna* c1115 LS, 1150–60 Dane, *-tun* eHy2 ib, *-ton'* 1195 CartAnt, *Bulintone* 1142–51, 1191 Dane, 'the farmstead, village associated with or called after Bula' from the OE pers.n. *Bula* and OE **tūn** with the OE medial connective particle **-ing-**. The same pers.n. occurs in **Bolingbroke**. A Priory was founded here at a place called *Lindelai* c1155 Dane, *-leya* eHy2 (1409) Gilb, 'the lime-tree wood' from OE **lind** and OE **lēah**.

Burgh le Marsh (LSR), *Burch* 1086 DB, l12th Dane, *Burg* 1086 DB, l12th Dane, *Burc* c1115 LS, 1175–81 Dane, *Burgh* Hy2 (1411) Gilb. It is *de Burgo in Marisco* (i.e. 'in the marsh') 1275 RRGr to distinguish it from **Burgh on Bain** (LSR), *Burg* 1086 DB, c1150 (e13th) *NCot*, *Burc* c1115 LS, 1153–54, eHy2 (e13th) *NCot*, *in Burgo* 1121–23, 1154–62 RA i, and is *in Burg super baine* Hy2 (e13th) *NCot*, from the R. Bain. Both are derived from OE **burh** 'a fortified place'.

Burnham (Thornton Curtis, LNR), *Brune* 1086 DB, *Brunne* 1190 (1301) Dugd vi, *Brunum* c1115 LS, *Brunnum* 1268 FF, 1303 Ch, *Burneham* 1382 *AddR*, from **brunnum**, the dat.pl. of ON **brunnr** 'a well, a spring, a stream', hence 'at the springs', which is topographically appropriate. For similar dat.pl. formations, cf. **Coatham** and **Newsham**, where a comparable later development of *-um* to *-ham* has taken place. Probably identical is **Burnham, High & Low** (Haxey, LWR), *Brune* 1086 DB, *Brunneham* c1184 (15th) Templar, *Brunham* 1179 P, l12th *AD*, *Ouerbrunham* 1295 *ib*, *Nedrebrunham* m13th ib, the DB spelling suggesting that this is also from **brunnum**. If so the *-um* developed early to *-ham*.

Burringham (LWR), *Burengham* 1196 ChancR, *Burringham* 1199 P, 1272 *Ass*, *Buringeham* 1218 Ass, *Burringeham'* 1223 RA ii, *Burningham* 1214 Cur. It has been suggested that this is perhaps 'the homestead, estate of the Burgrēdingas or the Burgrīcingas' from the gen.pl. *Burgrēdinga* or *Burgrīcinga* of OE *Burgrēdingas* or *Burgrīcingas*, a group-name meaning 'the family, the dependents of Burgrēd or Burgrīc' and OE **hām**.

Burtoft (Wigtoft, Hol), *Burtoft* 1086 DB, 1199 P, 1204 Cur, *-tofth* (sic) Hy2 (1316) Ch, 'the messuage, the curtilage near or belonging to a **burh** ('a fortified place')'. The second el. is ODan **toft**.

Burton (by Lincoln) (LWR), *Burton* 1086 DB, 1115 (p1269) *Bard*, 1160–70 RA iv, *-ton' iuxta Lincoln'* 1215 ib, *-tone* 1086 DB, *-tona* c1115 LS, p1125 (p1269) *Bard*, *-tuna* c1115 LS. **Burton, Gate** (LWR), *Bortone* 1086, *-ton* 1196 FF, *Burtuna* c1115 LS, *-tun (super Trentam)* 1163 RA i, *-tona* l12th RA iv, *Gaiteburton* 1199 (1330) Ch. **Burton Perwardine** (Kest), *Burtun* 1086 DB, 1185 Templar, 1212 Fees, *-ton* 1086 DB, 1170 P, *-tona* c1114 Dugd iv. **Burton upon Stather** (LWR), *Burtone* 1086 DB, *Bertona* 1100–8 France, *Burton'* 1199 P, 1202 Ass, *Burtonestathel* (sic) 1201 ib, *-statheher* (sic) 1208 FF,

-stathir' 1271 RRGr. All three mean 'the farmstead, village by the fortified place', from OE **burh** and OE **tūn**. The second must have been noted for the rearing of goats, the affix *Gate* being from ON **geit** 'a goat'. **Stather** is from ON **stǫthvar** the pl. of **stǫth** 'a landing place, a jetty'. **Pedwardine** is from the family of that name; Walter *Pudewardyn* held the manor in 1276 Ipm.

Burton Coggles (Kest), *Bertune, -tone* 1086 Db, *-ton'* 1184 P, *Byrtune* 1164 (l13th) *Stix, -ton(e)* 1291 Tax, *Birton'* 1210 Cur, 1254 ValNor, *Burton* 1185 Templar, *Burton in le Coggles* 1583 Admin, 'the farmstead, village by or belonging to a fortified place' from **byrh** the gen.sg. of OE **burh** and OE **tūn**. The affix **Coggles** is from ME **cogel** 'a round stone, a cobblestone'; presumably **Burton** was a place where cobble stones were obtained.

Burwell (LSR), *Buruelle* 1086 DB, *-welle* 1100–35 France, *Burewelle* 1110, c1150 ib, *-wella* c1115 LS, 1176 P, *-well'* 1184 ib, 'the spring by the fortified place' from OE **burh** and OE **wella**.

Buslingthorpe (LWR), *Esetorp* 1086 DB, *Esatorp* c1115 LS, *Buslingathorpa* Hy2 (1409) Gilb, *Buselingthorp* Hy2 (1291) Ch, c1200 RA iv. The DB and LS forms are probably from the ODan pers.n. *Æsi* and ODan **thorp** 'a secondary settlement'. The first el. was changed to the OFr pers.n. *Buselin*, that of the tenant c1115 LS.

Butterwick (Hol), *Butruic* 1086 DB, *Butrewich* eHy2 Dane, *Buttirwic* 1150–60 (1409) Gilb, *Buterewic* 1181 P, *Boterwic* 1194 CurR, *Buterwic* 1198 FF. **Butterwick, East** (LWR), *Butrewic* 1086 DB, Hy2 (1409) Gilb, 1208 ChancR, *Butterwyck'* c1189 (e14th) Selby, *-wyk'* e13th (e14th) ib, *Estbuterwyk'* 1282 FF. **Butterwick, West**, *Westbuterwyk'* 1305 Ass, *-buterwyk* 1306 Cl, **East** & **West Butterwick** are on opposite sides of the R. Trent. All three names are from OE **butere** 'butter' and OE **wīc** 'a dairy-farm'.

Byard's Leap (Cranwell, Kest), - *leap* 1724 Stukeley, commemorating a folk-tale of a witch and a horse called *Bayard* (OFr, ME **baiard** 'a bay horse') which in its fright made a prodigious leap, now marked by two sets of horse-shoes about fifty feet apart (for details see Jennifer Westwood, *Albion* ?18ff). The tale was certainly known much earlier for the place is recorded as *Bayardes leape of Ancaster hathe* [i.e. *heath*] 1601 Medium Ævum lxvi, 98.

Bytham, Castle (Kest), *æt Bytham* 1066–68 (c1200) ASWills, *Bitham* 1086 DB, c1128 (m12th) ChronPetro, *Biham* 1096–1100, 1130 P, 1202 Ass, *Byham* 1147–66 (1409) Gilb, 1242–3 Fees, *Bytham* 1254 ValNor, *Westbitham* 1086 DB, 1335 FF, *-bytham* 1288 Fine, *Magna Byham* 1230 Cur, 1265 RRGr, *castellum de Biham* 1219 Cur, 'the homestead in the broad valley' from OE **bythme** and OE **hām**. Forms in *Biham* etc. are due to Anglo-Norman influence. At various times the p.n. had different affixes, **West**, **Great** and **Castle**, each self-explanatory, to distinguish **Castle Bytham** from **Little Bytham**. **Bytham, Little** (Kest), *Bitham* 1086 DB, *Biamel* c1150 RA iii, *Byhamel* e13th *AD*, *Bihamel* 1210 P, 1212 Fees, *Byamell* 1428 FA, *Parua Bytham* 1412 *Anc*, *Litilbitham* 1464 Pat, *Estbytham* 1288 Fine. For the etymology see above. Forms in *-el* are from the OFr diminutive suffix **-el** 'little'.

C

Cabourne (LNR), *Caburne* 1086 DB, 1150–60 Dane, *-burna* c1115 LS, 1130 P, c1155 Dane, *Kaburna* 1157–63 ib, *Caburn'* 1199 P, 'the stream where jackdaws are found' from OE **cā** and **burna**, The stream is almost dried up today, so that it is impossible to determine its characteristic features as a **burna**.

Cadeby (Wyham, LNR), *Cadebi* 1086 DB, *Catebi* c1115 LS, *-by* c.1200 RA iv, 1212 Fees, 1245 FF, *North Cateby* 1287 Ass. It is sometimes *North* Cadeby in contrast to **South Cadeby** (an extinct village in Calcethorpe, LSR), *Catebi* 1086 DB, c1115 LS, 1157–63 (p1259) *Kirkst*, c1162 Dane, *-by* l12th (1409) Gilb, *Kateby* eHy2 (1409) ib. Both mean 'Kati's farmstead, village' from the ODan pers.n. *Kati* and ON **bȳ**. In **South Cadeby** the following f.ns. have been noted: *Katehou* lHy2 (1409) Gilb, *Catehowe* 1362 Ipm, *Cathowe* 1372 ib (from ON **haugr** 'a (burial) mound'), *Katedale* lHy2 (1409) Gilb (from ON **dalr** 'a valley') and *Catedyk* 1372 Ipm (from ON **dík** 'a ditch'); each has as first el. the same pers.n. *Kati* as in **Cadeby** itself, and presumably refers to the same man.

Cadney (LNR), *Catenai* (sic) 1086 DB, *Cadenai* c1115 LS, 1204 P, *-ei* Hy2 (1319) Dugd vi, *insula de Kadeneia* eHy3 CollTop, *Cadney* 1318 Pat, 'Cada's island of land' from the OE pers.n. *Cada*, a loan from PrW, being a hypocoristic form of PrW pers.ns. in *Cad-*, and OE **ēg**. Note that in eHy3 it is actually described as *insula*.

Cadwell Park (Tathwell, LSR), *Cathadala* Hy2 Dane, *Cattedale* Hy2 (1649) *Dods 75*, 1202 Ass, *-dala* 1194 P, *Catedal'* 1209–35 LAHW, *-dale* 1218 Ass, 'the (wild-)cat valley' from OE **cat(t)** and ON **dalr**, topographically appropriate.

Caenby (LWR), *Couenebi* (sic) 1086 DB, *Cafnabi* (checked from MS) c1115 LS, *Cauenebi* 1191 P, 1196 ChancR, 1201 P, *Kavenebi* 1203 Cur, 'Kafni's farmstead, village' from the ON pers.n. *Kafni* and ODan **bȳ**.

Caistor (LNR), *Castr* 975–78 ASCoins, *Castre* 1070–87 RA i, 1086 DB, *Caster* 1276 (1409) Gilb, *Caister* 1485 Pat, from OE **cæster** 'a Roman station'. It is also recorded as *Thwancastr(e)* 1190 (e13th), 1292 *NCot*, *Thwangcastr(e)* 1298 *Ass*, 1303 Ipm, the first el. being OE **thwang** 'a thong' in some unexplained transferred sense. This name persists occasionally until at least the end of the 18th century.

Calceby (LSR), *Calesbi* 1086 DB, c1115 LS, 1150–60, 1173–82 Dane, 1198 Cur, *Kalesbi* lHy2 (p1259) *Kirkst*, 'Kalf's farmstead, village' from the ODan pers.n. *Kalf* and ODan **bȳ**. The same pers.n. is also the first el. of the wapentake-name **Calceworth**, the district in which Calceby is situated. The gen.sg. pronounced [s] is Scand. in contrast to English [z], indicating that the name had been given by Danish speakers.

Calcethorpe (LSR), *Torp* 1086 DB, *Cheilestorp* c1115 LS, *Kailesthorpa* Hy2 (1409) Gilb, *-torp* l12th *KirkstInv i*, 1196 ChancR, *Keilestorp* lHy2 (p1259) *Kirkst*, *Kaylestorp* c1200 (1409) Gilb; apparently originally a simplex p.n. from ODan **thorp** 'a secondary settlement'. To this was prefixed the OE pers.n. *Cægel*, found also in a f.n. in the parish *Cheigelwang* 1157–63 (p1259) (from ON **vangr** 'a garden, an in-field') *Kirkst*. The modern form has presumably been influenced by that of **Calceby** and does not occur before the 16th century, note *Calsthorpe* 1535 VE iv. Calcethorpe is a depopulated village, the name surviving in **Calcethorpe House** & **Calcethorpe Manor House**.

Calceworth Wapentake (LSR), *Calsvad*, *Calsuad* 1086 DB, 1167, 1194 P, *Calswad* 1181 ib, *Calswat* c1115 LS, eHy2 Dane, *Calswath* 1168 *Kalswath'* 1201 Ass. The change to *-worth* has not been noted before *Calceworth* 1653 *ParlSurv*. The early forms are usually preceded or followed by some form of Latin *wapentacium*. **Calceworth** is derived from the ODan pers.n. *Kalf* and ON **vath** 'a ford'. This pers.n. is also the first el. of **Calceby**, in **Calceworth Wapentake**, and the reference must be to the same man. The site of the wapentake (ON **vápnatak**, late OE **wæpengetæc** 'a subdivision of a shire') meeting is not known, but was at a ford owned by its headman, perhaps in the vicinity of **Calceby**.

Cammeringham (LWR), *Camelingeham* (sic) 1086 DB, *Camringham* c1115 LS, *Cambrigeham* 1126 France, *Cambringeham* c1175, 1192 ib, *Kameringeham* 1219 WellesLA, *Cameringham* 1202 Ass; this is an OE **-ingahām** formation, denoting 'the homestead, estate of the family, the dependents of X'. The first el. is difficult but an unrecorded OE pers.n. **Cantmǣr* would fit the forms.

Candlesby (LSR), *Calnodesbi* 1086 DB, *Candlouebi* 1202 Ass, *Candlouby* 1212 Fees, *Canloueby* 1202 FF, *Kanlosb'* e13th RA vi, *Kandelesbi* 1202 Ass, probably from the OE pers.n. *Calunōth* and ODan **bȳ** 'a farmstead, a village', with the same pers.n. found also in **Candleshoe Wapentake** (LSR), *Calnodeshou* 1086 DB, c1115 LS, *-how* 1167 ChancR, *Calnothesho* 1167 P, *Candlesho* 1183 ib, *Candelesho* 1193 ib, *Kandelesho* 1199–1216 Abbr. The early spellings are usually preceded or followed by some form of Latin *wapentacium*. The second el. is ON **haugr** 'a mound'. The site of the wapentake (ON **vápnatak**, late OE **wæpengetæc** 'a subdivision of a shire') meeting place is not known for certain, but may well have been on Candlesby Hill.

Candleshoe Wapentake (LSR), see **Candlesby**.

Canwick (Kest), *Canewic* 1086 DB, 1146, 1163 RA i, *Kanewich* 1177, 1205 P, from the OE pers.n. *Cana* and OE **wīc** 'a dwelling, a specialised building, a dairy farm'.

Car Dyke (Kest), *Karesdic* l12th Dane, 1199–1215 *AddCh*, *-dich* 1255–80 *AD*, *-dik* 1276 RH, *Carisdik'* 1276 ib, *Karisdic* 1327 Ch, *Cardik* Hy2 (p1259) *Kirkst*, 1234 FF, *Caredich* 1135–54 (p1259) *Kirkst*, *-dic* 1161, Hy2 (l13th) *Stix*, 'Kárr's ditch' as suggested by the earliest run of forms. It is derived from the ON pers.n. *Kárr* and ON **dík** and was a Roman canal extending certainly from the **R. Witham** near Washingborough probably into Northampton-shire.

Careby (Careby, Aunby & Holywell, Kest), *Careby* 1189 (1332) Ch, 1201 FF, c1226 RA iii, 1226 Cur, 1227 Ch, 'Kari's farmstead, village' from the ODan pers.n. *Kari* and ODan **bȳ**.

Carlby (Kest), *Carlebi* 1086 DB, 1185 RotDom, *-by* 1146 Dugd i, *Karlebi* 1200 Cur, 1202 Ass, 'the farmstead, village of the free peasants', from ON **karl** and ON **bȳ** or 'Karli's farmstead, village' from the ON pers.n. *Karli* and ODan **bȳ**. The early spellings of the two are indistinguishable.

Carlton le Moorland (Kest), *æt Carlatune* 1066–68 (c1200) ASWills, *Carletune* 1086 DB, *-ton'* 1180–90 RA vii, 1185 Templar, 1203 Cur, *Carleton' in Moreland* 1293 RSu. The affix is self-explanatory. **Carlton Scroop** (Kest), *Carletune* 1086, *Carlentona* 1115 YCh iii, *Karleton* 1212 Fees, *Carleton Scrop* 1439 Pat. The *Scrope* family held land here, cf. Henry *Scrop* 1346 FA. **Carlton, Castle, Great & Little** (LSR), *Carlentun* 1086 DB, *-ton'* Hy2 (1409) Gilb, *- iuxta mare* l12th (Ed1) Barl, *Carletune* c1115 LS, *Karletun* c1110 France, *-ton'* 1195 P. **Castle Carlton** is *de castro de Carleton* 1219 Pat,

Castel Carleton 1266 ib; **Great Carlton**, *magna Carleton'* Hy2 (Ed1) *Barl*, and **Little Carlton**, *parua carl' iuxta mare* 1183–84 (Ed1) *Barl*. The affixes are self-explanatory. **Carlton, North & South** (LWR), *Carlentone* 1086 DB, -*tona* c1135 RA ii, *Carletune, -tone* 1086 DB, -*tune* c1115 LS, -*tona* 1141 RA i, *Karletona* a1140 ib ii, lHy2 Dane, *Nortcarletone* 1086 DB, *Suthcarleton'* 1272 *Ass*, 1294 *Barl*. The two settlements were distinguished as **North** and **South** from their situations. The former was also known as *Carleton' Wildeker* 1242–43 Fees and *Carletonkyme* 1310 RA ii, the latter as *Karleton Paynel* 1284–85 FA, from the families which variously held the vills. There is also a **Middle** or **Little Carlton**, *Mediæ Carleton* eHy3 (e14th) Selby, *parua Carleton'* e13 (Ed1) *Barl*, now completely depopulated. **Carlton** is a partially Scandinavianised form of OE **Ceorlatūn* 'the village of the free peasants, husbandmen' from OE **ceorl** 'a free peasant, a freeman below the class of noble' and OE **tūn**, with the first el. replaced by the cognate ON **karl**.

Carrington (Bolingbroke, LSR), was formed into a township in 1812 and took its name from its principal owner, Lord *Carrington*.

Casewick (Uffington, Kest), *Casuic* 1086 DB, *Kasewic* 1210–12 RBE, *Casewic* 1212 Fees, *Kesewic* 1226 Pat, 'the cheese farm' from OE **cēse** and OE **wīc**, with the first el. in a Scandinavianised form.

Casthorpe (Barrowby, Kest), *Kaschingetorp, Chaschingetorp* 1086 DB, *Chaschinthorp* Hy2 (1316) Ch, *Caschingtorp* l12th (e13th) *Castleacre*, 'Caschin's secondary settlement (of **Barrowby**)' from the pers.n. *Caschin* (recorded as such in DB) and ODan **thorp**. This pers.n. is usually taken to be from an unrecorded ON **Karski*, but the forms would better suit derivation from the Flemish pers.n. *Kasekin*, a hypocoristic form of the Latin saint's name *Nicasius*.

Castlethorpe (Broughton, LWR), *Castorp* 1086 DB, *Cheistorp* c1115 LS, *Kaistorp* 1224 FF, c1270 RA ii, *Keistorp* Hy3 (1311) Ch, the second el. is ODan **thorp** 'a secondary settlement', in this case probably of **Broughton**. The first el. is difficult, but we might consider a Scand. byname, either ON *Keikr* or ON *Keiss*. Forms in *Castlethorpe* do not appear till the 16th century.

Cawkwell (LSR), *Calchewelle* 1086 DB, -*wella* c1115 LS, *Calcwelle* 1185 Templar, 1203–6 RA i, *Kalcwelle* 1202 Ass, *Calkewell'* 1206 ib, from OE **calc** 'chalk' and OE **wella** 'a spring', topographically appropriate. The village lies in a hollow in the chalk, where there used to be many springs which have been ducted and the water taken away by the Water Authority.

Cawthorpe (Bourne, Kest), *Caletorp* 1086 DB, *-thorp* 1327 Ch, *Calthorp'* c1200 Semp, 1275 RH, 1282 Ipm. **Cawthorpe, Little** (LSR), *Calethorp* c1150, eHy2 (13th) *Alv*, 1202 Ass, 1205 Cur, *Calthorp'* l12th RA ii, *-thorpe* c1150 (1409) Gilb. Both mean 'Kali's secondary settlement' from the Scand. pers.n. *Kali* and ODan **thorp**. It is **Little** to distinguish it from the lost **Cawthorpe** (Covenham, LNR).

Caythorpe (Kest), *Carltorp* (sic), *Catorp* 1086 DB, 1178 P, *Cattorp'* 1185 RotDom, 1185 Templar, 1186 P, l12th (p1259) *Kirkst*, 'Káti's secondary settlement' from the ODan pers.n. *Káti* and ODan **thorp**. The DB spelling is presumably an error. The same pers.n. occurs also in **Cadeby**. Isolated spellings, *Caithorp* 1227 FF, 1315 Ipm, have been noted but these do not become common until the end of the 16th century.

Chapel Hill (Hol), *Chapel Hill* 1612, 1633, 1649 Admin, self-explanatory.

Chapel St Leonards (LSR), "the chapel of St Leonard" 1257 FF, *the chapell of seint Leonard in Mumby* 1503 LNQ xxii, *Chapyll s^t Lenerde* 1530 Wills iii, *Mumby chappell* 1535 VE iv, *Mumby Chapell* 1556 *Mad*, self-explanatory; it was originally a chapel of **Mumby**, dedicated to *St. Leonard*.

Claxby (LNR), *æt Cleaxbyg* 1066–68 (12th) ASWills, *Clachesbi* 1086 DB, *Clakesbi* 1150-60, 1186–1200 Dane, *-by* 1190 (1302) Dugd vi. **Claxby** (near Alford, LSR), *Clachesbi* 1086 DB, *Clakesbi* 1176, 1185, 1188 P, 1196 ChancR, 1202 Ass. **Claxby Pluckacre** (LSR), *Clachesbi* 1086 DB, *-bia* c1150 Dane, *Clakesb'* 1170-78 Revesby, *-bi* 12th *RevesInv*, *Claxeby* 1198 (1328) Ch, *Claxby Pluk Acre* 1227 Welles. All three mean 'Klak's farmstead, village' from the ODan pers.n. *Klak* and ODan **bý**. This pers.n. is recorded six times independently in DB in L. The affix **Pluckacre** is obscure,

Claypole (Kest), *Claipol* 1086 DB, 1196 ChancR, 1197 P, *Cleipol* 1185 Templar, 'the pool on clayey ground' from OE **clæg** and OE **pōl**.

Claythorpe (LSR), *Clactorp* 1086 DB, p1150 *HarlCh*, Hy2 Dane, 1200 CurP, 1202 Ass, *Clachetorp* 1166, 1167 P, *Claketorp'* 1203 Ass. The earliest example of the modern form is *Claythorpp* 1506 Ipm. The first el. may be the ODan pers.n. *Klak*, as in **Claxby**, though there is no trace of a gen.sg. Perhaps it is rather ODan **klakk** 'a hill'. The farm, which today represents

Claythorpe, lies on the slope above the **Great Eau**. The second el. is ODan **thorp** 'a secondary settlement', in relation to **Aby**.

Cleatham (LWR), *Cletham* 1066–87 (m12th) Dugd i, 1067 (m12th) RRAN, 1086 DB, c1115 LS, c1128 (12th) ChronPetro, 1189 (1332) Ch, probably 'the homestead, estate where burdock, goose-grass grows' from OE **clǣte** and OE **hām**.

Clee, Old (LNR), *Cleia* 1086 DB, *Cleiam* 1191 P, *Cleie* 1206 Ass, *Cle* c1115 LS, 1196 ChancR, 1206 P, *Clee* 1232 Welles, from OE **clæg** 'clay, clayey soil', topographically appropriate for the site of Old Clee.

Cleethorpes (LNR), *Thorpe* 1406 Pat, *Clethorpe* 1552 *Inv*, *-thorp* 1593 *ib*, 1606 Admin, *-thorpe* 1582 ib, *Clethorpes* 1588 *Inv*, *Clee thorpes* 1598 *ib*, 'the outlying settlement belonging to Clee', from the parish name **Clee** and ODan **thorp**, a late use of this word. It will be noted that the name appears in both singular *and* plural forms, the latter being no doubt because there were two very adjacent places *Hole* and *Itterby*, now part of Cleethorpes, with *Thrunscoe* a little to the south.

Clixby (LNR), *Clisby* 1086 DB, 1199 P, *Clisseby* 1177 ib, 1202 Ass, *Clipseby* 1196 ChancR, 1203 Ass, *Clifsebi* c1115 LS, 1202 Ass. The forms in *-fs(e)-* are errors for *-ss(e)-* due to the similarity of *f* and *s* in medieval manuscripts and spellings in *-ss(e)-* are the result of the assimilation of *-ps-* to *-ss-*. This is a difficult name, but is probably derived from the ON pers.n. *Klippr* and ODan **bȳ** 'a farmstead, a village'.

Coalbeach (Surfleet, Hol), *Caldebeche* Hy2 (1269) Ch, *-bech* a1269, c1274 *Spald ii*, 1277 *FF*, *-bache* 1327 Pat, from OE **cald** 'cold' and OE **bæce** 'a stream'; it was a grange of Spalding Priory.

Coates (LWR), *Cotes* 1086 DB, c1115 LS, 1157 (1407) Gilb, 1166 RBE, l12th Dane, *Cotis* c1115 LS, 'the cottages, the shelters' from the pl. of OE **cot**.

Coates, Great (LNR), *Cotes* 1086 DB, 1175 ChancR, 1204 FF, 1212 Fees, *Magna Cotes* 1272 *Ass*, *Grauncotes* Hy3 (e14) Selby, *Mikelcotes* 1329 *Ass*, *Great Cootes* 1562 *BT*, from OE **cot** 'a cottage, shelter' in the pl., to which was prefixed *Great* in contrast to the adjacent **Little Coates**. Forms in *Graun-* are from ME **graunt, graun** 'large, big' and those in *Mikel-* are from ON **mikill** 'big, great'. The spellings *Cotun* c1115 LS, *Kotun* 1182 P, *Cothum* 1196 ChancR, *Cotom* 1374 Peace are also recorded for **Great**

Coates and are from the dat.pl. **cotum** of OE **cot** 'at the cottages, etc.' and this form must have existed side by side with *Cotes*.

Coates, Little (LNR), *Sudcotes* 1086 DB, *Sut Cotum* c1115 LS, *Parva Cotes* 1177 P, 1226–28 Fees, *Littelcotes* 1377 Fine; the earliest spellings indicate that this is 'the cottages, shelters to the south', from OE **sūth** and **cot** in relation to Great Coates, the adjacent parish to the north. At an early date **sūth** was replaced by OE **lȳtel** 'little'. For the spelling *-um*, see **Great Coates**.

Coatham Nunnery (Brocklesby, LNR), *Cotes* 1086 DB, 1218 Ass, *Cotum* c1150, 1170 (e13th) *NCot*, 1219 FF, *Cotun* c1115 LS, *Nuncottum* 1268 *NCot*, from the OE dat.pl. **cotum** 'at the cottages, sheds or shelters' of OE **cot**, with the earliest spellings from the nom.pl. form. The weakly stressed syllable *-um* was later interpreted as *-ham*, for which cf. **Burnham**, **Howsham** and **Newsham**. A priory of Cistercian nuns was founded here c1150, hence **Nunnery**.

Cockerington, North & South (LSR), *Cocrinton(e)* DB, *Cocrinton'* a1168 Semp, *Cocringtuna* c1115 LS, *Cokerington'* eHy2 (13th) *Alv*, 1202 FF, *Kockerington'* c1163 (13th) *Alv, Cocrinton Sancte Marie* p1220 LAHW, *N: Cokerton* 1576 Saxton, *Cocrinton Sancti Leonardi* p1220 LAHW, *Southe Cokeringtom* 1547 Pat. The first el. is probably a British river-name **Cocker**, found in Cumberland, Durham and Notts, an older name for at least the lower reaches of the **R. Lud**, itself an OE river-name. **Cocker** is derived from a Celtic root meaning 'crooked', 'winding' topographically appropriate. Cockerington would then mean 'the farmstead, village associated with or called after the Cocker', with the OE medial connective particle **-ing-** and OE **tūn**.

Coleby (Kest), *Colebi* 1086 DB, 1170 P, 1175 ChancR, 1185 Templar, 1191, 1199 P. *-by* 1207 Cur. **Coleby** (West Halton, LWR), *Colebi* 1086 DB, 1181 P, 1202 Ass, *-by* 1113–28, 1210–12 RBE. Both are 'Koli's farmstead, village' from the ON pers.n. *Koli* and ODan **bȳ**.

Colsterworth (Kest), *Colstewrde* 1086 DB, *-uorde* 1086 ib, c1128 France, *-wrd'* Hy2 Semp, *-wurtha* 1178 P, *Colestwrth'* 1212 Cur. Forms in *Colster-* have not been found before *Colsterworth* 1291 Tax while forms without medial *-er-* continue sporadically until the 17th century. Even so it would appear that **Colsterworth** means 'the charcoal burners' enclosure' from OE **colestre** and OE **worth**.

Conesby (now in Scunthorpe, LWR), *Cunesbi* 1086 DB, *Cuningesbi* c1115 LS, 1199 P, *Cunyngesbia* Hy2 (1437) Pat, *Cunnyngesby* lHy2 (1409) Gilb, *Cuningebi* 1205 P, 'the king's village', from ODan **kunungr** and ODan **bȳ**, identical in origin with **Coningsby**.

Coningsby (LSR), *Cuningesbi* 1086 DB, c1200 Dane, *-by* 1162 (p1259) *Kirkst*, l12th *HarlCh*, *Kuningesbi* 1202 Ass, *Coningesbi* c1115 LS, 1198 (1328) Ch, *Conighesbi* c1115 LS, 'the king's village' from ODan **kunungr** and ODan **bȳ** 'a farmstead, a village', identical in origin with **Conesby**. It was held by the King in DB.

Conisholme (LSR), *Cunyngesholme* c1155 (1409) Gilb, *Cuningesholm'* a1185 (13th) *Alv*, 1196 FF, 1199 P, *Cunigeholm* c1190 RA v, 1202 Ass, from ODan **kunung** 'a king' and ON **holmr** 'higher raised ground in marsh', topographically appropriate.

Corby Glen (Kest), *Corbi*, *-by* l12th (1407) Gilb, *Corebi* 1156–57 YCh i, 1170 P, 1185 RotDom, Hy2 *AddCh*, 'Cori's farmstead, village' from the ON pers.n. *Cori* and ODan **bȳ**. The modern form of the p.n. arose in 1959, the affix being from the R. Glen which runs through the village.

Corringham (LWR), *Coringeham* 1086 DB, 1100–15 RA i, 1130 P, 1138–39 (1329) Ch, 1162 P, 1219 Ass, *Coringheham* c1115 LS, *Coryngeham* 1155–58 (1329) Ch, Hy2 (1427) Pat, *Coringham* 1086 DB, 1163 RA i, 'the homestead, the estate of the Coringas' from the gen.pl. *Coringa* of OE *Coringas*, a group-name meaning 'the family, the dependents of *Cora*' and OE **hām**.

Corringham Wapentake (LWR), *Coringeham* c1115 LS, 1130 P, 1138–39 RA i, 1168, 1170 P, 1202 Ass, named from Corringham where the wapentake (ON **vápnatak**, late OE **wæpengetæc** 'a sub-division of a shire') meeting was presumably held. The early forms are preceded by some form of Latin *wapentacium*.

Cotes, North (LNR), *Nordcotis* c1115 LS, *Northcotes* 1202 Ass, 1242–43 Fees, *Northecotes* 1226–28 ib, from OE **north** and OE **cot** 'a cottage, a hut' in the pl. There is no contrasting South Cotes; it is likely, therefore, that **North Cotes** was named in relation to **Fulstow**, the village to the south.

Counthorpe (Counthorpe & Creeton, Kest), *Cudetorp* 1086 DB, *Cunctorp* 1192 P, *Ciningtorp'*, *Cunitorp'* 1219 Cur, *Countorp* 1219 ib, *Cunetorp* 1219 Ass, *Cointorp* 1219 ib. The forms are too varied to suggest an etymology for the first el. The second is ODan **thorp** 'a secondary settlement (presumably of **Creeton**)'.

Covenham St Bartholomew & St Mary (LNR), *Covenham* a1067 (c1240) Whitby, 1086 DB, 1090–96 (c1240) YCh ii, 1100–15 (m13) Whitby, Hy1 (c1400) ib, 1136 (1312) YCh ii, *Couenham* 1086 DB, l12 RA v, 'Cofa's homestead, estate' from the OE pers.n. **Cofa* and **hām**. Later spellings, *Conam* 1427 Pat, *Coname* 1574 *AD*, etc. must represent a local pronunciation apparently not heard today but which is found in local documents into the 18th century. The full modern forms occur early — *Covenham Sancti Bartholomei* 1254 ValNor, *Couenham B. Marie* 1265 RRGr.

Cowbit (Hol), *Coubith* m13, lHy3, *Coubiht* 1267, *Koubith* lHy3 all (c.1331) *Spald ii*, *Coubyth* 1332 *SR*, *-bight* 1361 *Cor*, from OE **cū** 'a cow' and OE **byht** 'a bend, a bight', topographically appropriate for it denoting a bend in the R. Welland which partially encloses pasture for cows.

Cowbridge (Skirbeck, Hol), *Cubrygge* 1281 *Ass*, *Coubrigge* 1357 *Cor*, *Cowbrige* 1456 Cl, self-explanatory, from OE **cū** 'a cow' and OE **brycg** 'a bridge'.

Craiselound (Haxey, LWR), *Lund* 1086 DB, *Craslund* l12th *AD*, c1220 Bodl, *-lounde* 1289 *AD*; this was a simplex p.n. from ON **lundr** 'a grove', as with **East Lound** also in Haxey. The first el. added later is uncertain. It is also spelt **Graizelound**, as on the 1:50,000 O.S. map, note *GrasLund'* l12th *AD*, *-lund* 1329 (1389) Pat.

Cranmore (Deeping St James), *Cranemor'* 1282 Ipm, *Crannemore* 1349 Ipm, *Cranemore* 1381 ib, 1426 Cl, 'the marshland frequented by crane' from OE **cran** and OE **mōr**.

Cranwell (Kest), *Cranewelle* 1086 DB, 1149, 1178 (c1350) Rams, 1156 (p1269) *Bard*, 1180 P, 1185 Templar, 'the spring where cranes are found' from OE **cran** and OE **wella**. There are springs here to the south of the village.

Creeton (Counthorpe, Kest), *Cretun(e)*, *-tone* 1086 DB, *Creton'* 1201 Ass, *-tone* 1205 FF, *Crectone* (with *-ct-* for *-tt-*) 1166 RBE, *Cretton'* 1202 SelectPleas, *Creton'* 1204 Cur, perhaps 'Crēta's farmstead, village' from the OE pers.n. *Crēta* and OE **tūn**.

Croft (LSR), *Croft* 1086 DB, c1115 LS, 1178 (p1269) *Bard*, Hy2 Dane, 1202 Ass, from OE **croft** 'a small enclosed field'.

Crofton (Kest), *Crohcton'* (sic) 1204 Cur, *Croketon'* 1208, 1256 FF, 1275 RH, *Crocton* 1226, 1234 FF, *Croghton* 1303 Pat, *Crofton* 1556 Pat, *Crocton alias Crofton* 1660 *DCLB*, perhaps 'the farmstead, village where saffron grows' from OE **croh** and OE **tūn**. The change to **Crofton** is late and the reason is obscure.

Crosby (now in Scunthorpe, LWR), *Cropesbi* (sic) 1086 DB, *Crosseby* 1206 Ass, 1206, 1207 Cur, 1210 P, 'the village with a cross' from ON **kross**, late OE **cros** and ODan **bȳ**. The DB form is an error.

Crossholme (Bishop Norton, LWR), *Crosholm'* 1185 RotDom, 1197 FF, l12th RA ii, 1206 Ass, *Croxholm* c1225 (14th) *Queen's*, 'the raised land in marsh marked with a cross' from ON **kross**, late OE **cros** and ON **holmr** 'raised land in marsh, etc.'.

Crowland (Hol), *Cruglond'*, *-land* (9th), *Cruwlond* (l10th), *Cruland* (10th), *Crouland* (m11th) all c745 Guthlac (Felix), *Crulande* s.a. 963 (c1121), s.a. 1066 (c1121), s.a. 1076 (c1121) all ASC E, *Cruland* c1100 Saints, *Croiland* 1086 DB, *Croyland* 1114 Dugd ii, from an OE *crūw, *crūg 'a bend' and OE **land**, denoting land in a bend of the R. Witham.

Crowle (LWR), *Crull* c1070 (e14th) Selby, 1170–83 (c1200) CartAnt, c1084, 1087–1100, 1100–8, Hy1 (e14th) Selby, 1155 (c1200) CartAnt, *Crule* 1086 DB, c1184 (15th) Templar, probably originally a river-name OE *crull in the sense 'winding', i.e. etymologically related to Middle Dutch *krul*, 'curled hair', Mod English *curl*, and denoting a winding river or stream.

Croxby (LNR), *Crosbi* (sic), *Crocsbi* 1086 DB, *Crochesbi* c1115 LR, 1142–53 Dane, 1163 RA i, *Crokesby* m12 (l13th) *Stix*, *Croxebi* c1189 LAAS v, 'Krōk's farmstead, village' from the ODan pers.n. *Krōk* and ODan **bȳ**. For the same pers.n. see **Croxton**.

Croxton (LNR), *Croxestone* 1086 DB, *Crokeston'* 1190 P, *Crochestune* 1086 DB, *-tuna* c1115 LS, *Crocston'* 1195 P, *Croxston* c1150 (Ed1) *Newh*, 'Krōk's farmstead, village' from the ODan pers.n. *Krōk* and OE **tūn**. This is the only Anglo-Danish pers.n. hybrid p.n. in **tūn** in the whole of the North Riding of Lindsey. It probably represents an earlier Anglo-Saxon settlement taken over and partially renamed by the Danes. For the same pers.n. see **Croxby**.

Culverthorpe (Culverthorpe & Kelby, Kest), *Torp* 1086 DB, *Thorp* 1212, 1242–3 Fees, *Kellwarthorp'* 1275 RH, *Calewarthorp'* 1275 ib, *Calwarthorp'* 1276 ib, *Kilwardthorp* 1338 Ch, *Kilwarthorp* 1342 ib. This was originally 'the secondary settlement' from ODan **thorp**. By the third quarter of the 13th century at latest a pers.n. or surn. had been prefixed to the simplex form. It is, however, impossible to identify it since the forms are so varied, neither is it possible to suggest which settlement **Culverthorpe** was dependent upon.

Cumberworth (LSR), *Combreuorde* 1086 DB, *Cumberworda* c1115 LS, *-wurtha* c1175 Dane, *-worth* a1219 Welles, *Cumbrewrth* p1186 Dugd v, *-wurda* 1193 P, 'Cumbra's enclosure' from the OE pers.n. *Cumbra* and OE **worth.**

Cuxwold (LNR), *Cucualt* 1086 DB, *-wald* c1115 LS, 1163 RA i, *Cukewald'* 1146 RA i, 1166 RBE, lHy2 Dane, *Cokewald(')* 1242–43 Fees, perhaps from the OE pers.n. *Cuca* and OE **wald** 'a forest, an area of woodland on higher ground'. ME *cokkōu, cuk(k)ou* 'the European cuckoo' can be ruled out here, since it is only attested in surnames from 1191 and in independent use from 1300.

D

Dalby (LSR), *Dalbi* 1086 DB, c1115 LS, 1163 RA ix, *apud Dalbeiam* c1113 RRAN, *-bi* c1165 BuryF, c1180 Dane, 'the farmstead, the village in the valley' from ON **dalr** and ODan **bȳ**, topographically appropriate.

Dalderby (LSR), *Dalderby* 1147–51 (14th) Rams, 1221 Welles, *-bi* 1212 ib, *Dauderbi* l12th Dane, 1200 Cur, *-by* 1240 FF and is erroneously *Dalbi* c1115 LS; literally 'the farmstead, village of the small valley' from **dældar**, the gen.sg. of ODan **dæld**, and ON **bȳ**. This is topographically appropriate for the place is in a small valley running down to the R. Bain. Forms in *-u-* are the result of vocalisation of *-l-*.

Darby (Burton upon Stather, WRY), *Derbi* 1086 DB, 1210 P, 1212 Fees, *-by* 1275 RH, *Derebi* 1199, 1200 P, 1202 Ass, literally 'the farmstead, village of the animals, deer', from the gen.pl. of ON **djúr** and ODan **bȳ**, identical with Derby in Derbyshire.

Darwood (Woodhall), *Duuewda* lHy2 Dane, *Dufwudde* 1196–98 ib, *Dufwod* e13th *KirkstInv ii*, *-wode* 1210 (1252), 1252 Ch, 'the wood where doves are found' from OE **dūfe** and OE **wudu**. The name survives in **Darwood House.**

Deeping St James (Kest) & **St Nicholas** (Hol), **Deeping, Market** & **West** (Kest), *Depinge* 1086 DB, c1128 (12th) ChronPetro, *Deping* 1146 Dugd i, p1176 NthCh, *Deping'* 1202 Ass, 'the deep place' from OE **dēop** and the p.n. forming suffix **-ing**, referring to the situation of the Deepings in the fen. The self-explanatory affixes are recorded as *Deping Sancti Jacobi* c1221 Welles earlier *Estdeping* 1086 DB; *Markyddepyng* 1412 Pat, earlier *Estdeping' Sancti Guthlaci* 1254 ValNor; *West Depinge* 1086 DB.

Dembleby (Aunsby, Kest), *Denbelbi* (sic) 1086 DB, *-by* 1180–1200 (1409) Gilb, *Delbebi* (sic) 1086 DB, *Dembelbi* 1086 ib, *-by* p1114 Dugd iv, m12th (l14th) *Ped*, 1212 Fees, probably 'the farmstead, village by the pool' from ON ***dembil** and ODan **bȳ**. The stream here forms a distinct pool in the middle of the village.

Denton (Kest), *Dentune, -tone* 1086 DB, *-tona* 1140–54 BS, 1166 RBE, *-tuna* c1187 Dane, *Denton'* 1174 P, 1185 Templar, 'the farmstead, village in the valley' from OE **denu** and OE **tūn**.

Derrythorpe (Keadby with Althorpe, LWR), *Dudingthorp'* c1184 (15th) Templar, *Dudythorp'* 1279 *AD, Dodithorp'* 1263 FF, *Dodyngthorp'* 1329 *Ass*, from the OE pers.n. *Dudding* and ODan **thorp** 'a secondary settlement (presumably of **Keadby**)'. The use of -*o*- for -*u*- is not uncommon in ME scribal practice. The change to Derry- is late and is difficult to explain.

Dexthorpe (Dalby, LSR), *Dristorp, Dreistorp* 1086 DB, *Drextorp* c1180 BuryF, Hy2 (p1259) *Kirkst*, 1207 P, -*thorp* 1206 Ass, *Draaistorp'* 1208 FF. The first el. is apparently a pers.n. but it is impossible to suggest what it is; the second el. is ODan **thorp** 'a secondary settlement', presumably in relation to **Dalby**.

Digby (Kest), *Dicbi* 1086 DB, *Digby* 1160–65 RA ix, -*bi* 1185 Templar, *Diggeby* 1160–65 RA ix, 1194 P, 'the farmstead, village by the ditch' from ON **dík** and ON **bȳ**. The reference is probably to a drainage channel.

Doddington (Doddington & Whisby, Kest), *Dodinctone, Dodintune* 1086 DB, -*ington* 1178 P, 1254 ValNor. **Doddington, Dry** (Westborough, Kest), *Dudintun'*?1085–89, 1186–88 (14th) *Westm, Dodintone,* -*tune* 1086 DB, -*tona* 1135–54 (14th) *Westm,* -*ingtun'* 1157 (14th) *ib, Dridodyngton'* 1328 *FF*. Both are probably 'the farmstead associated with or called after Dodda or Dudda' from the OE pers.n. *Dodda* or *Dudda* with the OE medial particle -**ing**- and OE **tūn**. The first is often referred to as *Dodyngton Pygot* 1462 Pat, from the *Picot* family which held the manor here, compare William *Picot* 1205 Cur. The affix in **Dry Doddington** is self-explanatory.

Dogdyke (Kest), *Dockedic* Hy2 Dane, 1256 *HarlCh, Dokedic* l12th (l13th) *Stix*, 1229 FF, *Dockesdik'* 1241 Cl, 'the dyke where docks grow' from OE **docce** and OE **dīc** or ON **dík**.

Donington (Hol), *Duninctune, Donninctune, Donnintune* 1086 DB, *Doninton'* 1167 P, *Donyngton'* 1181 (m14th) *HC, Dunyngton* 1183 (m14th) *ib, Dunington* 1202 Ass. **Donington on Bain** (LSR), *Duninctune* 1086 DB, *Duningtun'* m12th (l13th) *Stix,* -*tona* 1199 (1330) Ch, 1200 ChR, *Dunnington'* 1202 Ass, *Donington'* 1200 (c1331) *Spald i, Donyngton' super Beyne* p1247 *HarlCh*; both probably mean 'the farmstead, village associated with Dunn(a)' from the OE pers.n. *Dunn(a)* with the OE connective particle -**ing**- and OE **tūn**. The affix **on Bain** is self-explanatory.

Dorrington (Kest), *Derintone* 1086 DB, -*ton'* 1170, 1173, 1180 P, *Diringtona* 1175 (1337) Ch, *Diringhton'* 1185 Templar, 'the farmstead, village called after or associated with Dēora' from the OE pers.n. *Dēora* with the OE connective particle -**ing**- and OE **tūn**. Forms in *Do*- are not found before the mid 16th century.

Dowsby (Kest), *Dusebi* 1086 DB, c1170 Semp, 1185, 1188 P, l12th *AddCh*, *Duseb'* 1185 Templar, 'Dūsi's farmstead, village' from the rare ODan pers.n. byname *Dūsi* and ODan **bȳ**.

Drayton (Swineshead, Hol), *Draitone* 1086 DB, *Dreitun* 12th HC, *Dreton'* 1199 CurR, *Drayton* 1280 Ipm, from OE **dræg** 'a portage, a dray' and OE **tūn** 'a farmstead, a village', but the sense of **dræg** here is uncertain.

Driby (LSR), *Dribi* 1086 DB, l12th Dane, 1200 CartAnt, *Driebi* 1130, 1162 P, Hy2 Dane, *Driby* 1202 Ass, 'the farmstead, village on dry ground', a hybrid p.n. from OE **drȳge** and ODan **bȳ**.

Dunholme (LWR), *Duneham* 1086 DB, c1115 LS, 1123–48 RA ii, 1146, Hy2 (1291) Ch, *Dunham* c1115 LS, c1160 Dane, probably 'Dunna's homestead, estate' from the OE pers.n. *Dunna* and OE **hām**. The topogaphy precludes OE **dūn** 'a hill' as first el. The interchange betwen -*ham* and -*holme* is common in L.

Dunsby (near Bourne, Kest), *Dunesbi* 1086 DB, 1190–1200 ASSR xlii, -*by* 1223 Welles, *Dunnesby*, 1223 Cur, eHy3 *AddCh*. **Dunsby** (Brauncewell, Kest), *Dunnesbi* 1086 DB, 1167 P. -*by* 1182 (1407) Gilb, 1210–12 RBE, *Dunesbi* 1170 P, -*by* 1182 (1407) Gilb. The name survives in **Dunsby House**. Each means 'Dunn's farmstead, village', a hybrid p.n from the OE pers.n. *Dunn* and ODan **bȳ**.

Dunstall (Corringham, LWR, site of extinct village), *Tonestale* 1086 DB, *Tunstal* c1115 LS, 1210 P, *Dunestal* c1115 LS, *Dunstal* 1185 Templar, -*stalle* 1190 P, 'the site of a farm, a farmstead', from OE **tūn-stall**.

Dunston (Kest), *Dunestune* 1086 DB, 1155, 1163 (p1259) *Kirkst*, -*ton'* 1188 P, 1196 CurP, 'Dunn's farmstead, village', from the OE pers.n. *Dunn* and OE **tūn**.

Dyke (Bourne, Kest), *Dic* 1086 DB, 1219 FF, *Dich* 1167 P, *Dik* 1234 FF, 1252 Ipm, 'the dyke' from ON **dík**. The village is situated on **Car Dyke**.

E

Eagle (Eagle and Swinethorpe, Kest), *Acley, -lei, Akeley, Aycle* 1086 DB, *Eicla* 1135–39, 1141 RA i, *Aicles* 1185 Templar, *Aicle* c1221 Welles, *Eycle* 1212 Fees, 'the oak wood or glade' from OE āc and OE lēah. The first el. OE āc was at an early date replaced by the cognate ON **eik**. The later development to *Egle* 1442 Pat, 1453 *LCCA* is presumably due to popular etymology.

Ealand (Crowle, LWR), *Aland* 1310 Selby, 1316 FA, 1332 *SR*, *Ealonde* 1574–75 *MinAcct* from ON **á** 'a river, a stream' and OE, ON **land** 'a tract of land', though **á** may well have replaced the cognate OE **ēa**.

East Ferry (LWR), see **Ferry, East**.

East Lound (LWR), see **Lound, East**.

Easton (Kest), *Estone* 1086 DB, *-ton'* 1174 P, 1189 Dugd v, 1200 Cur, 1202 FF, 'the eastern farmstead, village' from OE **ēast** and OE **tūn**; it may have been named in relation to **Stoke Rochford**.

Eastville (LSR), was formed into a township by Act of Parliament in 1812 and was earlier *Estfen* a1150, l12th (p1259) *Kirkst*, 1239 FF, 1296 *DuLa*, 'the east fen' from OE **ēast** and OE **fenn**, part of Bolingbroke Fen, compare **Midville** and **Westville**.

Edenham (Kest), *Edeham, Edeneham* 1086 DB, *Edenham* Hy1 (e14th) Bridl, 1115 (14th) *Bard*, 1145–53 (e14th) Bridl, a1176 *AddCh*, lHy2 *Anc,* 'Ēada's homestead, estate' from the OE pers.n. *Ēada* and OE **hām**.

Edlington (LSR), *Ellingetone* 1086 DB, *Hedlingtuna* c1115 LS, *Edlingtuna* c1115 ib, 1140–47 (p1269) *Kirkst, -tun'* eHy2 (l13th) *Stix, Edlyngton'* 1115 (14th) *Bard*, 1192 (m14th) *HC, Edlington'* 1125 (p1269) *Bard*, 'the farmstead, the village associated with or called after Ēad(w)ulf' from the OE pers.n. *Ēad(w)ulf*, with the OE medial connective particle **-ing-** and OE **tūn**.

Elkington, North & South (LSR), *Alchinton* 1086 DB, *-tona* 1136 (1312) Whitby, *Alkinton'* 1175–84 *AddCh*, 1196 ChancR, *Elkinton* 1100–15 (14th) Whitby, *Elchintona* 1145–48 (c1240) ib, *Elkingtona* 1100–15 (c1400) ib, *Nordhelkigtona* (sic) l12th (1409) Gilb, *Suthelkintona* 1160–69 Dugd vi. This is probably 'the farmstead, village associated with or called after Ēadlāc', from the OE pers.n. *Ēadlāc* and OE **tūn**, with the OE medial connective particle **-ing-**.

Ellers (Epworth, LWR), *the Ellers* 1327, 1332 *SR*, 1343 NI, 1377 Misc, 'the alder-trees' from the pl. of ON **elri**.

Elloe Wapentake (Hol), *Elleho* 1086 DB, 1168 P, 1202 Ass, *Elho* 1160 P, *Helho* 1167 ChancR, *Elho* 1188 ib, 'Ella's heel, spur of land' from the OE pers.n. *Ella* and OE **hōh**. The wapentake (ON **vápnatak** late OE **wæpengetæc** 'a sub-division of a shire') meeting-place was presumably near **Elloe Stone** (in Moulton parish), which is recorded in *Ellowestone Feild* 1608 *LRMB 211*. For details of the stone, see LNQ i, 141–44.

Elsham (LNR), *Elesham* 1086 DB, c1115 LS, 1190 P, *Ellesham* c1160 Dugd vi, c1162 RA ii, 112 Dane, 'Elli's homestead, estate' from the OE pers.n. *Elli* and OE **hām**.

Elsthorpe (Edenham, Kest), *Aiglestorp, Aighelestorp* 1086 DB, *Eylestorp'* 1212, 1223 Fees, *-thorp* 1242–43 ib, probably 'Ægel's secondary settlement (of **Edenham**)'. This is a difficult name, but the forms best suit the Continental Germanic pers.n. *Aigulf*, hence 'Aigulf's secondary settlement (of **Edenham**)'. The second el. is ODan **thorp**.

Enderby, Bag (LSR), *Andredebi, Andrebi* 1086 DB, *Anderbi* 1183 P, *-by* 1203 Ass, *Endrebi* c1115 LS, *-by* 1202 Ass, *Bag henderby* 1261 RRGr, *Bagenderby* 1291 Tax. **Enderby, Mavis** (LSR), *Endrebi* 1086 DB, c1115 LS, *Enderbi* 1142–53 Dane, 1170–98 Revesby, *-by* 1198 (1328) Ch, *Andrebi* Hy2 Dane, *Estendeby* 1198 (1328) Ch, *Malebisse Enderby* 1229 Cur, *Enderby Malebise* a1219 Welles. **Enderby, Wood** (LSR), *Endrebi* 1086 DB, 1195 FF, *Enderbi* lHy2 Dane, 1196–99 RA ii, c1200 NthCh, *-by* 1198 (1328) Ch, *Wodenderby* 1198 (1328) ib. Each probably means 'Eindrithi's farmstead, village' from the ON pers.n. *Eindrithi* and ODan **bȳ**. **Bag Enderby** is a small U-shaped village enclosing the church and off a lane to the North and this is no doubt the significance of **Bag** here, from ME **bagge** 'a bag' used in a transferred topographical sense with reference to the shape of the village; **Mavis** is from the *Malbisse* family, cf. Richard *Malebis* 1198 FF, which held the manor; **Wood** is self-explanatory.

Epworth (LWR), *Epeurde* 1086 DB, *-wurd* c1200 Dane, John *AddCh*, e13th AD, *Epwurth'* 1233 Lib, *Appewrda* m12th Dugd vi; the *A-* spellings are only found three times in a large collection, so they are to be ignored. The name probably means 'Eoppa's enclosure' from the OE pers.n. *Eoppa* and OE **worth**.

Eresby (Spilsby, LSR), *Iresbi* 1086 DB, *Eresb'* 1185 Templar, *-bi* l12th Dane, *-by* 1214–20 RA vi, 1238 RRG; the first el. is the ON pers.n. *Ȳrr*, the second el. ODan **bȳ** 'a farmstead, a village'.

Eskham (Marsh Chapel, LSR), *in Ascholmo* e13th (1409) Gilb, *Eskeholm* 1314 Ch, 1339 *LMR*, 'the raised land in marsh where ash-trees grow' from ON **askr**, **eski** and ON **holmr**. The interchange between *-holme* and *-ham* is common in L.

Evedon (Ewerby, Kest), *Evedune* 1086 DB, 1185 Templar, *Evdone* 1166 RBE, *Euedon'* 1196 FF, 1202 Ass, *-dona* 1196–1203 RA iii, 'Eafa's hill' from the OE pers.n. *Eafa* and OE **dūn**.

Ewerby (Ewerby & Evedon, Kest), *Grenebi, Grenesbi, Geresbi* (sic) 1086 DB, *Ieresbi* 1086 DB, *Iwareby* Hy2 Semp, *-bi* Hy2 Dane, 1185 RotDom, 1185 Templar, *Iwarby* p1184 Semp, 'Ivar's farmstead, village' from the ODan pers.n. *Ivar* and ODan **bȳ**. The DB forms are not supported by any later spellings and are presumably errors.

Ewerby Thorpe (Ewerby, Kest), *Oustorp* 1086 DB, 1212 Fees, 1223 Cl *Ouestorp'* c1190 (13th) *Castleacre, Oustthorp'* 1233 Cl, 'the secondary settlement to the east (of **Ewerby**)' from ON **austr** and ODan **thorp**. The modern form has not been noted before *Ewerby Thorpe* 1631 Admin.

F

Faldingworth (LWR), *Faldingeurde* 1086 DB, *Faldinguorda* c1115 LS, *-worda* c1160 Dane, *-word* 1163 RA i, *-wortha* c1155 (1411) Gilb, *-worth(e)* c1200 RA iv, probably 'the enclosure of the Faldingas' from *Faldinga* the gen.pl. of OE the group-name *Faldingas* 'the family, the dependents of *Falda*' and OE **worth**.

Fanthorpe (Louth, LSR), *Falmethorp* 1212 Fees, *Folmethorp'* 1235-53, 1273 RA v, 1277 *FF*, *-thorpe* 1314 LNQ xi, 1328 Banco, *Folmesthorpe* 1372 Misc. The first el. is difficult, but a plausible suggestion would be that it is the Continental Germanic pers.n. *Folcmar*, *Folmer*, which is attested in Flanders. The second el. is ODan **thorp** 'a secondary settlement'. The name survives today as **Fanthorpe Farm**.

Farforth (LSR), *Farforde* 1086 DB, p1196 Dudg v, l12th Dane, 1200 Cur, *Farefort* 1121–29 France, Hy2 Dane, 1170 P, perhaps 'the ford giving passage' from OE **fær** and OE **ford**. It carried the presumed Roman road from Horncastle towards Louth, as has recently been suggested.

Farlesthorpe (LSR), *Farlestorp'* 1160–75 RA iv, 1190 P, 1200 Cur, 1202 Ass, *Falestorp'* 1196 FF, 1200 ChR, 'Farald's or Farulf's secondary settlement', the first el. being either the ON pers.n. *Faraldr* or Old Swedish *Farulf* and the second ODan **thorp**.

Fenby (Ashby cum Fenby, LNR), *Fendebi* (sic), *Fenbi hundred* 1086 DB, *Fembi* (sic) c1115 LS, *Fenbi* 1190, 1192 P, *-by* 1231 Cl, *Fenneby* 1261 FF, 'the farmstead, the village in the fen', a hybrid p.n. from OE **fenn** and ODan **bȳ**. This is likely to be a partial Scandinavianisation of an earlier OE p.n. **Fenton* with a similar meaning, compare **Fenton**. The name survives in **Fenby Farm**.

Fenhouses (Swineshead, Hol), *Fenhus* 1234 FF, 1316 Ch, *Fenhuses* 1316 ib, *-houses* 1329 Ipm, 'the house(s) in the fen', from OE **fenn** and OE **hūs**.

Fenton (Kest), *Fentona* c1145 (p1269) *Bard*, 12th (p1259) *Kirkst*, *-tun* 1212 Fees, *-ton* a1219 Welles. **Fenton** (LWR), *Fentuna* c1115 LS, *-ton* c1225 *Queen's*, 1240 FF. Both mean 'the farmstead, village in the fen' from OE **fenn** and OE **tūn**, compare **Fenby**.

Ferriby, South (LNR), *Ferebi* 1086 DB, c1115 LS, *-by*, 1088–93 YCh i, 1207, *Feriby* 1175–81 Dane, l12 RA iii, *Suth feriby* Hy1 (e14th) Selby, 'the farmstead, village at the ferry' from ON **ferja** and ODan **bȳ**. It is **South** in contrast to **North Ferriby** on the opposite bank of the R. Humber.

Ferry, East (LWR), *Ferie* 1194 CurP, 1213 Abbr, *Estfery* 1288 *Ass*, *Fery By este Trente* 1288 *ib*, *Estkynardefery* 1287 *ib*, self-explanatory; it is on the east bank of the Trent opposite Owston; compare **Kinnards Ferry**.

Fillingham (LWR), *Figelingeham, Filingeham, Felingeham* 1086 DB, *Felingheham* 1103 France, *Figlingaham, Figlingheim* c1115 LS, *Filingeham* 1170 P, 1219 Ass, *Fillingeham* 1177, 1211 P, 'the homestead, estate of the Fyglingas' from *Fyglinga* the gen.pl. of OE *Fyglingas*, a group-name meaning 'Fygla's family, dependents', and OE **hām**. The form in *-heim* is from ON **heim** cognate with OE **hām**.

Firsby (LSR), *Friseby* 1125, c1145, 1147, 1159 (p1269) *Bard*, 1175–78 *Anc*, 1202 Ass. **Firsby, East** (LWR), *Frisebi* 1086 DB, 1185 Templar, lHy2 Dane, *-by* c1190 RA ix, *Frisabi* c1115 LS, *Frisbeia* 1137–39 YCh iii. Both mean 'the village of the Frisians' from OE **Frīsa** and ODan **bȳ**. These were presumably Frisians who accompanied the vikings in their settlement of eastern England, compare **Friesthorpe**. **West Firsby** is a depopulated settlement.

Fishtoft (Hol), *Toft* 1086 DB, a1155 (m14th) *HC*, 1166 P, 1192 (m13th) *HC*, 1202 FF, *Toftes* 1181 (m14th) *HC*, 'the messuage, the curtilage', occasionally in the pl. from ODan **toft**. The earliest reference to the p.n. *Fishtoft* is in 1416 on a stone in the parish church, recorded in 1634–42 Holles. The meaning of *Fish* is unknown. No family of that name has been noted here and it is at least possible that it is so called from a connection with fishing.

Fiskerton (LWR), *Fiscartune, -tone* 1086 DB, 1193 P, *Fischertune* c1115 LS, *-tona* c1128 (12th) ChronPetro, *Fikerton'* 1175–80 RA ix, 1178 P, a partial Scandinavianisation of OE **Fisceratūn* 'the farmstead, village of the fishermen' from OE **fiscere** and **tūn**, with the first el. replaced by the cognate ON **fiskari**.

Flaxwell Wapentake (Kest), *Flaxewelle* 1086 DB, 1175 P, *Flaxwelle* 1168 P, 1178 ChancR, 1185 RotDom, 'the spring where flax grows' from OE **fleax** and OE **wella**. The forms are preceded or followed by some form of Latin *wapentacium*. The site of the meeting-place of the wapentake (ON vápnatak, late OE **wapengetac** 'a subdivision of a shire') is not known.

Fleet (Hol), *Fleot* 1086 DB, *Flec* 1086 ib, 1160–70 (e13th) *Castleacre*, 1165 P, 1185 Templar, *Flete* e12 (14th) Rams, 'the inlet, the creek, the stream' from OE **flēot**; Fleet was formerly at the head of an arm of the sea. Note, the stream itself is referred to as *le Flete* 1316 Fleet.

Fleet Hargate (Fleet, Hol), *Herregate* 1276 RH, *Flete Hergate* 1316 Fleet, *Fletehergate* 1328 Banco, from OE **here**, ON **herr** 'an army' and ON **gata** 'a road', literally a road suitable for the passage of an army, hence probably 'the highway'; the parish name, **Fleet**, had been prefixed by the early 14th century.

Flixborough (LWR), *Flichesburg* 1086 DB, -*burc* c1115 LS, *Fliccheburc* 1163, 1176 P, *Flicheburc* 1165 ib, *Fli(c)keburc'*, *Flickesburc* 1202 Ass, a hybrid p.n. 'Flík's fortified place' from the ON pers.n. *Flík* and OE **burh**. It is highly likely that in a p.n. with **burh** as second el. the ON first el. *Flík* has replaced an earlier OE word or pers.n. An important Anglo-Saxon settlement site has recently been excavated here.

Folkingham (Kest), *Fulechingeham* 1086 DB, *Fukingeham* (sic) 1181 P, 1202 Ass, *Folchingeham* 1086 DB, *Folchingham* 1086 ib, c1140 Dane, *Folkyngham* 1115 (14th) *Bard*, -*ingham* p1125 (p1269) *ib*, a1176 AddCh, *Fokingeham* 1185 P, 'the homestead, estate of the Folcingas' from the gen.pl. *Folcinga* of the OE group-name *Folcingas* 'the family the dependents of *Folca*' and OE **hām**.

Fonaby (Caistor, LNR), *Fuldenebi* 1086 DB, *Fulmedebia* 1177 P, *Folmodebi* 1204 ib, *Felmetheby* 1226 Fees, *Folmetby* 1316 FA, *Folnetby* l12 (Edl) *Newb*. The inconsistency in the early spellings makes it difficult to propose an etymology for the first el., but we might tentatively suggest a Scand. pers.n. corresponding to Old Swedish *Folcmodh*. The second el. is ODan **bȳ** 'a farmstead, a village'.

Fordington (Ulceby with Fordington, LSR), *Fortintone* 1086 DB, *Forthintuna* c1115 LS, *Forthingtune* Hy2 Dane, -*ton'* 1212 Fees, *Forthingetun* e13th HarlCh, *Fordintun* 1173–82 Dane, *Fordington'* 1185 Templar, probably 'the farmstead, village associated with or called after Fortha' from the OE pers.n. *Fortha*, with the medial connective particle -**ing**- and OE **tūn**.

Fosdyke (Hol), *Fotesdic* 1195 P, 1212 Fees, -*dich* 1196 ChancR, 1200 Cur, -*dik* 1202 Ass, 'Fot's ditch, water-channel', a Scand. compound from the

ON pers.n. *Fótr* and **dík** 'a ditch, a water-channel'. The same pers.n. occurs in **Foston** and **Fotherby.**

Fosse Dyke (LWR), *Fossedic* eHy2 Dugd vi, c1155, 1155–60, 1160–66 Dane, *-dich* 1189–99 (1318) Ch, *fossatum quod Fossedik' appellatur* 1272 *Ass*, the name of the Roman canal from the Trent to Brayford Pool in Lincoln. It is derived from OE **foss** 'a ditch' and the tautological OE **dīc**. It is now called **Fossdyke Navigation.**

Foston (Kest), *Foztun(e)* (*-z-* = *-ts-*) 1086 DB, *Foston'* 1199 CurR, 1202 Ass, *Foteston'* 1205 P, *-tun* 1212 Fees, 'Fót's village' from the ON pers.n. *Fótr* and OE **tūn**, a hybrid Anglo-Danish p.n. which probably represents an earlier Anglo-Saxon settlement taken over and partially renamed by the Danes. The same pers.n. occurs also in **Fosdyke** and **Fotherby.**

Fotherby (LNR), *Fodrebi* 1086 DB, *Fotrebi* c1115 LS, a1184 (1409) Gilb, *-by* c1200 RA iv, *Foterby* Hy2 Dugd vi, a1170, probably 'Fot's farmstead, village', from the ON pers.n. *Fótr* (gen.sg. *Fótar*) and ODan **bȳ**. The same pers.n. occurs in **Fosdyke** and **Foston.**

Frampton (Hol), *Franetone, Frantune* 1086 DB, *-tona* Hy2 Dane' *-ton'* 1203 Abbr, *Francton* 1183 *HarlCh*, *-ton'* 1206 Cur, *Framton* 1202 Ass, perhaps 'Frameca's farmstead, village' from the OE pers.n. **Frameca*, a regular diminutive of OE *Fram*, and OE **tūn**.

Freiston (Hol), *Fristune* 1086 DB, *-tona* 1168 P, *-ton'* 1171, 1191, ib, 1198 FF, 1200 Cur, *Frestuna* 1158 *HarlCh*, eHy2 Dane, *-ton'* 1195 P, *Fryston'* 1183 (m14th) *HC*, 'the farmstead, the village of the Frisians', from OE **Frīsa, Frēsa** and OE **tūn**, probably a pre-viking p.n.

Freshney, R. (LNR), *portu de Fresken* 1258 BC, *portum de Freskeney* 1257 RH, "water of" *Freshney* 1279–80 Inqaqd, *Freskene aqua* 1279–80 IpmR, "water of" *Freskeney* 1280 Pat, 'the river with fresh water', from OE **fresc** and OE **ēa,** in the dat.sg. *æt frescan ēa* 'at the fresh river', identical with **Friskney.**

Friesthorpe (LWR), *Frisetorp* 1086 DB, *Frisatorp* c1115 LS, *Fristorp* 1146, c1155, 1163 RA i, 1189–95 ib iv, 'the secondary settlement of the Frisians' from the gen.pl. of OE **Frīsa** and ODan **thorp**. This no doubt denoted an isolated group of Frisians which accompanied the Danish settlers in L. Compare **Firsby.**

Frieston (Caythorpe, Kest), *Fristun* 1086 DB, Hy2 Dane, *-ton'* 1180 P, 1185 RotDom, 'the village of the Frisians' from OE **Frīsa**, **Frēsa** and OE **tūn**, identical with **Freiston** (Hol). The form of the name, without medial *-e-*, suggests it is a pre-viking p.n.

Friskney (LSR), *Frischenei* 1086 DB, *Freschena* c1115 LS, *Freskena* Hy2 Dane, *Freskenei* l12th Dane, *-eie* l12th RA ii, *-ay* 1196 FF, *Freschenei* a1168 Dugd vi, 'the river with fresh water', from OE **fresc** 'fresh' and OE **ēa** 'a river' in the OE dat.sg. *æt frescan ēa*, partially Scandinavianised; it is identical in origin with **R. Freshney**.

Frithville (LSR) was formed into a township by Act of Parliament in 1812 and was earlier *le Frith* 1322 Cl, 1322 Pat, 1323, 1325 Cl, from OE **fyrhth** in the sense 'fenland overgrown with brushwood'.

Frodingham (LWR, formerly a separate parish, now included in Scunthorpe), *Frodingham* c1128 (12th) ChronPetro, *Frodhingham* e13th (1311) Ch, *Frodingeham* 1224 Welles, 1291 Tax, *Frothigham* 1237 RRG, *Frothingham* 1259, 'the homestead, estate of the Frōdingas' from the gen.pl. *Frōdinga* of the OE group-name *Frōdingas* 'the family, the dependents of *Frōda*' and OE **hām**. Forms in *Froth-* are due to Scandinavian influence, as in **Frodingham** in the East Riding of Yorks.

Frognall (Deeping St James, Kest), *Frokenhale* c1139 (1332) *Deep*, 1348 Pat, *Froginhale* 1282 Ipm, 1288 *Ass*, *-hal'* 1327 SR, *Frogenale* 1473 *Deep*, 'the nook of land where frogs abound' from OE **frogga** and OE **halh**, dat.sg. **hale**.

Fulbeck (Kest), *Fulebec* 1086 DB, 1130 P, 1172–80 Dane, a1189 Semp, *-bech* 1146, 1163 RA i, *-bek* l12th Semp, 'the foul, dirty stream' from OE **fūl** and ON **bekkr**.

Fulletby (LSR), *Fullobi* (sic) 1086 DB, *Fuledebi* c1115 LS, *Fuletebi* c1115 ib, lHy2 Dane, *Fulleteby* 1175–81 ib, *Fulettebi* Hy2 ib, *Folettebi* 1167 P, 1208 FF, *Fulneteby* 1225 Welles, the first el. is obscure; the second is ODan **bȳ** 'a farmstead, a village'.

Fulnetby (Rand, LSR), *Fulnedebi* 1086 DB, *-by* 1234 FF, *Fulnetebi* c1115 LS, Hy2 (1406) Pat, *Fulnotebi* a1187 Dane, *Fulathebi* l12th ib, *Fulnethebi* 1196 ChancR. The first el. is obscure; the second is ODan **bȳ** 'a farmstead, a village'.

Fulney (Spalding, Hol), *Fuleneia* 1166, 1184 P, *Fulnea* 1175 ib, *Fulne* 1202 Ass, *Fulnee* c1230 (c1331) *Spald i*, 'the dirty stream' from OE **fūl** and OE **ēa**.

Fulsby (Kirkby on Bain, LSR), *Folesbi* 1086 DB, 12th *RevesInv*, 1200 FF, *-by* 1198 (1328) Ch, *Foleby* 1230 Cl, 'Foli's farmstead, village' from the ON pers.n. *Foli* and ON **bȳ**. The name survives in **Fulsby Wood House**.

Fulsthorpe, see **Thorpe** (Trusthorpe).

Fulstow (LNR), *Fugelestou* 1086 DB, 1183 P, *-stowe* 1180 ib, *Fughelstou* c1160 Dane, *Fulestou* 1147 RA iii, *Foulestow* Hy2 (1409) Gilb, probably from OE **fugol** 'a bird' and OE **stōw** 'a place, a place of assembly'. The first el. is less likely to be the OE pers.n. *Fugol*, for compounds of **stōw** with a pers.n. are rare and when they do occur they are usually hundred- or wapentake-names. It is later called *Foulestowe Harsyke* 1427 *LMR* and *Fulstow Beke* 1494 *ib*, from the *Arsic* and *Bec* families, holders of manors here.

G

Gainsborough (LWR), *Genesburuh* s.a. 1013, s.a. 1014 (m11th) ASC C, *-burc* 1167 P, *Gæignesburh* s.a. 1013, s.a. 1014 (e12th) ASC D, *Gainesburg* 1086 DB, m12th (l13th) *Stix*, *-burch* 1177 P, 'Gægn's fortified place' from the OE pers.n. *Gægn* and OE **burh**, no doubt from its site dominating the right bank of the R. Trent.

Gainsthorpe (Hibaldstow, LWR), *Gamelstorp* 1086 DB, *Gameltorp* c1115 LS, *Gamelestorp* 1180 P, 1196 ChancR, 1202 Ass, 1205 Cur, from the ODan pers.n. *Gamal* and ODan **thorp** 'a secondary settlement', perhaps of **Hibaldstow**. *Gamal* is recorded frequently in L in DB. The development to *Gains-* is late and obscure.

Garthorpe (LWR), *Gerulftorp* 1086 DB, *Gerold'torp* 1180 P, *Geraldtorp'* 1200 ib, *Gerlethorp* 1238, 1253 FF, *Gerlthorp* 1275 RH, *Gerthorp* 1275 ib. The forms from P are not supported by those from any other source and must be discounted. The name means 'Gerulf's secondary settlement' from the ODan pers.n. *Gērulf* and ODan **thorp.**

Gartree Wapentake (LSR), *Cheiretre* (sic) c1115 LS, *Geretre* 1168 P, *Gertre* 1178, 1193 ib, *Gairtre* 1200 ib, *Geirtre* 1202 Ass. The early forms are usually preceded or followed by some form of Latin *wapentacium*. The first el. is probably ON **geiri** 'a gore', used of a mark on a tree, the second el. is ON **tré** 'a tree'. It has been suggested that the reference is to a tree with a conspicuous mark on it indicating the site of the wapentake (ON **vapnatak**, late OE **wæpengetæc** 'a subdivision of a shire') meeting-place. Unfortunately the site is unknown.

Garwick (Heckington, Kest), *Gerewic* Hy2 (1316) Ch, e13th RA vii, 1298 Ipm, *-wik'* 1275 RH, *Gerwyk* 1315 (l15th) *BostCC*. The first el. may be the OE pers.n. **Gæra*; the second is OE **wīc** in one of its senses 'a dwelling, a specialised building, a farm, a dairy farm'.

Gautby (LSR), *Ganteby* a1129 (1336) Dugd vi, m12th (1336) ib, *-bi* 1196 FF (all *-n-* = *-u-*), *Goutheby* 1202 ib, *Gautebi* 1212 Fees, 'Gauti's farmstead, village' from the ON pers.n. *Gauti* and ODan **bȳ**.

Gayton le Marsh (LSR), *Gaiton'* 1202 FF, *Geiton'* 1206 Ass, *Geyton* 1222 Pat, *Gayton* 1236 RRG, *Gayton' in le Mersshe* 1378 Anc and cf. *mariscum de Gayton* l12th (Ed1) *Barl*. **Gayton le Wold** (LSR), *Gettune, Gedtune* (sic) 1086 DB, *Gayton* 1156–58 *HarlCh*, *Gaituna* c1155 Dane, *-tun* lHy2 ib, *-ton* 1156–58 *HarlCh*, 1185 Templar, *Westgayton* 1236 RRG, *Gatton on the Wold* (sic) 1557 InstBen, the DB form being clearly an error. Both names were probably originally 'the farmstead, village where goats are kept' from OE **gāt** and OE **tūn**. The first el. was replaced by the cognate ON **geit**. The affixes are self-explanatory.

Gedney (Hol), *Gadenai, Gadenay* 1086 DB, *-ai* 1130 P, *Gedenei, -ai* 1194 CurP, 1212 Fees, *-ey* 1231 FF, probably 'Gǣda's island of land' from the OE pers.n. *Gǣda* and OE **ēg**.

Gelston (Brandon, Kest), *Cheuelestune* (sic) 1086 DB, *Genelesdon'* (-n- = -u-) 1198 Abbr, *Geueleston'* 1200 CurR, 1202 Ass, 1208 FF, probably 'Giǫfull's village' from the ON byname *Giǫfull* and OE **tūn**, a hybrid Anglo-Danish p.n. which probably represents an earlier Anglo-Saxon settlement taken over and partially renamed by the Danes.

Gilby (Pilham, LWR), *Gillebi* 1138–39, 1139 RA i, *-by* 1220–32 *Foster*, 'Gilli's farmstead, village' from the ON pers.n. *Gilli* and ODan **bȳ**.

Glanford Brigg (LNR), *Glanford'* 1183 P, *pontem de Glaunford* 1203 P, *punt de Glanford'* 1218 Ass, *pontem de Glaunford'* 1259 Cl, *Glaunford Brigge* 1318 Pat, *Glamfordbrigges* 1331 ib. **Glanford** is almost certainly derived from OE **glēam** 'revelry, etc.' and OE **ford** 'a ford', hence 'the ford where sports are held'; forms in *Glaum-* and *Glaun-* are Scandinavianised, showing the influence of ON **glaumr**. To this was later added Brigg, from ON **bryggja** 'a jetty, a quay', but which here refers to a bridge over the R. Ancholme, as the Latin forms clearly show.

Glen, R. (Kest), *aqua de Glenye* 1276 RH, *Glen* 1365, 1366 Pat, *le Glene* 1390 *DuLaCh*. This is probably a Celtic r.n., identical with R. Glen in Northumberland, meaning 'the clean one' from PrW ***glen**, a reference to a clear stream.

Glentham (LWR), *Glantham, Glandham* 1086 DB, *Glentham* 1086 ib, eHy2 (1409) Gilb, 1163 *And*, 1183–84 RA iv, *Glentheim* c1115 LS, *Glenteham* 1185 Templar. **Glentham** is presumably to be taken with **Glentworth**, the first el. of each having similar forms. This is perhaps an OE **glente** probably 'a kite'. If so Glentham would mean 'the homestead, estate frequented by kites', the second el. being OE **hām**.

Glentworth (LWr), *Glentewrde, -uurde, urde* 1086 DB, *Glenteworda* c1115 LS, *-wurde* a1150 Dane, *-worthe* 1155–60 ib, *-worde* 1160–66 ib, *-worth'* 1202 Ass. For the first el. see **Glentham**; the second is OE **worth**, hence 'the enclosure frequented by kites'.

Gokewell (Broughton, LWR), *Gaukeuell'* 1185 Templar, *Goucuella* l12th CollTop, *Goukewell'* e13th YCh vi, 1212 Fees, probably 'the spring frequented by cuckoos', a hybrid name from ON **gaukr** and OE **wella**. The site of the Priory here was called *Eskadal'* a1175, Hy2 Goke, *Aschedale* 1487 Yarb, 'the valley where ash-trees grow' from ON **eski** and **dalr**.

Goltho (LSR), *Golthowe* 1209–35 LAHW, *-hawe* c1221 Welles, *Gouthawe* 1272 *Ass*, *Golthag'* 1307 *Kirkst*, *-haugh* 1308 Inqaqd, *-hagh* 1323 Ipm, probably 'the enclosure where marigolds grow' from OE **golde** and OE **haga**. It is now depopulated.

Gonerby, Great & Little (Kest), *Gunfordebi* 1086 DB, 1130 P, *Gunnefordeb'* 1185 Templar, *Gunnewordebi* 1086 DB, *Gunwordebi* 1163 RA i, *Gynewardebeia* 1146 ib, *-bi* 1200 Abbr, *Gunwarbie Magna* 1634 *Foster*, *Little Gonerby* 1605 Admin, probably 'Gunnvarth's farmstead, village' from the ON pers.n. *Gunnvarthr* and ODan **bȳ**. The forms in *-ford-*, however, might imply that we are concerned with ON *Gunn(f)rothr*, which was later modified through confusion of its second el. with common name el. OE (Anglian) *-ward*, ON *varthr*. **Little Gonerby** is represented today by **Little Gonerby Farm**.

Gosberton (Hol), *Gosebertcherche* 1086 DB, 1180 P, *-chirche* 1086 DB, 1229 Welles, *Gozeberdecherca* 1086 DB, *Goseberdechirche* 1177 P, *Goseberchirche* c1180 (13th) *Castleacre*, from the Continental Germanic pers.n. *Gosbert* and OE **cirice** 'a church'. Forms in *Gosseberdkyrk* c1200 (1407) Gilb, *Goseberdkirke* 1210–12 RBE, *Gosberkirke* 1212 Fees, from ON **kirkja** 'a church', replace those in *-chirche* which continue however to be used into the 18th century. The change to *-ton* has not been found before the late 15th century, as in *Gosburton* 1487 Pat, and there are numerous later references such as *Gosberton alias Gosberkirk* 1696 Foster. For a similar replacement of *cirice* by *kirkja* see **Algarkirk**.

Gosberton Cheal (Gosberton, Hol), *æt Cegle* 852 (12th) ASCharters, *Ceila* 1086 DB, *Cheile* 1179 P, *Cheyle* 1237 FF, 1244 Ipm, probably derived from OE *cegel 'a pole', perhaps referring to a pole or post serving as a boundary marker. The parish name, **Gosberton**, was prefixed later.

Goulceby (LSR), *Colchesbi* 1086 DB, *Colkesbi* 1193 P, *Golkesby* 1135–54, eHy2 (l13th) *Stix*, 1231 FF, *-bi* 1212 Fees, c1221 Welles, *Golckesbi* 1185 Templar, *Kolkesbi* 1194 P; if initial *C-* and *K-* are the correct forms then this is from the ON pers.n. *Kolkr* with ODan **bȳ** 'a farmstead, a village'. The first el. has the Scand. gen.sg. in *-s*, which survives as [s] in the present-day pronunciation, indicating that the name must have been given by Scand. speakers.

Goxhill (LNR), *Golse* 1086 DB, 1182 P, *Golsa* 1086 DB, c1115 LS, c1141 BMFacs, *Gausa* 1148–52 LAAS vi, *Gosla* c1145 Dane, *Gousle* 1135–40 (e14) YCh ii, *Gousel* 1127–35 (e14) YCh iii, *Gousele* 1163 RA i; this is identical with Goxhill in the East Riding of Yorkshire. It is a most difficult name and no certain solution can be offered.

Graby (Aslackby, Kest), *Greibi* 1086 DB, eHy2, l12th Dane, *-bye* 1210–12 RBE, *-bi* 1219 Ass, *Greyby* 1236 Cl, perhaps 'Grey's farmstead, village' from ON **grey** 'a bitch', used as a nick-name, and ODan **bȳ**. However, the first el. presents semantic problems and it seems safer to derive it from OE **grǣg** 'grey', hence 'the grey farmstead, village'.

Grainsby (LNR), *Grenesbi* 1086 DB, 1146 RA i, c1150 Dane, 1198 CurR, *Greinesbi* c1115 LS, p1150 *HarlCh*, 1218 Ass, *Greynesby* 1242–43 Fees, *Grainesbi* 1166 RBE, 'Grein's famstead, village' from the ON pers.n. *Grein*, ODan *Grēn* and ODan **bȳ**.

Grainthorpe (LSR), *Germundstorp, Germundtorp* 1086 DB, 1195 FF, *Ghermudtorp* (sic) c1115 LS, 1208 FF, *Germundthorp* 1156–58 *HarlCh*, *Germuntorp* 1187 (1409) Gilb, 'Germund's secondary settlement' from the Continental Germanic pers.n. *Germund* and ODan **thorp**. Note, *Alv* f.97v in a later hand states that "Alan' Comes Britannie feoffauit Germundus de terris de Germthorp et de aduocacōem ecclesie ei'dem ville".

Grange de Lings (LWR), *grangeam super Lynges* 1325 FA, *grangiam de Lynges iuxta Ryson* (i.e. **Riseholme**) 1329 Ass, *Lyngges Grange* 1332 Pat, literally 'the grange of the heathers' from ON **lyng**. It was a **grange** of Barlings Abbey.

Grantham (Kest), *Grantham, Grandham, Granham, Graham* 1086 DB, *Graham* c1128 France, 1130 P, 1180–83 *MiD*, 1201 Ass, *Grantham* 1227 Cl, 1232 Cur. The complete lack of forms in *Grante-* do not support a pers.n. OE *Granta* as first el., as has been suggested. Perhaps the first el. is OE *grand 'gravel' which is topographically appropriate. The second el. is OE hām 'a homestead, an estate'. The numerous forms in *Graham* are due to Norman influence.

Grasby (LNR), *Grosebi, Grosbi* 1086 DB, *Grossebi* c1115 LS, 1166 P, *Gressebi* 1165 ib, 1202 Ass, *Greseby* 1212 Fees, perhaps from ON grjót 'gravel, stones', topographically appropriate here, and ODan bȳ 'a farmstead, a village'. However, this does not explain the forms in *Gro-*, unless they are errors for *Gre-*.

Grayingham (LWR), *Graingeham, Grangeham* 1086 DB, *Graingeham* c1146 RRAN, *Grahingaham* 1157 France, *Greingheham* c1115 LS, *Greingeham* 1196, 1208 ChancR, from the gen.pl. *Grǣginga* of OE *Grǣgingas*, a group-name meaning 'the family, the dependents of *Grǣg(a)*' and OE hām 'a homestead, an estate'.

Greatford (Kest), *Griteford* 1086 DB, *Greteford* 1086 ib, 1178 P, *Gretford* 1191, 1200 ib, 1202 Ass, 'the gravelly ford' from OE grēot and OE ford, topographically appropriate.

Grebby (Scremby, LSR), *Gredbi* (sic), *Greibi* 1086 DB, *Grebbi* 1212 Fees, 1218 Ass, *Grebby* 1317 Ipm, from ON grjót 'gravel, stones', topographically appropriate, and ODan bȳ 'a farmstead, a village'.

Greenfield (Aby, LSR), *Grenefeld* a1150, c1150, 1150–60 Dane, p1150 *HarlCh*, p1160 Dane, 'the green open land' from OE grēne and OE feld.

Greetham (LSR), *Grandham* (sic), *Gretham* 1086 DB, 1232 Cur, 1242–43 Fees, 1254 ValNor, *Greham* 1166–75 Dane, *Graham* l12th ib, *Greteham* 1233 Welles, 'the homestead, the estate on gravelly land' from OE grēot and OE hām, topographically appropriate. Forms with loss of medial -*th*- are due to Anglo-Norman influence.

Greetwell (LWR), *Grentewelle* (sic) 1086 DB, *Gretwella* c1115 LS, lHy2 Dane, -*well* c1220 RA iv, *Gretewelle* 1121 (1308) Ch, 1163 RA i, 'the gravelly spring' from OE grēot and OE wella, topographically appropriate.

Grimblethorpe (LSR), *Grimchiltorp* c1115 LS, *Grimkiltorp* c1162 Dane, Hy2 (1409) Gilb, *Grimkeltorp'* l12th (m13th) *NCot*, *Grimcheltorp* eHy2 Dane, 'Grīmkel's secondary settlement', from the ODan pers.n. *Grīmkel* and ODan **thorp**. The name survives in **Grimblethorpe Hall**.

Grimoldby (LSR), *Grimalbi* 1086 DB, *Grimolbi* c1115 LS, Hy2 (1324) Ch, Hy2 (1409) Gilb, lHy2 Dane, 1202 FF, *Grimoldbi* 1086 DB, *Grimoldeby* c1170 (1409) Gilb, *-bi* 1185 P, *Grimoldesbi* 1187 ib, 'Grimaldi's farmstead, village' from the ODan pers.n. *Grimaldi* and ODan **bȳ**.

Grimsby, Great (LNR), *Grimesbi* 1086 DB, c1115 LS, 1130 P, *-by* 1155–56 RBE, 1192 P, *Grymesby* c1151 RA i, *magnam Grymesby* 1293 *Ass*, *mekill Grimesby* 1481 *GrimsCB i*, *Grete grimesby* 1462 ib, 'Grím's village' from the ON pers.n. *Grímr*, ODan *Grīm*, recorded several times in L in DB, and ODan **bȳ**. **Grimsby** is referred to in the Icelandic saga, *Orkneyinga saga* c1120 (c1300) in the phrase *í grims bæ mithivm* "in the middle of Grimsby". It is **Great** in contrast to **Little Grimsby**; *mekill* is derived from ON *mikill* 'great'. **Grimsby, Little** (LNR), *Grimesbi* 1086 DB, c1115 LS, *Grymesby* 1160–66 (1409) Gilb, *Parva Grimesbia* c1115 LS, *Litell Grymesby* 1462 Pat, identical in origin with **Great Grimsby**.

Grimsthorpe (Edenham, Kest), *Grimestorpe* 1166 RBE, *-torp'* lHy2 *Anc*, 1212 Fees, *Grimesthorp* 1189 (15th) Bridl, 1242–43 Fees, 'Grīm's secondary settlement (of **Edenham**)' from the ODan pers.n. *Grīm* (as also in **Great & Little Grimsby**) and ODan **thorp**. *Grim* occurs in DB in L.

Gunby (LSR), *Gunnebi* 1086 DB, 1171 P, c1200 Dane, e13th *HarlCh*, 1205 P, *-b'* 1185 Templar. **Gunby** (Gunby and Stainby, Kest), *Gunnebi* 1086 DB, 1200 P, 1202 Ass, *-by* 1212 Fees, *Gunebi* 1201 ChancR. Both mean 'Gunni's farmstead, village' from the ON pers.n. *Gunni* and ODan **bȳ**. The same pers.n. occurs in **Gunness** and **Gunthorpe**.

Gunnerby (Hatcliffe, LNR), *Gunresbi* 1086 DB, c1115 LS, *Gunreby* a1182 (13th) *Alv*, *Gunnerby* 1242–43 Fees, 'Gunnar's farmstead, village' from the ODan pers.n. *Gunnar* and ODan **bȳ**.

Gunness (LWR), *Gunnesse* 1199, 1200, 1202 P, 1202 Ass, 1210 P, 1210–12 RBE, 'Gunni's ness, headland' from the ON pers.n. *Gunni* and ON **nes** 'a ness, a headland'. There is a marked promontory in the R. Trent here. The same pers.n. occurs in **Gunby** and **Gunthorpe**.

Gunthorpe (Owston Ferry, LWR), *Gunetorp* c1200 Dane, *Gunthorp'* 1279 *AD*, 1279 *FF*, 1288, 1289 *Ass*, 'Gunni's secondary settlement' from the ON pers.n. *Gunni* and ODan **thorp**. The same pers.n. occurs in **Gunby** and **Gunness**.

Guthram Gowt (Deeping St Nicholas), *Goderamscote* 1295 *Ass*, 1315 (l15th) *BostCC*, *Godramcote* 1325 (c1331) *Spald i*, cf. *Goderamesende* 1199 (c1331) *Spald ii*, 'Godram(n)'s cottage' from the Continental Germanic pers.n. *Godram(n)* and OE **cot**, the second el. later being confused with OE **gotu** 'a sluice', as in *Guddram Gote* 1552 Sewer.

Gwash, R. (Kest), *Wass* l12th Dugd vi, *aquam q' vocatur Was* 1275 RH, *aquam de le Wasshe* 1550–52 *MinAcct*, *Gwash* 1586 Camden. For additional forms see *The Place-Names of Rutland*, EPNS 1994, p. 2. This is probably from OE **wæsse** 'riverside land which floods and drains quickly', originally applied to a piece of land and subsequently transferred to the river, topographically appropriate for the **Gwash** before the construction of Rutland Water Reservoir. The river was subject to severe flooding, especially around Ryhall in Rutland, where it has formed two oxbow lakes. The modern quasi-Welsh spelling **Gwash** is not found before Camden, who may well have invented it himself.

H

Habertoft (Willoughby with Sloothby, LSR), *Halbertoft* 1166 P, *Halbirtoft'* 1259 *HarlCh*, *Halbertoft* 1294 *Anc*, *-thoft* 1327 *SR*, *Habirthoft* 1259 FF, probably 'Hallbjǫrn's messuage, curtilage' from the ON pers.n. *Hallbjǫrn* and ODan **toft**.

Habrough (LNR), *Haburne* (sic) 1086 DB, *Haburc* c1115 LS, c1150 Dane, *-burg'* 1187 P, 1202 Ass, *-burgh* 1281 QW, 'the high fortified place' from OE **hēah** and OE **burh**, the first el. having been replaced by the cognate ON **hár** 'high'.

Haceby (Newton, Kest), *Hazebi* 1086 DB, *Hatsebi* 1115 RA i, *Haceby* eHy2 (1411) Gilb, *Hascebi* 1161 P, 1194 CurP, *Hazebi* 1166 P, *Hacebi* 1172 ib, 1198 Cur, probably 'Hadd's farmstead, village', from the ON pers.n. *Haddr* and ODan **bȳ**. For the modern pronunciation of the name compare **Laceby**.

Hackthorn (LWR), *Haggethorn* 968 (l13th) RamsChron, 1193 P, *Hagetorne* 1086 DB, *-thorn* 1202 Ass, *Hachethorna* c1115 LS, *Hachetorna* c1115 ib, *Haketorn* 1156–85 (p1269) *Bard*, c1160 Dane, *Hachetorn* lHy2 ib, *Hakethorn* lHy2 ib, 'the hawthorn' apparently from an OE **haca-thorn**, a side-form of the more common **haguthorn**, which would have given Hawthorne today. Presumably it was named from a prominent tree.

Haconby (Kest), *Haconesbi, Hacunesbi, Haconebi* 1086 DB, *Hacunebi* 1135–54 Dane, 1164, 1201 P, *Hakunebi* 1170, 1185 ib, *Hakonebi* 1199 CurP, 'Hákon's farmstead, village' from the ODan pers.n. *Hákon* and ODan **bȳ**.

Haddington (Auborn, Kest), *Hadinctune* ?1085–89 (14th) *Westm*, 1086 DB, *Hadingtun* 1160–76 BS, 1190–1200 RA viii, *-ton'* e13th *AddCh*, probably 'the farmstead, village associated with or called after Had(d)a' from the OE pers.n. *Had(d)a* (or *Hæddi*) with the OE medial connective particle **-ing-** and OE **tūn**.

Hagnaby (LSR), *Hagenebi* 1086 DB, c1150 RA vi, 1193 P, *Hagenesbia* 1142 NthCh, *Haghenebi* m12th Revesby, *Hagnebi* 1170–78 ib. **Hagnaby** (Hannah cum Hagnaby, LSR), *Haghnebi* c1200 Dane, 1202 Ass, *-by* e13th *HarlCh*, 1228 Welles. Both mean 'Haghni's farmstead, village' from the ODan pers.n. *Haghni* and ODan **bȳ**.

Hagworthingham (LSR), *Haberdingham* 1086 DB, *Aburdingeham* 1166 P, *Hacberding(e)ham* 1086 DB, *Hawordingheham* c1115 LS, *Hagworthyngham* 1115 (14th) *Bard*, *-ingham* 1147 (p1269) *ib*, *Hagwrthingham* l12th (p1259) *Kirkst*, *Agewordingheheim*, *Hagwordingeheim* c1115 LS, *Hagwurdingeh'* 1166, 1180 P, *Hagworthingeham* 1202 Ass. This is apparently the gen.pl. *-inga* of an OE group-name in **-ingas** ('the family, the people of X') with OE **hām** 'a homestead, an estate' as second el. The forms are difficult but an unrecorded OE pers.n. ***Hagubeard*, which would be cognate with Old High German *Hagabarth* and ON *Hagbarthr*, might be suggested as first el. Hence the name would mean 'the homestead, the estate of the family, the people, of Hagubeard'. Forms in *-heim* are from ON **heim** cognate with OE **hām**.

Hainton (LSR), *Hainton(e)*, *-tune* 1086 DB, Hy2 (1409) Gilb, *-tona* c1160 (1409) ib, *-ton'* eHy2 (m13th) NCot, *Heintuna* c1115 LS, *-ton'* 1163 RA i, 'the enclosed farmstead' from OE **hægen** and OE **tūn**.

Hale, Great & Little (Kest), *Hale* 1086 DB, 1194 CurP, *Hales* 1094 France, *Hal* 1166 RBE, Hy2 (1316) Ch, 1202 FF, *Magna Hale* 1204 Cur, *Mikelhal* 1256 FF (from ON **mikill** 'big, great'), *Litlehale* 1180 P, *Parva Hale* a1204 RA vii, 'at the nook of land' from the dat.sg. **hale** of OE **halh**. The affixes are self-explanatory.

Hallington (LSR), *Halintun* 1086 DB, *Haligtune* c1115 LS, *Halington* m12th, Hy2 Dugd v, *-ton'* 1200 ChR, *Hallington'* 1202 Ass, 'the farmstead, village associated with or called after Hal(l)a', with the OE medial connective particle **-ing-** and OE **tūn**, the first el. being an unrecorded OE pers.n. ***Hal(l)a** cognate with Old High German *Heilo*.

Halstead Hall (Stixwould, LSR), *Haustede*, *Halstede* Hy2 (l3th) *Stix*, *Hallestede* 1172–80 Dane, *-sted* 1275 RH, from OE **hallstede** literally 'the place, the site of a hall'.

Haltham on Bain (LSR), *Holtham* 1086 DB, Hy2 (p1259) *Kirkst*, *-am* 1162 (p1259) *ib*, *-eim* c1115 LS, *-aim* 1163 Dane, *-haim* eHy2 (p1259) *Kirkst*, 'the homestead, the estate in the wood' from OE **holt** and OE **hām**. Forms in *-eim*, *-aim* and *-haim* are from ON **heim** cognate with **hām**.

Haltoft End (Freiston, Hol), *Halketoft* eHy2 (13th) *Kirkst*, c1180 Dane, 1193 P, 1200 Cur, 1202 FF, *Alketoft* eHy2 Dane; the first el. is uncertain, but it is perhaps from OE **halc**, ME **halke** 'a corner, a nook', the second being ODan **toft** 'a messuage, a curtilage'.

Halton, East (LNR), *Haltune* 1086 DB, *-tun* c1115 LS, c1155 Dane, *-ton'* 1202 Ass, 1224 FF, *Esthalton* 1415 WillsPCC, from OE **halh** 'a nook of land', here in the sense 'a piece of dry ground in marsh' and OE **tūn** 'a farmstead, a village', topographically appropriate. **Halton, West** (LWR), *Haltone* 1086, *-ton* c1115 LS, 1158 France, *Hauton* 1194 (Hy4) GCB, 1219 Welles, *Halghton'* 1219 Fees. **West Halton** is also derived from OE **halh** and OE **tūn** but in this case the 'nook' refers to the situation of the village lying in a nook in the ground rising from the R. Trent to the cliff. The affixes **East** and **West** are self-explanatory.

Halton Holegate (LSR), *Haltun* 1086 DB, c1190 de l'Isle, *-tona* 1142–51 Dane, *-tone* 1166 RBE, *Hauton* c1135 Dane, *-tona* Hy2 ib, *Hauton Holgate* 1576 Saxton. Identical with **East & West Halton**, The village lies in a small valley in the rising ground on the edge of the fens. Sporadic forms in *-u-* are due to vocalisation of *-l-*. The affix **Holegate** 'the road running through the hollow', from OE **hol** and ON **gata**, is descriptive of the situation of the village.

Hameringham (LSR), *Hameringam* 1086 DB, 1158 *HarlCh*, *Hamringheheim* c1115 LS, *Hameringeham* 1188, 1190, 1194 P, 'the homestead, the estate of the Hamoringas' from the OE gen.pl. *Hamoringa* of the OE group-name *Hamoringas* probably 'the dwellers by the hill', the first part of which would then be OE **hamor** 'a hill'. The place is on a hill.

Hammond Beck, New & Old (Hol), *Hamundebek* 1315 (c1331) *Spald i*, *Hamondbek* 1315 *BostCC*, *Hamonde Bek* 1489 Thompson, 'Hamond's stream' from the ME pers.n. *Hamond* (OFr *Hamond*) and ON **bekkr**.

Hanby (Lenton, Kest), *Handebec* 1210 P, 1212, 1242–43 Fees, *-bek'* 1258 FF, perhaps 'Handi's stream' from the ON byname *Handi* and ON **bekkr**, identical with **Hanbeck**, a lost village in Wilsford parish. The change to **Hanby** has so far not been noted before the 19th century.

Hannah (Hannah cum Hagnaby, LSR), *Hanei* 1153–69 Dane, *-eg'* 1195 P, 1196 ChancR, *-eye* 1228 Welles, *-ai* eHy2, Hy2 Dane, perhaps 'the island of land where cocks are found' from OE **hana** in the gen.pl. and OE **ēg**. Alternatively, the first el. may be the OE pers.n. *Hana*, as in **Cold Hanworth**.

Hanthorpe (Morton, Kest), *Hermodestorp* 1086 DB, *Hermetorp* 1166 RBE, Hy2 LN, 1202, 1219 Ass, *Hermthorp'* c1200 Semp, probably 'Hermóth's secondary settlement (of **Morton**)' from the ON pers.n. *Hermóthr* and ODan **thorp**.

Hanworth, Cold (LWR), *Haneurde, -worde* 1086 DB, *-worda* c1115 LS, c1160 Dane, *-wort* c1155 (1409) Gilb, *-wurth'* 1185 RotDom, *-worth'* c1215 RA iv, *Calthaneworth* 1322 Ipm, *Calde Haneworth* 1325 FA. **Hanworth, Potter** (Kest), *Haneworde* 1086 DB, *-wrda* 1135–54 (p1259) *Kirkst*, 1156–57 (Ed2) YCH i, *-wurd'* 1195 P, *-wrthe* 1196–1203 RA vii, *Potterhaneworth* 1327 Banco. Both mean 'Hana's enclosure' from the OE pers.n. *Hana* and OE **worth**. The first is **Cold** presumably from its exposed situation; there were medieval pottery kilns at **Potter Hanworth**.

Hardwick (LWR), *Harduic* 1086 DB, *-wyk* Hy2 (1409) Gilb, *Hertwic* 1184 (p1259) *Kirkst*, *Herdewic* 1185 Templar, 1202 Ass. **Hardwick Grange** (Swineshead, Hol), *Herdewyk* 1316 Ch, *Herdwik'* 1327 *SR*, 1338 Cl, *West herwyk* 1395 Works. Both are derived from OE **heorde-wīc** 'a herd farm', probably denoting the part of a manor devoted to livestock rather than to arable farming. In 1395 **Hardwick Grange** is described as *vacheriam Abbatis de Swyneshed*, i.e. a dairy-farm.

Hareby (LSR), *Harebi* 1086 DB, 1154–60 RA i, 1170 P, 1185 Templar, Hy2 RA ii, 1199 Revesby, 'Hari's farmstead, village' from the ON byname *Hari* and ODan **bý**.

Harlaxton (Kest), *Herlavestune* 1086 DB, *Herlauestun'* 1174 P, 1185 Templar, *-tona* 1180–83 *MiD*, *-ton'* 1185 Templar, 1218 Ass, probably 'Hiǫrleif's farmstead, village' from the ON pers.n. *Hiǫrleifr* and OE **tūn**. The second el. of the pers.n. shows anglicisation, ON *-leifr* having been replaced by the corresponding OE *-láf*. This was almost certainly an established Anglo-Saxon settlement taken over and partially renamed by the Danes.

Harmston (Kest), *Hermestune* 1086 DB, *-ton'* 1178, 1181 P, *Heremodestone* 1086 DB, Hy2 (1316) Ch, *-tun'* 1196–1203 RA vii, probably 'Hermóthr's farmstead, village', from the ON pers.n. *Hermóthr* and OE **tūn**. This was no doubt an earlier OE p.n. partially renamed by the Danes.

Harpswell (LWR), *Herpeswelle* 1086 DB, *Harpeswella* c1115 LS, 1185–87 Dane, *-well'* 1203 Ass, *Harpewell'* 1196 ChancR, perhaps from OE **hearpere** 'a harper' and OE **wella** 'a spring', the second *-r-* being lost through dissimilation.

Harrington (LSR), *Haringtun* Hy2 Dane, c1200 RA vi, *Haryngtona* lHy2 (1409) Gilb, *Harinton'* 1198 Cur, 1202 Ass, *-tun* l12th Dane, perhaps 'the farmstead, village associated with or called after Hearra', with the OE medial connective particle **-ing-** and OE **tūn**. The first el. would then be the OE pers.n. *Hearra, Hærra*, which is recorded independently in the form *HÆRRA* as the name of an Exeter moneyer in the reigns of Harthaknut and Harald Harefoot.

Harrowby (Londonthorpe, Kest), *Herigerbi* 1086 DB, *Herierbi* 1155–60, 1172 Dane, 1185 Templar, *Herierebi* 1155–60 Dane, perhaps 'Hergeirr's farmstead, village' from the rare ON pers.n. *Hergeirr* and ODan **bȳ**. However, from *Herierdebi* 1202 Ass, *-by* 1228 Ch to *Herierdeby* 1412 FA are a number of references with medial *-d-*. If these are significant then the first el. would probably be the OE pers.n. *Heregeard*. No certainty is possible. **Harrowby** is a joint parish with **Londonthorpe**, as **Londonthorpe and Harrowby Without**, the latter with reference to its relationship to Grantham.

Hartsholm (Skellingthorpe, Kest), *Hertesholm* 1135–54, 1147, m12th, eHy2, 1178 (p1269) *Bard*, *-holme* 1331 Ch, probably 'Hjǫrt's island of land, raised land amidst the marsh' from the gen.sg. *Hartar* of the ON byname *Hjǫrtr* and ON **holmr**.

Hasthorpe (Willoughby with Sloothby, LSR), *Haroldestorp* 1086 DB, *Hardisthorp'* 1259 HarlCh, *Hardesthorp* 1281 QW, 1317 Ipm, 'Harald's secondary settlement' from the ODan pers.n. *Harald* and ODan **thorp**, presumably of **Willoughby**.

Hatcliffe (LNR), *Hadeclive* 1086 DB, 1226–19 Fees, *Haddecliue* c1184 (15th) Templar, c1200 RA iv, *-cliua* 1219 Welles, *Hateclive* 1328 Ipm, 'Hadda's (steep) slope' from the OE pers.n. *Hadda* and OE **clif**, which is topographically appropriate.

Hatton (LSR), *Hatune* 1086 DB, *Hattuna* c1115 LS, 1154 *HarlCh*, c1160 (p1259) *Kirkst, Hatton'* 1212 Fees, 'the farmstead, the village on the heath' from OE **hæth** and OE **tūn**.

Haugh (LSR), *Hage* 1086 DB, l12th Dugd v, 1200 Cur, *Haga* a1150, eHy2 Dane, *Haghe* 1204 Cur, 'the enclosure' from OE **haga**.

Haugham (LSR), *Hecham* 1086 DB, 1188 P, *Hacham* c1150 (13th) *Alv*, c1180 *MiD, Hagham* 1191, 1212 Fees, 'the high homestead, estate' from OE **hēah** and OE **hām**, topographically appropriate.

Haverholme (Ewerby, Kest), *Insulam Hafreholm* 1139 Dugd vi, *insulam Haferholm* 1139 (1634) *Dods 144*, *Haverholm* 1139–55 YCh i, 1174–81 (1337) Ch, *insulam de Haverholm* 1175 (1337) ib, 1198 Cur, 'the island of land where oats grow' from ON **hafri** and ON **holmr**. In 1137 the site was given by Alexander, Bishop of Lincoln, to the Cistercians of Fountains Abbey who later left Haverholme for Louth Park. The gift was then made to the Gilbertines who settled there in 1139.

Haverstoe Wapentake (LRY), *Hawardeshou* 1086 DB, c1115 LS, 1238–41 Fees, 1275 RH, *Hawardeho* 1230 P, *Hawardhou* 1242–43 Fees, 'Hāwarth's (burial) mound' from the ODan pers.n. *Hāwarth* and ON **haugr**, a Scand. compound. The forms are preceded or followed by some form of Latin *wapentacium*. The pers.n. *Hāwarth* is also the first el. of **Hawthorpe** and of **Hawerby** (in the same wapentake) and both names no doubt refer to the same man. The site of the meeting-place of the wapentake (OM **vápnatak**, late OE **wæpengetac** 'a sub-division of a shire') is almost certainly a round barrow in the parish of Hawerby at TF 254 977 close to the road from Grainsby to Wold Newton, but which has recently been almost levelled by ploughing.

Hawerby (Hawerby cum Beesby, LNR), *Hawardebi* 1086, 1196 ChancR, 1202 *HarlCh*, *Hawardabi* c1115 LS, *-by* 1244 RRG, 1254 ValNor, 'Hāwarth's farmstead, village' from the ODan pers.n. *Hāwarth* and ODan **bȳ**; *Hawarth* is also the first el. of **Haverstoe**, the wapentake in which Hawerby is situated and it is highly likely that both refer to the same man who would have been the head-man of the wapentake. This pers.n. is also the first el. of **Hawthorpe**.

Hawthorn Hill (Coningsby, LSR), *Hauthorn'* e13th (p1259) *Kirkst*, *Houtorn* Hy3 *HarlCh*, *Hawthorn* 1510 LNQ xiii, from OE **haguthorn** 'the hawthorn, the whitethorn', no doubt named from a prominent tree.

Hawthorpe (Irnham, Kest), *Awartorp* 1086 DB, *Hawardtorp* eHy2 *AddCh*, *Hawertorp* c1160 Semp, *Hawrtorp* eHy2, c1160 Dane, *Hauerthorp* e13th *AddCh*, 'Hawarth's secondary settlement (of **Irnham**)' from the ODan pers.n. *Hawarth* and ODan **thorp**. The pers.n. *Hawarth* is found also in **Haverstoe Wapentake** and **Hawerby**.

Haxey (LWR), *Acheseia* 1086 DB, *Haxei* m12th Dugd vi, Hy2 (1478) Pat, *Haxey, -ai* l12th *AD*, *-aie* c1200 (1409) Gilb, *-eye* 1219 Cur, probably 'Haki's island of land' from the ON pers.n. *Haki*, with the ME gen.sg. in *-es*, the Scand. gen.sg. in *-s* having replaced the original Scand. *-a*, and ON **ey**.

Healing (LNR), *Hechlinge, Heghelinge* 1086 DB, c1115 LS, *Hegelinge* 1086 DB, 1166 RBE, 1235 Dugd vi, *Heiling'* eHy2 (e13) *NCot*, 1199 Memo, *Helinges* 1212 Cur. 'The followers, the people of Hægel' from the OE pers.n. *Hægel* and the OE suffix -**ingas**. **Healing** is in origin a group-name denoting a body of people bound by kinship or lordship, *Hægel* being the name of the leader. **Healing** became a p.n. when the *Hægelingas* settled in what is today **Healing**. It is the only such p.n. formation found in the North Riding of Lindsey. The name has the same etymology as **Hayling** in Hampshire.

Heapham (LWR), *Iopeham* 1086 DB, *Iopheim* c1115 LS, *Epham* 1167 P, *Hepham* 1196 ChancR, 1202 Ass, from OE **hēope** 'hips' or **hēopa** 'the dog rose' and OE **hām** 'a homestead, an estate'.

Heckington (Kest), *Echintune* 1086 DB, *Hechintone* 1086 ib, *Hekyngton'* 1115 (p1269) *Bard*, -*ingtona* p1125 (c1269) *ib*, *Hekintun* l12th Semp, *Heckingtuna* p1184 ib, 'the farmstead, village associated with, called after Heca' from the OE pers.n. *Heca* with the OE medial connective particle -**ing**- and OE **tūn**.

Heighington (Kest), *Hyctingetun', Hictingtun* Hy2 (p1259) *Kirkst, Hictinton* lHy2 (p1259) *ib*, *Hickinton'* 1242–43 Fees, perhaps 'the farmstead, village called after or associated with Hyht' from the OE pers.n. *Hyht* with the OE connective particle -**ing**- and OE **tūn**.

Helpringham (Kest), *Helpricham, Helperincham* 1086 DB, *Helpringham* 1138 NthCh, *Helprincheham* c1180 *AddCh*, *Helpringeham* 1213, 1224 FF, 1219 Ass, 1227 Welles, 'the homestead, the estate of the Helprīcingas' from the gen.pl. *Helprīcinga* of the OE group-name *Helprīcingas* 'the family, the followers of *Helprīc*' and OE **hām**.

Helsey (Mumby, LSR), *Helleseye* 1259 *HarlCh*, 1272 *Ass*, 1316 RA ix, 1340 *Barl*, -*eie* 1294 *Anc*, -*ay* 1317 Ipm, *Helsey* 1327 ib; the forms are late and the etymology is difficult. The second el. is OE **ēg** 'an island, raised land in marsh' and the first would appear to be ON **hjallr** 'a shed for drying fish' and also 'a ledge'. The exact meaning of the name must remain obscure, though 'ledge' does not appear topographically appropriate here.

Hemingby (LSR), *Hamingebi* (sic) 1086 DB, *Heninghebi* (sic) c1115 LS, *Hemingbi* 1160–75 RA vi, 1172 Dane, *Hemmingebi* 1185 RotDom, Hy2 Dane, 'Heming's farmstead, village' from the ODan pers.n. *Heming* and ODan **bȳ**.

Hemswell (LWR), *Helmeswelle* 1086 DB, 1185–87 Dane, *-wella* c1115 LS, c1145 Dane, *-well'* 1185 Templar, 1196 ChancR, 'Helm's spring' from the OE pers.n. *Helm* and OE **wella**.

Heydour (Kest), *Haidure* 1086 DB, *Heidure* Hy2 (1329) Dugd v, 1202 Ass, *Haydure* c1200 AASR xxvii, *Heidur'* 1201 Cur, *-dore* 1202 Ass, 'the high gap' from OE **hēah** and OE **duru** 'a door, a gap, a pass', the name of the gap in the ridge west of the village.

Hibaldstow (LWR), *Hibaldestowa* 1066–87 (m12th) Dugd i, 1087–88 RA i, c1115 LS, *-stou* 1150–60 Dane, 1163 RA i, *Hiboldestou(e)* 1086 DB, c1128 (12th) ChronPetro, 'the burial-place, the place dedicated to St Hygebald', the second el. being OE **stōw**. Saints c1000 states *Thonne resteth sancte Higebold on Lindesige on thare stowe the is genemnod Cecesege neah thære ea the is genemnod Oncel* "Then St. Higebold was buried in Lindsey at that place which is called Cecesege near the river which is called Ancholme". The earlier name *Cecesege* means 'Cec's island of land' from the OE pers.n. *Cec* and OE **ēg**.

Hilldyke (Boston/Sibsey, Hol/LSR), *Hylldyk'* a1155 (m14th) HC, *Hilledic* 1179 RevesbyS, l12th (13th) *Kirkst*, 1206 OblR, *-dich* 1210 FF, self-explanatory, from OE **hyll** 'a hill' and OE **dīc**, ON **dík** 'a ditch, a water-channel', later 'an embankment'. According to BostHistS 2, 34 it was part of the "kings highway" from Boston to the R. Humber.

Hill Wapentake (LSR), *Hille* 1086 DB, 1168, 1195 P, *Hylle* 1086 DB, 1242–43 Fees, *Hilla* c1115 LS. The early forms are usually preceded or followed by some form of Latin *wapentacium*. The meaning is 'the hill', from OE **hyll** but the site of the meeting-place of the wapentake (ON **vápnatak**, late OE **wæpengetac** 'a sub-division of a shire') is not known.

Hirst Priory (Belton, LWR), *Hyrst* Hy1 (13th), m12th (13th) *Nostell*, *Hirst* c1184 (15th) Templar, *Hurst in Axiholm* 1241 Lib, from OE **hyrst** 'a wooded hill', the site of an Augustinian Priory, a cell of Nostell Priory, founded in the reign of Henry I.

Hoffleet Stow (Wigtoft, Hol), *Holflet* 1175, 1176 P, c1180 (13th) *Castleacre*, 1195 P, 1202 Ass, *-fliet* 1202 P, from OE **hol** 'a hollow' and OE **flēot** 'an inlet, a creek, a stream', presumably denoting a stream flowing in a hollow. **Stow** has been added later and in south Lincolnshire has the meaning 'a dam'.

Hogsthorpe (LSR), *Hocgestorp* 1173–82 Dane, *Hoggestorp* 1180–90 ib, 1195 P, 1196 ChancR, 1198 P, 'Hogg's secondary settlement', a hybrid name from the OE pers.n. *Hogg* and ODan **thorp**, probably of **Mumby**.

Holbeach (Hol), *Holobec, -bech, Holebech* 1086 DB, *Holbecha* 1133–39 RRAN, *Holebec* 1160–70 RA vii, *-beche* 1170 P, 1194 CurP, *-bech* 1182 (c1331) *Spald i*, perhaps from OE **hol** 'hollow' and OE **bæc** 'a back', as has recently been suggested. Holbeach has a raised site and a meaning 'the concave ridge' is topographically appropriate.

Holbeach Hurn (Holbeach, Hol), *Holebechehyrne* 1328 Banco, 1408 Pap, *Holbech'hirne* 1329 *Ass, Holbechirne* 1338 Pat, *Holbechirn* 1340 ib, from the parish-name **Holbeach** and OE **hyrne** 'a corner', 'a spit of land in a river-bend', topographically appropriate. In 1408 Pap it is described as "the sea-girt island of" *Holbeche-hyrne*. **Hurn** is often added to the names of villages in Holland.

Holbeck (Ashby Puerorum, LSR), *Holebec* 1198 (1328) Ch, 112th *RevesInv*, 1270 *Anc*, 'the stream running in a hollow' from OE **hol** and OE **bece** or ON **bekkr**. It may well be that the second el. was originally **bece** and that this was replaced by **bekkr**.

Holdingham (Kest), *Haldingeham* 1202 Ass, *Haldingham* 1202 ib, 1230 RA ii, 1230 Cur, 'the homestead, estate of the Haldingas' from the gen.pl. *Haldinga* of the OE group-name *Haldingas* 'the family, the dependents of Halda' and OE **hām**.

Holland, *Hoilant, Hoiland* 1086 DB, *-landia* 1088–93 YCh i, *-landa* 1130 P, *-land'* 1156, 1182 ib, *Hoylande* 1093–1136 RA vii, 1202 Ass, *-landa* Stephen (m14th) *HC, -land* 1200 ChR, 'the tract of land, the district by a hill-spur or characterised by hill spurs', from OE **hōh** 'a heel, a spur of land' and OE **land**. The bulk of early spellings have *-oi-* or *-oy-* and these are the result of Anglo-Norman influence, apparently an attempt to recognise the presence of the long vowel in OE **hōh**.

Holland Fen (Hol), *marisco de hoyland* 112 (113th) *Stix, - de Hoiland* 1202 P, "marsh of" *Hoyland* 1253, 1255 Pap, 1280 Ipm, *Holandefen* 1331 (c1350) Rams, self-explanatory. Part of Holland Fen was known as **Eighthundred Fen**, *Hauthundr'fen* 1241 Cl, *Eythundrefen* 1272 *Ass, marisco octo hundredorum* 1276 (c1331) *Spald i, Eyghthundredfen* 1348 Pat, literally 'the fen of the eight hundreds'. The eight hundreds (a local division of land) which shared common rights in this fen were those of Algarkirk, Frampton, Kirton, Skirbeck, Sutterton, Swineshead, Wigtoft and Wyberton, all except Skirbeck in Kirton Wapentake.

Holme (LWR), *Holme* 1067–69 (m12th) HC, c1128 (12th) ChronPetro, *Holm* 1086 DB, c1115 LS, c1140 *AD*, 1212 Fees, from ON **holmr** 'an isle', but usually 'higher ground amidst the marshes'.

Holme Hill (Cleethorpes, LNR), *Sotholm* 1182 P, *Sutholm'* 1212 FF, c1300 Guis, *Holm* 1275 RH, *Holme* 1276 ib, *Holm' Hyll* 1508 *GrimsCB ii*. The earliest forms indicate that this is 'the southern piece of higher ground amidst the marsh' from OE **sūth** and ON **holmr**. From 1275 onwards the name appears only in a simplex form till **Hill** was added in the 16th century. It is now no more than a mound, the hill having been dug out for building material.

Holton cum Beckering (LSR), *Houtone* 1086 DB, *-tuna* c1115 LS, *-ton'* 1198 Cur, c1200 RA v, 1202 Ass. **Holton le Clay** (LNR), *Holtun, -tone* 1086 DB, *Houtona* c1115 LS, *-ton* 1201 Cur, 1212 Fees, 1240 RRG, 1242–43 Fees, *Howlton in le Claie* 1615 Admin. **Holton le Moor** (LNR), *Hoctun(e)* 1086 DB, *-ton'* 1168 P, *Houtuna* c1115 LS, *-ton* 1181 P, c1200 RA iv, *Howeton'* 1202 Ass, *Houton in Mora* 1327 *SR*. Each of the **Holtons** means 'the farmstead, village on a heel or spur of land' from OE **hōh** and OE **tūn**, topographically appropriate. The first is distinguished by the name of the neighbouring **Beckering**; the second as **le Clay** since it is on the clay; the third as **le Moor** which is self-explanatory.

Holywell (Careby, Kest), *Helwella* 1147–54 YCh iii, *-well* 1149–50 ib, *Helewel* c1150 RA iii, *-well* 1190 YCh iii, 1200 Cur, probably 'the wishing well' from OE **hæl** 'omen, good fortune' or OE **hǣlu** 'health, healing' and OE **wella**. The development to **Holy-** is late and is no doubt due to popular etymology. The name survives as **Holywell Hall**. There is a prominent spring here.

Honington (Kest), *Hundintune, Hondintone* 1086 DB, *Hundingtun'* 1135–54, 1150–60, a1185 all (13th) *Stix*, 1200 Cur, *-ingtune* 1172, lHy2 Dane 'the farmstead, village associated with or called after Hund(a)' from the OE pers.n. *Hund(a)* with the OE medial connective particle **-ing-** and OE **tūn**.

Horbling (Kest), *Orbelinge* 1086 DB, *Horbelinge* 1086 DB, c1120 (13th) *Castleacre*, *Horbelinga* Hy2 Dane, *Horbeling* eHy2 ib, 1185 Templar,

Horblinge c1160 Semp, 'the family, the followers of Billa', from the OE pers.n. *Billa* and the OE suffix -**ingas**. To this was prefixed **horh** 'filth, dirt', 'mud', no doubt descriptive of the situation of the settlement, and a comparable p.n. formation to **Quadring**. For further details of group names, see **Healing**. The same group, the *Billingas*, also gave their name to **Billingborough**, an adjacent village, while the same group-name occurs in **Billinghay**.

Horkstow (LNR), *Horchetou* (sic) 1086 DB, *Horchestou* c1115 LS, *Horkestowe* 1115 (14th) *Bard*, 1233 Fees, 1254 ValNor, *Horkstowe* 1278 RRGr, from OE ***horc** 'a shelter' and OE **stōw** 'a place, etc.', presumably a place used as a shelter.

Horncastle (LSR), *Hornecastre* 1086 DB, -*castra* 1130 P, *Horncastre* 1147–54 YCh ii, m12th (l13th) KirkstPsalt, -*castra* 1148–54 YCh iii, -*castr'* 1150–60 *Anc*, 1158 P; it is recorded once on an AS coin as *HORN* 979–85; the earliest references so far noted to -**castle** are *Horncastell* c1360 Gough, 1386 Pat. The name means 'the Roman town on a horn-shaped piece of land (between the R. Bain and R. Waring)', from OE **horn, horna**, used topographically of a projecting horn-shaped piece of land, especially one formed in a river-bend, and OE **cæster**. **Horncastle** is almost certainly to be identified with *Bannovallum* 7th (13th) Ravenna, a PrW (Celtic) name meaning 'the strong spur (of land)'. It seems hardly coincidental that OE **horn, horna** 'peak, horn' translates the first element of the Celtic name, ***banno-**; **Horncastle** must have been given by people who knew the meaning of both words.

Horncastle Wapentake (LSR), *Hornecastre* 1086 DB, 1198 P, -*castra* c1115 LS, 1168, 1188, -*castr'* 1166 ib, 1185 RotDom. The early forms are usually preceded or followed by some form of Latin *wapentacium*. The wapentake (ON **vápnatak**, late OE **wæpengetæc** 'a subdivision of a shire') is named from **Horncastle**, where its meeting-place presumably was.

Horsington (LSR), *Horsintone* 1086 DB, 1166 RBE, -*intun* c1140 Dane, -*inton'* 1180 P, *Horsingtun* 1142–53 Dane, m12th (l13th) *Stix*, 'the farmstead, village associated with or called after Horsa' from the OE pers.n. *Horsa* with the OE medial connective particle -**ing**- and OE **tūn**.

Hough on the Hill (Kest), *Hag, Hache* 1086 DB, *Hacg* Hy2 (1318) Dugd vi, *Hach* 1202 Ass, 1204 P, *Hagh'* 1208 FF, 'the enclosure' from OE **haga**. The affix is self-explanatory.

Hougham (Kest), *Hacham* 1086 DB, 1163 RA i, *Hacam* 1086 DB, 1123–48 RA ii, *Hakham* 1208 FF, *Hagham* 1210 RBE, 1218 RA ii. This may well be 'the homestead, estate belonging to **Hough on the Hill**' from **Hough** and OE **hām**, as has elsewhere been proposed. It is possible that the second el. is rather OE **hamm** 'land hemmed in by water; a river-meadow' since the place is in a bend of the R. Witham.

Houghton (Grantham, Kest), *Hogtune, Hogetune, Hochtune, Hoctune* 1086 DB, *Hoctona* 1130, 1179 P, -ton' 1178, 1193 ib, 'the farmstead, village on a heel, a spur of land' from OE **hōh** and OE **tūn**. The name is now represented by **Houghton Farm**.

Howell (Asgarby, Kest), *Welle, Huuelle* 1086 DB, *Huwella* 1165 P, *Huwell'* 1166 ib *Huwelle* 1185 Templar, *Huel* (sic) 1195 FF, *Howell'* 1169 P, *-welle* 1195 ib, *Houwell'* 1175–84 AddCh. The first el. is obscure; the second is OE **wella** 'a spring' which is recorded as *Howell Well* c1650 *Terrier*.

Howsham (Cadney, LNR), *Usun* (sic) 1086 DB, *Husum* c1115 LS, 1177 P, *Housom* 1375 Works, 'at the houses', from the dat.pl. of either OE **hūs** or ODan **hús**, the weakly stressed syllable *-um* being subsequently interpreted as *-ham*. This is a common formation in Denmark and it is likely that this name is of Danish origin, cf. **Burnham**, **Coatham** and **Newsham**.

Hubbert's Bridge (Frampton, Hol), *the bridge over the great dreane called Hubards bridge* 1653 *Sewer*, cf. *Hobarts Hurne* 1529 Wills ii, *Hubbert Syke* 1547 Sewer i. It was named from the *Hubbert* family, cf. John *Hubbert* 1552 Sewer i. *Hurne* is from OE **hyrne** 'an angle, a corner of land', while *Syke* is from OE **sīc** 'a stream (especially one in flat marshland)' or ON **sík** 'a ditch', later 'a piece of meadow along a ditch or stream'.

Humber, R. (LWR/LNR), forms in L documents include: *usque Humbrae fluminis* 731 Bede, *Humbre* 731 ib, *be suthan Humbre* s.a. 827 (c900) ASC A, *ofer Humbre muthan* s.a. 867 (c900) ib, *oth Humbre stream* c890 (10th) OEBede, *of Humbre* 971 (12th) BCS 1270 (S 782), *Hunbran ea* s.a. 942 (c1000) ASC B, *to Humbran muthe* s.a. 993 (1121) ib E, *into Humbran muthan* s.a. 1013 (1121) ib, *into Humbran* s.a. 1066 (1121) ib, *innan Humbran* s.a. 1069 (1121) ib, *Humbra ea* s.a. 942 (c955) ASC A. **Humber** is a pre-English r.n. and may well be pre-Celtic too, since no convincing etymology in Celtic can be suggested. It probably belongs to the group of r.ns. referred to as Old European, compare **Swallow**.

Humberston (LNR), *Humbrestone* 1086 DB, *Humbrestan* Hy2 Dane, 1223 Cur, *Humberstein* c1115 LS, 1180 P, 1203 FF, *-stain* 1164–81 (l13) YCh v, 'the stone by the R. Humber' from the river-name and OE **stān**; forms in *-stein, -stain* are from the cognate ON **steinn**. According to Holles (1634) the stone was "a great Boundry blew Stone".

Humby, Great & Little (Ropsley, Kest), *Humbi* 1086 DB, 1220 Cur, 1233 FF, 1255 Cl, *Hunby* 1303 FA, *Humbye Parva alias Little Humbye* 1539 LP xiv. It is impossible to offer a convincing etymology of the first el.; the second is ODan **bȳ** 'a farmstead, a village'.

Hundleby (LSR), *Hundelbi* 1086 DB, eHy2 (l13th) *Stix*, 1188 P, Hy2 Dane, *-bia* 1141–54 ib, 'Hundulf's farmstead, village' from the ON pers.n. *Hundulfr* and ODan **bȳ**.

Hundle Houses (Wildmore Fen, LSR), *Hunildus* eHy2 (p1259) *Kirkst*, *Hunnildhus* Hy2 (p1258) *ib*, *Hunildhus* 1210 (1252) Ch, 'Hūnhild's house' from the OE feminine pers.n. *Hūnhild* and OE **hūs**.

Hundon (Caistor, LNR), *Humendone, Hundidune* (sic) 1086 DB, *Huneduna* c1115 LS, l12 Dane, *-dun* 1212 Cur, *Hunduna* 1212 Fees, *-dune* 1275 RH. In spite of the erratic DB forms, this is probably 'Hūna's hill' from the OE pers.n. *Hūna* and OE **dūn**.

Hungerton (Wyville, Kest), *Hungretune* 1086 DB, *-tun'* Hy2 (l13th) *Stix*, *Hungertuna* 1106–23 (1333) Ch, *-ton'* 1185 RotDom, 1242–43 Fees, 'the farmstead, village with poor ground' from OE **hungor** 'hunger, famine' and OE **tūn**.

Huttoft (LSR), *Hotoft* 1086 DB, c1115 LS, 1155–58 (1334) Ch, 1156 (p1269) *Bard*, 1160–75 RA vi, l12th ib, a hybrid p.n. from OE **hōh** 'a heel, a spur of land', topographically appropriate, and ODan **toft** 'a curtilage, a messuage'.

Hykeham, North & South (Kest), *Hicham* ?1085–89 (14th) *Westm*, 1086 DB, 1138 NthCh, 1163 RA i, *Hicaham* 1115 (13th) RRAN, *Hiccham* 1160–65 NthCh, *Northhicam* 1086 DB, *Est Hykam* 1303 FA, *Suthicham* 1212 Fees, perhaps 'the homestead, estate where the blue tit-mouse is found' from OE **hice** and OE **hām**, but this is really uncertain. **North Hykeham** is occasionally distinguished as **East**. The affixes are self-explanatory.

I

Immingham (LNR), *Imungeham* (sic) 1086 DB, *Immingeham* c1115 LS, 1205 ChR, *Imingeham* 1200 FineR, *Immingham* Hy1 (c1240) YCh ii, 'the homestead of the Immingas', from the gen.pl., *Imminga*, of the OE group-name *Immingas* 'the family, the dependents of *Imma*' and OE **hām**. This is a p.n. which probably belongs to an early period of Anglo-Saxon settlement in the area.

Ingham (LWR), *Ingeham* 1086 DB, c1115 LS, 1146 RA i, 1191 P, 1206 ChR, *Ingaham* 1163 RA i, *Ingham* Hy2, lHy2 Dane. This name has been traditionally interpreted as 'the homestead, estate of Inga' from the OE pers.n. *Inga* and OE **hām**. However, like Ingham in Norfolk and Suffolk, it is probably better explained as an ancient cultic p.n., OE **Ing(a)hām* (from Germanic **Ingwia-haima*) 'the homestead, estate of the devotees of the deity Ing'.

Ingleby (Saxilby, WRY), *Englebi* 1086 DB, c1115 LS, c1170 Dane, *Englabi* c1115 LS, *Engelbi* 1150–60 RA iv, lHy2 Dane, *Ingelby* 1154–72 (1407) Gilb, 'the village of the English' from the gen.pl. **Engla** of OE **Engle** and ODan **bȳ**. It was earlier distinguished as **North Ingleby**, *North Engelby* 1286 *Ass* and **South Ingleby**, *Suthengelby* 1286 *Ass*. The former is represented today by **Ingleby Hall Farm**, the latter by **Ingleby Grange**. This was presumably an isolated village of English in a heavily settled Danish area.

Ingoldmells (LSR), *in Guldesmere* (sic) 1086 DB, *Ingoluesmera* 1095–1100 AC, *in Golvesmeles* (sic) 1144–55 (m13th) Pontefract, *Ingolvesmeles* 1147–55 (m13th) ib, *Ingoldesmeles* 1179 ChancR, *Ingaldemeles* 1178 (p1269) *Bard*, *Ingoldmelis* l12th RA vi. 'Ingólf's sand-banks' from the ON pers.n. *Ingólfr* and the pl. of ON **melr**. Forms in *-uld, -old, -ald* show confusion with Continental Germanic names in *-ald, -old* or with ON names like *Harald* and *Thorald* due to weakening of medial syllables in ME; this was almost certainly facilitated here by the existence of early ME *Ingald, -old* from ON *Ingialdr*. In some early forms initial *In-* has been mistaken for the Latin preposition *in* and twice the second el. has been confused with *mere*.

Ingoldsby (Kest), *In Goldesbi* 1086 DB, *Ingoldesbi* 1086 ib, 1176 P, *-by* a1184, l12th Semp, *Yngoldesbi* a1183 Dane, 'Ingiald's farmstead, village' from the ODan pers.n. *Ingiald* and ODan **bȳ**.

Irby in the Marsh (LSR), *Irebi* c1115 LS, c1180 BuryF, 1191 P, l12th Dane, *-by* 1198 (1328) Ch. **Irby upon Humber** (LNR), *Iribi* 1086 DB, *Irebi* 1086 ib, c1115 LS, 1166 P, *Yrebi* 1185 Templar, l12th RA ix. Both mean 'the farmstead, the village of the Irishmen' from ON Íra, gen.pl. of Íri 'an Irishman' and ODan bȳ, the reference being to isolated settlements of Norwegian vikings from Ireland or perhaps to Irishmen who accompanied the vikings to England. The affixes are self-explanatory.

Irnham (Kest), *Gerneham* 1086 DB, *Erneham* 1090–1100, 1100–08 YCh vi, *Irnam* 1100–08 ib, *Irenham* 1130–66, 1159 (p1269) *Bard*, *Yrnham* 1150–66, 1175–88 YCh v, *Yrneham* 1166–91 ib, probably 'Georna's homestead, estate' from the OE pers.n. *Georna* and OE hām.

K

Kate's Bridge (Baston, Kest), *Catebrigg* 1245 FF, 1276 RH, 1295 Ass, *Katebrigg'* 1275 RH, 1295 (l14th) *Spald i*, 'Káti's bridge' from the ON pers.n. *Káti* and OE **brycg** in a Scandinavianised form or from the cognate ON **bryggja** itself. The same pers.n. occurs also in **Cadeby** and **Caythorpe**. The modern form has not been found until the 18th century and is due to popular etymology.

Keadby (LWR), *Ketebi* c1184 (15th) 1185 Templar, 1199 P, 1316 YD iv, 'Kæti's or Keti's farmstead, village' from the ODan pers.n. *Kæti, Keti* and ODan **bȳ**. An exact parallel to this name is the Danish p.n. **Kædeby** (*Keteby* 1231).

Keal, East & West (LSR), *Cale* 1086 DB, *Cal'* c1115 LS, *Cales* c1135 Dane, *Chales* 1142–53 ib, *Kela* 1146–53 ib, *Kales* 1177 RA vi, *Kele* 1166 RBE, *Estrecale* 1086 DB, *Oustcal'* c1115 LS, *Austercales* 1142 NthCh, *Estrekales* 1199 (1330) Ch, *Westrecale* 1086 DB, *Westerkales* 1185 Templar, *-keles* l12th (1409) Gilb, 1189–98 RA vi. The early interchange between *-a-* and *-e-* is due to the influence of Anglo-Norman scribal practices. **Keal** is no doubt 'the keel' from OE **kjǫlr** 'a keel' used topographically of 'a ridge' (as also in **Keelby**) appropriate for both places. **East** and **West Keal** are already differentiated in DB, the affixes being derived from ON **eystri** or OE **ēasterra** 'more easterly' and ON **vestri** or OE **westerra** 'more westerly', respectively, later simplified to **East** and **West**. Forms in *Oust-* and *Auster-* show contamination by Anglo-Scandinavian **oust** 'east' and ON **austr**.

Keal Cotes (West Keal, LSR), *Cotes* c1160 (p1259) *Kirkst*, c1200 RA vi, 1254 Cl, *Kelecotes* 1396 Peace, 'the cottages, the sheds' from the pl. of OE **cot**, belonging to **Keal.**

Keddington (LSR), *Cadinton(e)* 1086 DB, *Kedinton'* 1182 P, *-tune* Hy2 Dane, *Chedingtuna* c1115 LS, *Kedyngtona* c1150 (1409) ib, *-ington'* 1180 P, l12th RA ii, perhaps 'the farmstead, village associated with or called after Cedd(a)' from the OE pers.n. *Cedd(a)* with the OE medial connective particle **-ing-** and OE **tūn**. The initial consonant has been Scandinavianised from *Ch-* to *K-*.

Keelby (LNR), *Chelebi* 1086 DB, c1115 LS, *Kelebi* 1143–47, p1182 Dane, *-by* c1150 (e13th) *NCot*, *Keilby* c1215 RA ii, 'the farmstead, village on the ridge' from ON **kjǫlr** 'a keel', in the sense 'a ridge', and ODan **bȳ**, topographically appropriate for the site of the village. Cf. **Keal**.

Keisby (Lenton, Kest), *Chisebi* 1086 DB, *Kisebi* eHy2 Dane, c1150, Hy2 *AddCh*, 1150–60, a1184 Semp, *Kysebi* Hy2 *AddCh*, 'Kisi's farmstead, village' from the ON byname *Kisi* and ODan **bȳ**.

Kelby (Culverthorpe, Kest), *Chillebi*, *Chelebi* 1086 DB, *Kellebi* Hy2 Dane, 1199 P, 1202 Ass, 1212 Fees. The first el. is probably the OE pers.n. *Cēol* which would normally be pronounced *Ch-*, but has become *K-* as a result of Scandinavian influence. The second el. is ODan **bȳ** 'a farmstead, a village'.

Kelfield (West Butterwick, LWR), *Chalchefeld* 1154 (e14th) Selby, *Calkefeld* eHy2 Dane, *Kelkefeld* eHy2 (1409) Gilb, 1179 P, Hy2 Dane, from OE **calc** 'chalk' and OE **feld** 'open land'.

Kelsey, North (LNR), *Chelsi* (sic) 1086 DB, *Calisei* 1094 France, *Chaleseia* c1115 LS, 1146 RA i, *Keleseye* 1123–47 RA iv, *-ey* c1150 (1409) Gilb, *Norchelsei*, *Nortchelesei* 1086 DB, **Kelsey, South** (LNR), *Sudkeleseia* 1171, 1204 P. The first el. of Kelsey is obscure, but appears to be the gen.sg. *-es* of an OE pers.n. The second el. is OE **ēg** probably in the sense of 'dry or higher ground in marsh'. The two villages were distinguished as **North** and **South** already at the time of DB.

Kelsey Hall (Great Steeping, LSR), *Kelsayhall* 1507 Cl, named from a family called *Kelsey*, compare William *de Kellessay in Steping'* 1299 RA ii, Ralph *de Kelsay* 1327 SR.

Kelstern (LSR), *Cheilestorne* 1086 DB, *Kailesthern'* 1196 ChancR, *Keylsterne* 1210 (1252) Ch, *Chelestorne* 1086 DB, *Chelestuna* (sic) c1115 LS, *Kelesterne* 1150–60 *Anc*, 1185 Templar. The early forms in *-ei-*, *-ai-* suggest that the first el. is the OE pers.n. *Cægel*, as in **Calcethorpe**; the second el. is OE **thorn** 'a thorn-tree'. The initial consonant has been Scandinavianised from *Ch-* to *K-*.

Kesteven, *condenso syluæ quæ uulgo Ceostefne nuncupatur* ("the thickets of the wood called Kesteven by the common people") c1000 Æthelweard, *Chetsteven* 1086 DB, *Ketsteuene* 1185, 1194 P. The first el. is PrW ***ceto-** 'a wood', the second ON **stefna** 'a meeting' here in a transferred sense 'a district with a meeting', probably an administrative district.

Ketsby (South Ormsby, LSR), *Chetelesbi* 1086 DB, Hy2 Dane, *Chetlesbi* c1115 LS, *Ketelsbi* c1150 France, *Ketlesbi* 1185 P, 'Ketil's farmstead, village', from the ON pers.n. *Ketil* and ODan **bȳ**.

Kettleby (Bigby, LNR), *Kitlebig* (sic) 1066–68 (12th) ASWills, *Chetelbi* 1086 DB, *Ketelbi* 1196 P, -*by* 1225 Cur. The first el. has been traditionally taken to be the Scand. pers.n. *Ketil* (cf. **Ketsby**), but the absence of any indication of the genitive in the early forms is curious. We may instead be concerned with the appellative ON **ketill** 'a kettle' used topographically. The name would then mean 'the farmstead, village at a kettle-shaped hollow', the second el. being ODan **bȳ**, cf. the lost p.n. *Ketælscogh* in Maribo Amt on Falster in which **ketill** is used topographically. **Kettleby Thorpe** *Torp* 1086 DB, c1115 LS, 1166 P, *Thorp* 1232 Cur, *Thorp' iuxta Kettelby* 1306 FF, named from **Kettleby** and ODan **thorp** 'a secondary settlement'. This is the only major p.n. in the North Riding of Lindsey derived from **thorp** and recorded in DB.

Kettlethorpe (LWR), *Ketlethorp'*, c1225 (14th) *Queen's*, *Ketelthorp* 1254 ValNor, *Ketelestorp* 1249 RRG, *Ketlesthorpe* 1241 RRG, from the same ODan pers.n. *Ketil*, as in **Ketsby** and perhaps **Kettleby**, and ODan **thorp** 'a secondary settlement'.

Kexby (LWR), *Cheftesbi* 1086 DB, *Keftesbi* 1194 P, 1202 Ass, 1207 Cur, 1219 Ass, *Chestesbi* (*-s-* = *-f-*) 1086 DB, 1212 Fees, obscure.

Killingholme, North and **South** (LNR), *Cheluingeholm* 1086 DB, 1180 P, *Chiluingeholm* c1115 LS, *Kiluingeholm* c1141 BMFacs, c1155 Dane, *Killingeholm* 1194 P, *Kiluingholm* 1143–47 Dane, *North Kiluingholm* 1160–66 ib, *Sud Kiluingholm* 1160–66 IB. The first part of this name is the gen.pl. *Cēolwulfinga* of the OE group-name *Cēolwulfingas*, later *Cēolfingas* with shortening of the medial syllable, 'the family, the dependents of *Cēolwulf*'. The final el. cannot originally have been **holmr** an ON word, since p.ns. composed of group-names are confidently believed to belong to an early stratum of name-giving in England, i.e. long before the Danes settled in north L. The final el. is, therefore, likely to have been OE **hām** 'a homestead', hence 'the homestead of the *Cēolwulfingas*', **hām** being replaced by ON **holmr**. The two places were early distinguished as **North** and **South**.

Kingerby (LNR), *Chenebi* (sic) 1086 DB, *Chiniereby* 1139–40 AC, *Kyneierbeia* (checked from MS) 1135–64 RA iv, *Kinierbia* 1212 Fees,

Kynyerby 1276 RH, *Kinierebia* c1162 RA iii, probably 'Cynegeard's farmstead, village' a hybrid p.n. from the OE unrecorded pers.n. **Cynegeard* and ODan **bȳ**.

King Street (Kest), *le Kingestrete* 1507–9 *MinAcct*, *Kingstrete* 1550–52 *ib*, self-explanatory. It is also known as *Stonystrette* 1530–32, *Stonestrete* 1507–9, *Stonystrette* 1530–32 all *MinAcct*. This is the name of the Roman road running almost due north from Chesterton (Romano-British *Durobrivae*) to Bourne and then north-west to rejoin Ermine Street at Ancaster.

Kingthorpe (Apley, LSR), *Chinetorp* 1086 DB, c1115 LS, *Kynthorpa* 1187 (1409) Gilb, *Kinthorp* l12th (Ed1) *Newh*, *Kinctorp* 1212 Cur, *Kuningkestorp* 1202 Ass, *Cunnigetorp'* 1209 FF. The early forms of the name suggest that it means 'the royal secondary settlement' from OE **cyne** 'royal' and ODan **thorp**. The 1202 and 1208 forms suggest it is 'the king's secondary settlement'. If these latter forms are correct then a very early reduction of the medial syllable must have taken place.

Kinnards Ferry (Owston Ferry, LWR), *Kinardferi* eHy2 (1632) *Dods 135*, *Kinardeferi* eHy2 (1409) Gilb, *-fere* 1185 Templar, *-ferie* l12th *AD*, c1200 Dane, 'Cynehard's ferry' from the OE pers.n. *Cynehard* and ON **ferja**, the name of the ferry across the R. Trent at Owston.

Kirkby (Kirkby cum Osgodby, LNR), *Kyrchebeia* 1146 RA i, 1162 RA iv, *Kirkebi* m12 Dugd vi, *-by* 1214 RA iv, c1221 Welles, 1291 Tax. **Kirkby, East** (LSR), *Cherchebi* 1086 DB, *-bi* 1142 NthCh, *Kirchebi* 1170–80 RA vi, 1180–90 NthCh, *Kirkeb'* 1185 Templar, *-by* Hy2 RA ii, *Estkirkeby* m12th (l13th) KirkstPsalt. **Kirkby Green** (Scopwick, Kest), *Cherchebi* 1086 DB, *Kirkebi* 1175 (1337) Ch, 1185 Templar, *-by* Hy2 (1407) Gilb, *Kirkeby super le grene* 1409 RRep. **Kirkby la Thorpe** (Kest), *Cherchebi, Chirchebi* 1086 DB, *Kyrcheby* 1163 RA i, *Kyrkeby* 1196–1203 RA iii, 1196 FF, *Kirkebi* 1196 ChancR. **Kirkby on Bain** (LSR), *Cherchebi* 1086 DB, c1115 LS, *Kyrkebi* c1150, 1179 *DuDCCh*, *Kirkebi* c1152 LAAS vi, 1162 Dane. **Kirkby Underwood** (Kest), *Cherchebi* 1086 DB, *Cherquebi* (sic) c1140 Dane, *Kyrchebi* 1140–60 *AddCh*, 1168 P, *Kirchebi* 1167 ib, *Kyrkebi* 1182 ib. All mean 'the village with a church' from ODan **kirkju-bȳ**, a compound appellative normally given to villages in which the Danes found a church on their arrival. These must have been existing villages taken over and renamed by the new settlers. The affixes **East** and **on Bain** are self-explanatory. **Green** refers to 'a village green'. **la Thorpe** is a mistake on the part of the O.S. It should read **Laythorpe** (see **Laythorpe**) the name of the settlement on the south side of The Beck. The affix appears early, note *Kirkeby* "by" *Laythorp* 1263 FF and an isolated form *Kirkebye la Thorpp* 1537–39 LDRH. SC p. 229 (1602) states *Kirky Lathhrope - This Kyrkby ys now all one w*[th] *the other, by meanes of an union.* **Underwood** is literally '(the place) under the wood' from OE **under** and OE **wudu.** There is still extensive woodland west of the village.

Kirkstead (LSR), *Kirkestede* 1139 Dugd v, 1154, 1158 *HarlCh*, c1162 Dane, 1167–68 RBE, *Chirchesteda* 1157 P, *Chirkested'* 1185 RotDom, a partially Scandinavianised form of OE **cirice-stede** 'the site of a church' with the replacement of OE **cirice** by the cognate ON **kirkja.** It was the name given to the Cistercian abbey founded there in 1139.

Kirmington (LNR), *Cheritone* (sic) 1086 DB, *Chernigtuna* c1115 LS, *Chirringtune* 1155–60 Dane, *Kirningtun* 1143–47 ib, *Kirningeton* 1285 Cl, *Kermintton* 1200 ChR. The early spellings are so varied that it is impossible to suggest what the first el. is, except that it is probably an OE pers.n. in composition with OE **-ing-** and OE **tūn,** hence 'the farmstead, village associated with or called after X'.

Kirmond le Mire (LSR), *Cheuremont* 1086 DB, *Chevermunt* 1090–96 (15th), a1170 (c1240) Whitby, *Caprimonte* 1100–15 (15th) ib, *Capremonte* 1136 (1312) ib, *Cheuermunt* 1202 Ass, *Keuermunt* 1150–55 Dane, *Keuermunde* Hy2 (m13th) *NCot, Kirmond in the myre* 1607 Camden. This is a French name probably transferred from one of the Chevremonts in France and means 'the goat hill'. Initial *K-* shows that we are concerned with the Norman-Picard variant of this name (the Central French variant had initial *Ch-*). The initial *Ch-* here probably merely reflects AN scribal practice in early (up to 1200) forms, though in 15th century copies it can possibly be regarded as a reflection of the influence of Central French usage. The basic form is doubtless represented by *Keuermunt* 1150–55, which is directly paralleled by such Norman p.ns. as **Quevremont, Quievremont** (Seine-Maritime). Some of the early spellings are in Latinised forms. The affix refers to the wet ground in the valley below the hill.

Kirton (Hol), *Chirchetune* 1096 DB, *-ton'* 1166 P, *-tone* 1459 Cl, *Kirketone* 1155–56 RBE, *-ton'* c1156–57 *HarlCh*, 1170 P, *Kircheton'* 1171 ib. **Kirton in Lindsey** (LWR), *Chirchetone* 1070–87 RA i, 1086 DB, *-tona* 1087–88, 1100–15 RA i, 1146 RRAN, *-tune* 1090 RA i, *-tun'* 1156 P, *Kirchetona, Chirketone* 1146 RA i, *Kirketona* 1087–88 ib. Both are from OE **cirice** 'a church' and OE **tūn** 'a village', **cirice** being replaced by the cognate ON **kirkja.**

Kirton Holme (Kirton, Hol), *Kyrketonholme* 1316 Ch, *Kyrkton Holme* 1388 WillsPCC, *Kirketon holme* 1401 AD iii, from the parish name, **Kirton**, and ON **holmr** 'raised land amidst the marshes'.

Kirton Meeres (Kirton, Hol), *Merys* 1313 Pat, *Meres* 1326 ib, 1327 *SR*, 1379 *FF*, *Kyrton meres* 1527 Wills ii, presumably 'the pools', from pl. of OE **mere**. The parish name, **Kirton**, was prefixed later.

Kirton Wapentake (Hol), *Chirchetone* 1086 DB, *-ton'* 1185 RotDom, *Cerchetone* 1130 P, *Kirketon* 1168, 1186 ib, *Kyrketon'* 1177 ib, named from **Kirton** (Hol); the forms are preceded or followed by some form of Latin *wapentacium*. The meeting-place of the wapentake (ON **vápnatak**, late OE **wapengetæc** 'a sub-division of a shire') must have been at **Kirton** itself.

Knaith (LWR), *Cheneide* 1086 DB, *Chneya* Hy2 (1268) Ch, *Kney* e13th *HarlCh*, *Cneie* 1225 Welles, *Cneye* 1227 Ch, *Knayth* c1225 (14th) *Queen's*, probably 'the landing-place by the bend (in the R. Trent)' from OE **cnēo** 'a knee' used in a transferred topographical sense 'a bend' and OE **hæth**, appropriate to the situation of the village.

Kyme, North & South (Kest), *Chime* 1086 DB, 1165 P, *Kyme* c1115 LS, 1157 (1407) Gilb, *Kyma* p1169 Dane, *Kime* 1150–55 ib, 1150–60 Semp, *Chimba* 1130, 1156 P, *Chimbe* 1174–64 BS, *Kymba* 1183–84 RA iii, eHy2 (1409) Gilb, *Kimbe* 1182 P, *Nortchime* 1086 DB, *Northkime* 1220 Cur, *Suthkyme* 1316 FA. It has been suggested that **Kyme** is derived from OE **cymbe* 'a depression, a hollow'. The settlements at the **Kymes** lie on areas of higher ground (above the 25' contour) north and south of a shallow depression. The two settlements are distinguished as **North** and **South**.

Kyme Eau (Kest), *aqua de Kyme* e13 (1639) LNQ xvii, *ripam de Kime* 1241 Cl, *aq' de Kyme* 1315 (l15th) *BostCC*, *le Ee de Kyme* 1342 Orig, 1343 Cl, 1376 Works, named from the p.n. **Kyme** and OE **ēa** 'a river, a stream'.

L

Laceby (LNR), *Leuesbi* 1086 DB, 1130 P, 1132 (1403) Pat, *Leyseby* c1115 LS, 1204 FF, *Laifsebi* lHy2 Dane, *Leissebi* 1168 P, 'Leif's farmstead, village' from the ON pers.n. *Leifr* and ODan **bȳ**. It is very likely that spellings in *-ss-* are assimilated forms of *-fs-*. The gen.sg. pronounced [s] is Scand. in contrast to · English [z], indicating that the name had been given by Danes.

Lambcroft (Kelstern, LSR), *grangiam de Lambecroft* 1212 Fees, *Lambcroft* 1327 *SR*, *Lamcroft* 1329 *Ass*, 1332 *SR*, self-explanatory, from OE **lamb** 'a lamb' and OE **croft** 'a small enclosed field'. It was a grange of Louth Park Abbey.

Langham (Mumby, LSR), *Langholm'* 1217 (Ed1) *Barl*, 1219 Ass, 1232 Cl, *Langeholme* 1272 *Ass*, *-holm* 1294 *Anc*, 'the long island of land, raised ground in marsh' from OE **lang** or ON **langr** and ON **holmr**.

Langoe Wapentake (Kest), *Langehou* 1086 DB, *-ho* 1130, 1168 P, *Langhou* c1155 Dane, 1196 ChancR, *Langho* 1166 P, 'the long mound' from ON **langr** and ON **haugr**. The forms are preceded or followed by some form of Latin *wapentacium*. The meeting-place of the wapentake (ON **vápnatak**, late OE **wæpengetæc** 'a subdivision of a shire') is not known.

Langrickville (LSR) was formed into a township by Act of Parliament in 1812 and was named from **Langrick**, *magna langraca* 1162 (p1259) *Kirkst*, *Langerak' both'* (i.e. ODan **bōth** 'a booth, a temporary shed') *in aqua de Widhem* 1243 Cl, *Langrake* 1260 *Kirkst*, 1270 FF, 'the long stretch of water' from OE **lang** and OE **rǣc**, with reference to the R. Witham.

Langtoft (Kest), *Langetof* (sic) 1086 DB, *-toft* 1167, 1170, 1191 P, 1200 Cur, 'the long messuage, curtilage' from OE **lang**, ON **langr** amd ODan **toft**, with reference to a straggling village. It is possible that it lies on a Roman branch road from **King Street** leading into the fens.

Langton (LSR), *Langetune* 1040–41, 1077 (l13th) RamsChron, *-tone* 1086 DB, *Langhetuna* c1115 LS, *Langetun(a)* c1180, l12th Dane. **Langton by Partney** (LSR), *Langetune* 1086 DB, *Langhetona* c1160 Semp, *Langeton'* 1180, 1199 P, *-tun* c1200 RA iv. **Langton by Wragby** (LSR), *Langetone* 1086 DB, *-tuna*, *Langhetuna* c1115 LS, *Langetona* 1147 (p1269) *Bard*, *-tun* 1150–55

Dane, *Langtona* c1155 (1411) Gilb, *Nord Langeton* m13th (p1259) *Kirkst*. It is also *Humbelloc Langeton* 1252 Ch, *Humlok* - 1304 *FF*, *Humbloklangton'* 1467 *DCAcct*. Each means 'the long village' from OE **lang** and OE **tūn**. Recently, it has been pointed out that all three **Langtons** in Lindsey are associated with Roman roads. This common feature, it is suggested, may well indicate a settlement strung out along a pre-existing road and such a suggestion is no doubt correct. **Low Langton** is *Suth Langeton* John (p1259) *Kirkst*, *Suthlangeton* m13th (p1259) *ib* from its situation in relation to **Langton by Wragby**, which is itself sometimes **North** for a similar reason. The alternative affix for the latter, *humblok* etc., is from ME **hemlok(e)** 'hemlock', no doubt from the growth of the plant there.

Langworth (Barlings, LWR), *Langwath* 1170, Hy2 (1291) Ch, 1202 Ass, 1210 FF, and note the reference to a bridge here in *Reginaldum custodem pontis de Langwath'* 1202 Ass. **Langworth Grange** (Coningsby, LSR), *Langwat* eHy2 (p1259) *Kirkst*, *Langwath* e13th *KirkstInv ii*, *grangiam . . . de Langwath* 1210 (p1259) *Kirkst*, 1223 Cur, 1225 (p1259) *Kirkst*. Both mean 'the long ford' from OE **lang**, ON **langr** and ON **vath**. The development to **-worth** is late. **Langworth Grange** was a **grange** of Kirkstead Abbey.

Laughterton (Kettlethorpe, LWR), *Lahtreton'* 1213–23 RA ii, *Lahterton'* 1272 *Ass*, *Lachterton* c1225 (14th) *Queen's*, 1253 Cl. The first el. is obscure; the second is OE **tūn** 'a farmstead, a village'. The name has been identified with *Leugttricdun* 675–92 (12th) BCS 840 (S 1806). This identification is quite uncertain, since **Laughterton** is not situated on a hill, which is to be assumed for *Leugttricdun*, since the second el. there is OE **dūn** 'a hill'.

Laughton (Aslackby, Kest), ? *æt Lohtune* 1066–68 (c1200) ASWills, *Loctone* 1086 DB, *-tona* 1139–54 *AD*, a1177 Semp, *-ton'* a1170, l12th ib, *Lochtun* c1160 *AddCh*, 'the enclosure, farmstead that can be locked' from OE **loc** and OE **tūn**. The earliest reference does not certainly belong here.

Laughton (LWR), *Lacestone, Lastone* (corrected from *Lestone*), *Lactone* 1086 DB, *-ton'* 1185 Templar, 1204 Cur, 1205 P, *Lactuna* c1115 LS, *-tun* 1212 Fees, from OE **lēac-tūn** 'a leek enclosure', 'a herb garden'. The DB forms are clearly errors.

Lawress Wapentake (LWR), *Lagvlris* 1086 DB, *Lagolfris* c1115 LS, *Laulris* c1155 Dane, 1170 P, *Lauelris* 1202 Ass, *Lauris* 1168 P. The early forms of the name are preceded by some form of Latin *wapenacium*. **Lawress** means 'Lag-Ulf's coppice' from the ON personal name **Lag-Ulfr* and ON **hrís**.

The pers.n. means literally 'Law Wolf' with Law prefixed, as a nickname, to Wolf, as in similar names in Iceland. Lag-Ulf must have been a prominent lawman here and the wapentake (ON **vápnatak**, late OE **wæpengetæc** 'a sub-division of a shire') meeting must have been held at a coppice belonging to its lawman, though the site is not known.

Laythorpe (Kirkby la Thorpe, Kest), *Ledulftorp, Leduluetorp* 1086 DB, *Leilthorp* Hy2 (c1331) *Spald i*, 1202 FF, *-torp* 1185 Templar, *Lailtorp'* 1196–1203 RA iii, *Layltorp'* 1196 FF. 'Leithulf's secondary settlement (no doubt of **Kirkby la Thorpe**)' from the ON pers.n. *Leithulfr* and ODan **thorp**. The subsequent development is obscure. The name is no longer used independently; see **Kirkby la Thorpe**.

Lea (LWR), *Lea* 1086 DB, *Le* c1115 LS, 1150–60 Dane, *Lee* 1135–54 Dugd v, 1163 *And*, 1196 Cur, from OE **lēah** 'a wood, a glade, a clearing'; there is still a stretch of ancient woodland in the parish, cf. *boscum de Lee* 1135–54 Dugd v.

Leadenham (Kest), *Ledeneham* 1086 DB, *Ledenham* 1178 P, 1185–87 Dane, Hy2 (1409) Gilb, 1185 Templar, l12th Dane, probably 'Lēoda's homestead, estate' from the OE pers.n. *Lēoda* and OE **hām**.

Leake, Old (Hol), *Leche* 1086 DB, *Lech'* 1180–90 NthCh, 1191 P, *Lec* lHy2 Dane, *Leke* l12th (1409) Gilb, *Lecke* c1200 RA vii, *Leik* 1221 FF, probably originally 'the brook' from OE **lece** influenced or replaced by ON **loekr**, a word of similar meaning.

Leasingham (Kest), *Lessingham, Leuesingham* 1086 DB, 1189 (1341) Semp, 1197, 1200 P, 'the homestead, estate of the Lēofsigingas' from the gen.pl. *Lēofsiginga* of the OE group-name *Lēofsigingas* 'the family, the followers of *Lēofsige*' and OE **hām**.

Legbourne (LSR), *Lecheburne* 1086 DB, *-burna* Hy2 (1314) Ch, *-burn'* 1175 ChancR, *Leceburna* 1190–93 Dane, *Lekeburna* m12th *HarlCh*, *-burne* c1150 (1409) Gilb, from OE **lece**, which is derived from OE *lecan* 'to drip', and OE **burna** 'a stream'. The name would mean something like 'the trickling stream', which is topographically appropriate. Part of the reach between Little Cawthorpe and Legbourne is actually used as a bridle way.

Legsby (LSR), *Lagesbi* (sic) 1086 DB, *Legesbi* c1150 (1409) Gilb, lHy2 Dane, *Leggesby* 1187, Hy2 (1409) Gilb, l12th Dane, 'Legg's farmstead, village' from the ON byname *Leggr* and ODan **bȳ**. On the boundary between Legsby and Linwood is *Leggeshou* c1150, *Legeshou*, Hy2, c1200, *Leggeshow* Hy2 all (1409) Gilb 'Legg's mound, burial mound' presumably named from the same man and ON **haugr**.

Lenton (Lenton, Keisby & Osgodby, Kest), *æt Lofintune* 1066–68 (c1200) ASWills, *Lavintone, Parva Lavintune* 1086 DB, *Lavintunia* c1150 *Anc*, *Lauinton*' 1166 P, 1185 Templar, *Lauingtun*' p1167, Hy2 (l13th) *Stix*, perhaps 'the farmstead, village called after or associated with Lāfa' from the OE pers.n. *Lāfa* with the OE medial connective particle **-ing-** and OE **tūn**. The ASWills form is probably an error. The change to **Lenton** is late and has not been noted before *Lavington al. Lenton* 1723 SDL.

Leverton (Hol), *Levretune* 1086 DB, *Leuerton*' 1167 P, 1202 Ass, *Leverton*' 1205 Cur, probably 'the farmstead, village where rushes, reeds, yellow irises grow' from OE **læfer, lēfer** and OE **tūn**.

Limber, Great (LNR), *Lindbeorhge* 1066–68 (c1200) ASWills, *Linberge, Linberghā, Limberge* 1086 DB, *Linberga* c1115 LS, 1223 Cur, *Limberge* 1086 DB, 1193 P, *Magna Linberga* c1115 LS. **Limber, Little** (Brocklesby, LNR), *Limberge* 1086 DB, *parua Limbergia* c1155 Dane, 1269 *HarlCh*. **Limber** is 'the hill where lime-trees grow' from OE **lind** and **beorg**. It was early distinguished as **Great** and **Little**.

Lincoln, *Lindon* c150 Ptolomey, *Lindo* 4th (8th) AntIt, *Lindum colonia* l7th (13th) Ravenna, *in Lindocolino* 731 Bede, *Lindcoln* 975–78 ASCoins. The original name is derived from PrW *linn 'a pool', with reference to the broad pool in the R. Witham, now known as Brayford (Pool). To this was added the British form of Latin *colonia* after the establishment of time-expired legionaries here in succession to the earlier fortress.

Lincolnshire, *Lindcolnescire* 1016 (m11th) ASC C, *Lincolne scire* 1016 (p1050) ASC D, *Lincolna scire* 1065 (l12th) ib, *Lincole scire* 1086 DB, from **Lincoln** and OE **scīr** 'a district', comprising the Parts of Lindsey, Kesteven and Holland. It was an English creation after the reconquest of the Danelaw in the earlier 10th century and must have included at least the areas under the control of the Danish armies with their headquarters at Lincoln and Stamford.

Lindsey, *in prouincia Lindissi, - lindisi, - . . . Lindisfarorum* 731 Bede, *on Lindesse* 838, 873 (c900) ASC A, *in Lindisse, on Lindese* c890 (10th) OEBede, *on Lindesige* 838 (c1050) ASC D, *Lindesege* c890 (10th) OEBede. The first el. of Lindsey is a derivative of PrW *linn 'a pool', as in **Lincoln**. To this was later added OE **ēg** 'an island of land', though which "island" is referred to is uncertain. The most likely meaning of **Lindsey** is 'the island of the people of Lincoln' or 'of the pool'.

Linwood (Blankney, Kest), *Lyndewode* 1135–54. c1230 (p1259) *Kirkst, Lindwod* eHy2 (p1259) *ib.* The name survives as **Linwood Hall Farm**. **Linwood** (LNR), *Lindude* (sic) 1086 DB. *Lindwda* c1115 LS, *-wode* p1182 Dane, 1200 Cur. Both mean 'the lime-tree wood' from OE **lind** and OE **wudu**.

Lissington (LSR), *Lessintone* 1086 DB, *Lissigtuna* c1115 LS, *Lissingtun* eHy2 (m13th) *NCot, -ton'* c1200 RA v, *Lissinctona* Hy2 Dane. The first el. is difficult to determine, but it has been suggested that the name means 'the farmstead, village associated with or named after Lēofsige', from the OE pers.n. *Lēofsige* with the OE medial connective particle **-ing-** and OE **tūn**. The development of *-fs-* to *-ss-* is due to assimilation.

Listoft (Hogsthorpe, LSR), *Lystoft'* 1327 *SR*, 1348 *FF*, 1389 IngCt, *Listoft'* 1332 *SR*, 1340 *Barl*, perhaps 'the curtilage, messuage at the edge, border (of a settlement, cultivated area, etc.)', from ODan **list** 'strip, edge', **lista** 'edge, border' and ODan **toft**.

Lobthorpe (North Witham, Kest), *Lopintorp* 1086 DB, 1202 Ass, *Leipintorp* 1185 Templar, *Lopingthorp* 1198–1205 RA ix, *Loupintorp* 1202 Ass, *Loupingtorp'* 1212 Fees, probably 'Hlaupingi's secondary settlement (presumably of **North Witham**)' from the ON pers.n. **Hlaupingi* and ODan **thorp**.

Londonthorpe (Londonthorpe & Harrowby Without, Kest), *Lundetorp* 1086 DB, l12th Dane, 1202 Ass, *Lundertorp* 1086 DB, 1172–80 Dane, c1200 RA ix, *-thorp'* l12th Semp, literally 'the secondary settlement of the grove' from ON **lundr**, gen.sg. **lundar**, and ODan **thorp**. Apart from an occasional form *Lundentorp'* 1237 Fees, *Londynthorpe* 1374 *AddCh*, the modern spelling, **London-**, is not common till the 16th century.

Long Eau (Saltfleetby, LSR), *aqua del Haa* Hy3 (Hy4) *GCB, Ha* Ed1 (Hy4) *ib, le Aa* 1397 *Anc*, 14th *AD*, 1590 *Sewers*, 'the stream, the river' from ON á. **Long** was added later, but already in 1577 Harrison commented on the fact that this was "of a longer race" than other streams in the area.

Lound (Toft with Lound and Manthorpe, Kest), *Lund* 1086 DB, l12th Dane, 1202 Ass, 1202 P, 'the small wood, the grove' from ON **lundr**.

Lound, East (Haxey, LWR), *Lund* 1086 DB, l12th *AD*, *Lunda* c1200 Dane, *Lunde* 1279 *FF*, *Estlund* l12th, eHy3 *HarlCh*. As with **Craiselound**, also in Haxey parish, this was originally a simplex p.n. from ON **lundr** 'a grove', to which was prefixed **ēast** indicating its situation east of **Haxey** itself.

Louth (LSR), *Hludensis monasterii* s.a. 790 (c1100) ASC F, *Ludes* 1086 DB, *Ludam* 1093, 1126, 1139 RA i, *Luda* c1115 LS, 1146 RA ii, *Lude* 1160–75 RA vi, the earliest spelling *Louthe* being 1234 FF, *Luth'* 1219 Cur, 1245 FF. **Louth** takes its name from the **R. Lud**, the development of *-d* to *-th* being due to Scand. influence.

Louthesk Wapentake (LSR), *Ludes* 1086 DB, 1168 P, *Ludesc* c1115 LS, *Ludesca* c1155 Dane, *Ludhesche* 1175 P, *Luthesk* John Abbr, *Ludeske* 1202 Ass. The early forms are preceded or followed by some form of Latin *wapentacium*. The name is derived from **Louth** and ON **eski** 'a place growing with ash-trees', though it is very likely that **eski** has replaced OE **æsc** 'the ash-tree at Louth', denoting the site of the meeting-place of the wapentake (ON **vápnatak**, late OE **wæpengetæc** 'a subdivision of a shire').

Louth Park (LSR), *de Parcolude* 1129 (m15th) ChronLP, *de Parco Lude* 1148–68 RA i, 1189 (l12th) CartAnt, 1198 Cur. All the references are to the abbey in the park, the name of which is self-explanatory.

Loveden Wapentake (Kest), *Lovedun* 1086 DB, *Louedone* 1168 P, -*don'* 1169, 1193 ib, 'Lufa's hill' from the OE pers.n. *Lufa* and OE **dūn**. The forms are preceded or followed by some form of Latin *wapentacium*. The meeting-place of the wapentake (ON **vápnatak**, late OE **wæpengetæc** 'a subdivision of a shire') was on **Loveden Hill**, the site of an Anglo-Saxon cemetery.

Lud, R. (LSR), *aquam que uocatur Ludena* c1163, eHy2, l12th all (13th) *Alv*, *Ludhena* 1314 Ch, *Ludna* Hy3 (13th) *Alv*, *Luthena* c1200 (13th) *ib*, *Lude* e13th, Hy3 (13th) *ib*, 'the loud one' from OE **hlūde**, a derivative of OE **hlūd**. The forms in *Ludena* are from the r.n. and OE **ēa** or ON **á** 'a river', as in **Ludney**.

Ludborough (LNR), *Ludeburg* 1086 DB, 1253 Ipm, *-burc* c1115 LS, *Ludburc* 1177 P, *Lutheburc* 112 RA iv, *-burg'* 1253 Ipm, *Loutheburgh* 1297 Pat, probably 'Luda's fortified place' from the OE pers.n. *Luda*, well-evidenced in English p.ns., and **burh**; later forms have been influenced by those for **Louth** (LSR). Alternatively, the meaning might be 'the fortified place belonging to or associated with Louth'.

Ludborough Wapentake (LNR), *Ludeburc* c1115 LS, *-bur* 1265 Misc, *Ludburc* 1200 P, *-burg'* 1254 ValNor, *Lutheburg* 1291 Tax, *-burgh'* 1298 Ass, named from **Ludborough**, presumably where the wapentake meeting was held. The forms are preceded or followed by some form of Latin *wapentacium*. The wapentake (ON **vápnatak**, late OE **wæpengetæc**), was a subdivision of a shire.

Luddington (LWR), *Ludintone* 1086 DB, *-inton'* 1180, 1182 P, 1200 Cur, *-ington'* Hy3 (e14th) Selby, 1254 ValNor, 'the farmstead, village associated or called after Luda' from the OE pers.n. *Luda*, probably also first el. of **Ludborough** and of **Ludford**, with the OE connective particle **-ing-** and OE **tūn**.

Ludford, Magna & Parva (LSR), *Ludefort* a1070 (c1240) Whitby, c1078 (15th) ib, *Ludesforde* 1086 DB, *-fort* c1115 LS, *Ludeforde* 1086 DB, c1115 LS, 1160–70 RA v, *Magna Lufford* c1221 Welles, *Ludford Maior* 1254 ValNor, *Parua Ludforda* 1228–30 (1409) Gilb. It is also *Longlutheford* 1402 FA, *Longludforth* 1465 Fine, a name often used today, *long* denoting a long straggling village. The name probably means 'Luda's ford' from the OE pers.n. *Luda* and OE **ford**. The same pers.n. probably occurs also in **Ludborough** and **Luddington**. The site of the ford is not known, but it has recently been suggested that a north-south ford must be presumed and that the ford probably carried a Roman road, for there was an extensive Romano-British settlement here.

Ludney (Grainthorpe, LSR), *Ludena* c1115 LS, Hy2 Dudg v, l12th (13th) *Alv*, *Luthena* m12th, Hy2 (1649) *Dods 75*, 1202 Ass, named from the **R. Lud**.

Lusby (LSR), *Luzebi* 1086 DB, *Luceby* 1115 (14th) *Bard*, 1125, 1147 (p1269) *ib*, Hy2 RA ii, *Lusceby* m12th (p1269) *Bard*, 1185 Templar, probably 'Lút's farmstead, village' from the ON pers.n. *Lútr* and ODan **bý**.

Lutton (Hol), *Luctone* 1086 DB, *Luttona* 1111 (c1331) *Spald i*, c1120 (13th) *Castleacre*, *Lutona* 1123 France, *Luton* 1170 P, *Luttunia* c1150 (13th)

Castleacre, Lutton' 1177 P, probably 'the farmstead, village by the pool' from OE **luh** and OE **tūn**. It is also called **Sutton St Nicholas**, note *Sutton Sᵗ Nicholas al's Lutton* e17th *HDMan*.

Lymn, R. (LSR), *Lime* m12th, 1178, l12th all (p1269) *Bard, a Limna* 1234 MLM, *Lyme* l12th (p1269) *Bard, Nouum Limme* Hy2 (p1269) *ib, novam Lim'* 1219 FF. This is a Celtic r.n., a derivative of PrW **lemo-* 'an elm', meaning 'the river where elm-trees abound'. **New Lymn** was the name of a diversion of the river to improve the scour through Wainfleet Haven. The old river was also called *yᵉ lytylle lyme* Hy8 *Map, the Little Lymme* 1576 *Monson*.

M

Mablethorpe (LSR), *Maltetorp* (sic) 1086 DB, *Maltorp* (sic) c1115 LS, *Malbertorp* 1086 DB, lHy2 Dane, 1190–1200 RA vi, *Maubertorp* 1176 P, l12th Dane, 'Malbert's secondary settlement' from the Continental Germanic pers.n. *Malbert* and ODan **thorp**. The forms in -*u*- are due to vocalisation of -*l*-.

Maidenwell (Farforth, LSR), *Welle* 1086 DB, *Madewelle* 1209–35 LAHW, *Maidewelle* 1230 P, *Maidenwell'* 1212 Fees, *Maydenwell'* 1242–43 ib, originally a simplex p.n. 'the spring' from OE **wella**, to which was prefixed OE **mægden** 'a maiden, a young unmarried woman' (in both the short and full form), though the significance of *maiden* is not known. There are two large pools here.

Maltby (Raithby cum Maltby, LSR), *Maltebi* 1086 DB, c1115 LS, lHy2 Dane, 1219 Ass, -*by* 1157–94 (e14th) Werb. **Maltby le Marsh** (LSR), *Maltebi* 1086 DB, c1115 LS, l12th Dane, *Maltesbi* 1086 DB, *Mautesbi* 1176 ChancR, -*by* 1219 Welles. Both mean 'Malti's farmstead, village' from the ODan pers.n. *Malti* and ODan **bȳ**. The affix in the second is self-explanatory. Forms in -*u*- are due to vocalisation of -*l*-.

Manby (LSR), *Mannebi* 1086 DB, c1115 LS, 1166–75 Fulstow, lHy2, c1200 Dane, -*by* c1150 (1409) Gilb, 1183 Dane, Hy2 (13th) *Alv*. **Manby** (Broughton, LWR), *Mannebi* 1086 DB, a1175, 1175, 1205–23 Goke, 1209 P. Both mean 'Manni's farmstead, village' from the ON pers.n. *Manni* and ODan **bȳ**. The pers.n. occurs also in **Manthorpe**.

Manley Wapentake (LWR), *Manelinde* (sic), 1086 DB, -*li* c1115 LS, *Maneslei* 1130 P, *Manelea* 1167 ib, *Manlea* 1166, 1193 ib, -*le* 1171 ib, 1202 Ass, -*let* 1185 RotDom, -*led* e13th (1311) Ch. The early forms are usually preceded or followed by some form of Latin *wapentacium*. The second el. of **Manley** appears to be OE **lēah** 'a wood, a glade, a clearing', but some of the earliest spellings seem to suggest it could be ON **hlíth** 'a slope'. The first el. may be the same as that of **Manby** in the same wapentake, i.e the ODan pers.n. *Manni*, but no certainty is possible. The site of the meeting-place of the wapentake (ON **vápnatak**, late OE **wæpengetæc** 'a sub-division of a shire') is not known.

Manthorpe (Belton, Kest), *Mannetorp* 1185 Templar, Hy3 (1407) Gilb, 1212 Fees, *Manethorpe* 1230 FF. **Manthorpe** (Toft, Kest), *Mannethorp* 1066–68 (c1200) ASWills, *-torp* 1086 DB, 1168 ChancR, 1185 Templar. Both mean 'Manni's secondary settlement' from the ODan pers.n. *Manni* and ODan **thorp**. *Manni* occurs also in Manby.

Manton (LWR), *Malmetun* 1066–87 (m12th) Dugd i, 1067 (12th) RRAN, c1128 (12th) ChronPetro, c1140 *AD*, *-tune* 1086 DB, 1154–62 YCh x, *-tuna* c1115 LS, 'the farmstead, village on sandy soil', from OE **malm** and OE **tūn**.

Mar Dike (Saltfleetby St Peter, LSR), *Maredic* 1183, l12th Dane, *le maredic* l12th, e13th, p1250 (Hy4) *GCB*, *Mardik* c1200 RA v, 'the boundary ditch, bank' from OE **(ge)mǣre** and OE **dīc**, ON **dík**. This is the name of the seaward end of the Roman road, Margary 273.

Mareham le Fen (LSR), *Marun* 1086 DB, *Marum* 1135–54, 1172 Dugd v, 1170–98 Revesby, l12th Dane, c1200 NthCh, *Mareham in the ffenne* 1644 LAAS ii, 'at the pools, the ponds' from the dat.pl. **mǣrum** of OE **mǣr(e)**. The change to **-ham** has not been noted before the 17th century, nor has the affix **le Fen**, which distinguishes **Mareham le Fen** from **Mareham on the Hill**.

Mareham on the Hill (LSR), *Meringhe* 1086 DB, *Maringes* 1114–3 (14th) Rams, c1160 Semp, 1196–99 RA ii, *Maringa* Hy2, lHy2 Dane, *Maringe* 1147–51 (14th) Rams, 1166 RBE. This is an OE group-name, *Meringas*, *Mǣringas* 'the dwellers by the ponds, pools' from OE **mere**, **mǣr(e)** and OE **-ingas** in its developed sense 'dwellers at, people who live at'. There are several small ponds south of the the church. The development to **-ham** has not been noted before the 19th century. The earliest record of the affix so far found is *Maring of the hill* 1517 DIn, compare **Mareham le Fen**.

Markby (LSR), *Marchesbi*, *Marchebi* 1086 DB, c1115 LS, 1195 P, c1200 RA iii, *Markebi* 1177 P, Hy2, 1193 Dane, 1198, *-by* a1168 Semp, probably 'Marke's farmstead, village' from the ODan pers.n. *Marke*, which was borrowed from Low German, and ODan **bȳ**.

Marsh Chapel (LNR), *Fullestowe merske* e13th Holywell, *Fulestowmersk* 1277–92 *ib*, *Foulestowemersh'* 1358 FF, *Mersch Chapel* 1347 Pat, *Marshchapell* 1457 *Harm*, 'the marsh belonging to Fulstow', from the parish-name **Fulstow** and OE **mersc**, later named from the *chapel* there.

Marston (Kest), *Merestune, -tone, -ton* 1086 DB, *-ton'* 1180 P, *Merstun* p1160 Dane, *-tona* 1166 RBE, l12th Semp, *Merston* 1171 P, 'the farmstead, village in the marsh' from OE **mersc** and OE **tūn**. The village lies low beside the R. Witham.

Martin (Kest), *Martuna* 1135–54 (p1259) *Kirkst, -tona* 1162 (p1259) *ib*, 1185 Templar, 1196 Cur, *-tona* l12th Dane. **Martin** (LSR), *Mertona* 1040–41 (l13th) ECEE (?spurious), *Martone* 1086 DB, *-tuna* c1115 LS, 1162 (p1259) *Kirkst, -tona* 1150–60 Dane, *-tun* 1154 *HarlCh*. Each means 'the farmstead, village by the pool' from OE **mær(e)**, **mere** and OE **tūn**. Cf. **Marton**.

Marton (LWR), *Martone* 1086 DB, *-tuna* c1115 LS, *-tun'* 1154–66 RA i, *-ton'* 1176, 1177 P, 1185 Templar, 'the farmstead, village by the pool' from OE **mær(e)** and OE **tūn**. The form *Martineuuelle* 1054–57 (12th) Eyns belongs here, *-uuelle* referring to **Well Wapentake** in which **Marton** is situated.

Mawthorpe (Willoughby with Sloothby, LSR), *Malthorp* 1242–43 Fees, 1281 QW, 1290 Ipm, 1308 Pat, perhaps 'Malti's secondary settlement' from the ON pers.n. *Malti* and ODan **thorp**, presumably of **Willoughby**. The same pers.n. appears in **Maltby**. The modern spelling is not found before the 16th century and is the result of the vocalisation of *-l-* to *-u-*.

Melholme (North Cockerington, LSR), *Medelholme* eHy2, Hy2, c1200, p1240, *Methelholm* lHy2, Hy3 all (13th) *Alv*, a Scand. compound from ON **methal** 'middle' (presumably betweem **North Cockerington** and **South Somercotes**) and ON **holmr** 'higher ground in marsh'.

Melton Ross (LNR), *Medeltone* 1086 DB, *Meltuna* c1115 LS, *-tona* 1146 RA i, *-ton'* 1200 Cur, *Mealtun* c1160 Dane, *Meuton'* 1204 Cur, *Melton Roos* 1375 *MiD*. **Melton** is a partial Scandinavianisation of Middleton 'the middle farmstead, village' from OE **middel** and **tūn** with ON **methal** 'middle' replacing **middel**. Forms such as *Mealtun, Meuton'* are due to Anglo-Norman influence. It is not clear to which places *Middle* refers. The *de Ros* family held one fee in Melton in 1303 FA and has been noted here as early as 1265 Misc, hence *Ross*.

Melwood, High & Low (Owston, LWR), *Methelwde* lHy2 Dane, *-wode* 1180–90 ib, *-wude* e13th *AD*, *-wod* 1275 RH, 'the middle wood' from ON **methal** (apparently between **Owston** and **Epworth**) and OE **wudu**, a hybrid p.n.

Mere (Branston, Kest), *Mere* 1185 Templar, 1203 Ass, 1212 Fees, 'a pool, a pond' from OE **mere**.

Messingham (LWR), *Mæssingaham* 1066–68 (12th) ASWills, *Messingeham* 1067–69 (12th) HC, 1086 DB, 1181, 1197 P, *Massingeham* c1115 LS, 1166 RBE, 'the homestead, the estate of the Mæssingas' from *Mæssinga*, the gen.pl. of the OE group-name *Mæssingas* 'the family, the dependents of *Mæssa*' and OE **hām**.

Metheringham (Kest), *Medric(h)esham* 1086 DB, *Medringham* 1135–54 (p1259) *Kirkst*, 1202 FF, *Metringham* 1190 (1301) Dugd vi, 1202 Ass, *Mederingeham* 1193 P, 1202 Ass. This is either 'Mēdrīc's homestead, estate' or 'the homestead, estate of Mēdrīc's people'. It is not clear whether we are concerned with a simple genitive formation or with a group-name in **-ingahām**. The first el. is the OE pers.n. **Mēdrīc*, which is cognate with *Mederic(h)us*, the name of a fourth century Alamannic prince.

Mickleberry Hill (Mumby, LSR), *Mikelberg', -berch'* c.1220 (Ed1) *Barl*, *Mikilbergh'* 1332 SR, *Mikkelbergh* 1340 *Barl*, 'the big hill' from ON **mikill** and ON **berg**.

Midville (LSR), was formed into a township in 1812 by Act of Parliament, cf. **Eastville, Frithville** and **Westville**.

Millthorpe (Pointon, Kest), *Milnetorp'* l12th Semp, 1202 Ass, 1212 Cur, *-thorp'* l12th Semp, 'the secondary settlement with a mill' from OE **myln** and ODan **thorp**. Presumably it was a dependent settlement of **Pointon**.

Miningsby (LSR), *Melingesbi* 1086 DB, *Minigesbia* 1142 NthCh, *Miniggesby* m12th (l13th) KirkstPsalt, *Mithingesbia* 1142 NthCh, *-by* 1198 (1328) Ch, *-bi* l12th Dane, *Midhingesbi* 1154–58 (1330) Ch, *Midingesbi* 1199 (1330) ib, *Mitingesb'* 1185 Templar, *Mitinghesbi* l12th Dane. This is a very difficult name with a great variety of early spellings and the best suggestion that can be made is that the first el. is an ON pers.n. *Mithjungr*, the second being ODan **bý** 'a farmstead, a village'. The change of *-th-* to *-n-* has parallels in other p.ns.

Minting (LSR), *Mentinghes, Mentinges* 1086 DB, a1129 (1336), m12th (1336) Dugd vi, 1201 Cur, *-inges* 1123–29 (c1331) Spald i, c1221 Welles, *Minthinges* 1140–50 Dane, an OE group-name meaning 'the family, the people of Mynta' from the OE pers.n. *Mynta* and the OE suffix **-ingas**. For more details of this formation see **Healing**.

Minting Park (Minting, LSR), see **Thorley**.

Monksthorpe (Great Steeping, LSR), *Monkethorp'* 1347 *HarlCh*, *Monkthorp* 1348 Dugd v, *Monkethorpe* 1418 Pat, 'the secondary settlement of the monks (of Bardney Abbey)' from ME **monke** and ODan **thorp**, a late example of the use of **thorp**.

Moorby (LSR), *Morebi* 1086 DB, 1170–98 Revesby, *-by* c1200, e13th RA vi, *Morbi* 1204 P, 1219 Fees, from OE **mōr**, ON **mór** in the sense 'a moor' and ODan **bȳ** 'a farmstead, a village'. The village is on the slope of the Wolds.

Morton (LWR), *Mortune* 1086 DB, *Morton'* 1223 Cur, 1237, 1241 RA ii, 1276 RH; it lies low beside the R. Trent. **Morton** (Kest), *Mortun(e)* 1086 DB, *-tunie* 1135–54 Dane, *-tuna* 1138 NthCh, *-ton'* 1185 RotDom, 1191 P, c1200 Semp. The village is on low-lying ground on the edge of the fen. **Morton** (Thorpe on the Hill, Kest), *Morton* 1242–43 Fees, 1275 RH, 1284–85 FA. Each means 'the farmstead, village in marshy land' from OE **mōr** and OE **tūn**.

Mosswood (Belton, LWR), *Mosewode* c1184 (15th) Templar, 1298 Pat, *Moswod'* Hy2 (e14th) Selby, *-wud'* 1204 ChR, 'the wood where moss, lichen grows' from OE **mos** and OE **wudu**.

Moulton (Hol), *Multune* 1086 DB, *-tuna* 1154–58 (1330) Ch, *Muleton'* 1165 P, 1166 RBE, l12th Dane, *Moltona* 1154–56 RA i, *Moleton'* 1166, from either the OE pers.n. *Mūla* and OE **tūn** 'a farmstead, a village' or OE **mūl** 'a mule' and OE **tūn**, the first explanation being perhaps more likely.

Moulton Eaugate (Moulton, Hol), *Egate* lHy3, 1329 (c1331) *Spald ii*, *Eagate* 15th *AddR*, *Eyegate* 1608 *AOMB 395*, 'the way, road to the river' from OE **ēa** and ON **gata**, with the parish name, **Moulton**, being prefixed later.

Muckton (LSR), *Machetone* (sic) 1086 DB, *Muketun* c1110 France, lHy2 Dane, *-tune* c1160 RA vi, *-ton'* 1212 Fees, 'Muca's farmstead, village' from the OE pers.n. *Muca* and OE **tūn**.

Mumby (LSR), *Mundebi* 1086 DB, *Monbi* c1115 LS, *Mumbi* c1115 ib, 1150–60 Dane, 1156–58 *HarlCh*, c1175 Dane, c1200 RA vi, 'Mundi's farmstead, village' from the ON pers.n. *Mundi* and ODan **bȳ**.

N

Navenby (Kest), *Nauenebi* 1086 DB, 1163–6 AC, 1170 P. 1170–75 Dane, 1199 P, *Navenebi* 1086 DB, 1188 P, 1196 RA viii, 'Nafni's farmstead, village' from the ODan pers.n. *Nafni* and ODan **bȳ**.

Nene, R. (Kest), forms in L documents include: *to Nen* s.a. 963 (c1121) ASC E, *Neen* 1154 (c1200) CartAnt, 1206, 1216, 1247 (c1500) *CrowReg, Nene* 1232 (c1331) *Spald ii*, 1268 Pat. This is identical with the **R. Neen** in Shropshire-Worcestershire and is a Celtic r.n., but the meaning is obscure.

Ness Wapentake (Kest), *Nesse* 1086 DB, 1185 RotDom, 1200 P, *Nes* 1168, 1190 ib, 'the headland' from ON **nes**. The forms are preceded or followed by some form of Latin *wapentacium*. The site of the meeting-place of the wapentake (ON **vápnatak**, late OE **wæpengetæc** 'a sub-division of a shire') is not known.

Nettleham (LWR), *Netelham* 1086 DB, c.1101 RA i, c1115 LS, 1126, 1139, 1149 RA i, 1161 *DC, Nettleham* 1086 DB, 'the homestead, estate where nettles grow' from OE **netel(e)** and OE **hām**. For the significance of nettles, see **Nettleton**.

Nettleton (LNR), *Neteltone* 1086 DB, *-tune* c1115 LS, *-tun* 1150–60 Dane, *Nettiltona* c1150, 1187 (1409) Gilb, *Netleton(')* 1175 ChancR, 'the farmstead, village where nettles grow' from OE **netel(e)** and OE **tūn**. Before the widespread use of fertilisers the presence of nettles indicated a concentrated phosphate content in the soil suggesting that the ground where they grew had been a site of human settlement.

Newball (Stainton by Langworth, LSR), *Neuberie* (sic) 1086 DB, *-bele* c1110 France, c1175 Dane, *-bell'* 1204 Cur, *Neobole* c1115 LS, *apud Niwebelam* c1142 Templar. The DB form is apparently 'the new fortified place' from OE **nīwe, nēowe** and OE **burh**, but in all the rest the second el. has been replaced by ODan **bōle** 'a dwelling, a homestead'.

Newham (Thornton le Fen, LSR), *Neuham* m12 (13th) KirkstPsalt, eHy2, Hy2 (p1259) *Kirkst*, 1210 (1252) Ch, 'the new homestead, estate' from OE **nīwe, nēowe** and OE **hām**.

New Holland (Barrow upon Humber, LNR), *the modern hamlet of the New Holland, where a large Inn was built on the Humber bank about ten years ago* 1828 White. A Note in LNQ ii, no. 96 quotes from the *Hull Advertiser*, Dec. 8th, 1848, which it is claimed throws light on the origin of the name, — "On the 4th instant, in Caister [died], Mr. Thomas Lamley . . . from whom New Holland first received its name, he having landed there a cargo of smuggled goods".

Newland (Lincoln), *noua terra* 112 Semp, *le neuland* Hy2 (13th) *Kirkst*, *Neue-*, *Neweland* 1182 P, 1206 Ass, 'land newly brought into cultivation', from OE **nīwe** and OE **land**.

Newport (Lincoln), *Neuport*' 1123–45, 1163 RA ii, 1185 Templar, 'the new market' from OE **nīwe** and OE **port**.

Newsham (Brocklesby, LNR), *Neuhuse* 1086 DB, -*hus* 1143–47, 1177 Dane, -*hous* 1236–47 *HarlCh*, *Newehus* c1141 BMFacs, *Neosum* c1115 LS, *Neusum* 1222 Cur. There are two alternative forms for **Newsham**. Those represented by *Neuhuse* and *Neuhus* are from the nom.sg. or nom.pl. of **Nīwehūs* 'the new house(s)'. Those forms represented by *Neosum, Neusum* etc. are from the dat.pl. **æt nīwan hūsum* 'at the new houses'. It is the latter which has given the modern **Newsham**, the weakly stressed ending having been interpreted in the 16th century as *ham,* cf. **Burnham, Coatham** and **Howsham**. *Neusum* is a type of name common in Denmark and it is reasonable to accept **Newsham** as being of Danish origin.

Newstead (Uffington, Kest), *de Nouo Loco* 1210 FF, *de Novo Loco* 1242–43 Fees, 1254 ValNor, *Newsted* 1219 FF. **Newstead Priory** (Cadney, LNR), (*de*) *Novo -*, *Nouo Loco* 1199 ChR, *Novus Locus* 1254 ValNor, *Newsted(e)* 1227 Ch, 1327 Pat. Each means 'the new monastery' from OE **nīwe** and OE **stede** 'a place, a site', also 'a holy place, a monastery'. The first was an Augustinian Priory founded at the end of the 12th century at a bridge over the R. Gwash. The second was a Gilbertine Priory founded there by the reign of Henry II at a place called *insula de Rucholm* Hy2 (1319) Dugd vi, 'the rough island of land, raised land in marsh' from OE **rūh** and ON **holmr**. *Rucholm* survived as a f.n. until at least 1767 *Stubbs*.

Newton (Newton and Haceby, Kest), *Neutone* 1086 DB, -*tona* eHy2 Dane, -*tun*' 1185 Templar, *Niweton*' 1168, 1190 P, *Neweton*' 1199 CurR. **Newton on Trent** (LWR), *Neutone* 1086 DB, *Neotune* c1115 LS, *Newetun*' 1154–66 RA i, *Niweton*' 1194 P, *Newentone* 1155–62 RA i, 1158–62 (1329) Ch, on the bank of the **R. Trent. Newton, Toft** (LNR), *Neutone* 1086 DB, -*tona* c1160 Dane, 1170–75 RA iv, *Newetuna* c1115 LS, *Niwetun* 1170–75 RA iv, *Newton'* 1210–15 ib, *Toft Neuton* 1324 Pat. It is near to **Toft next Newton. Newton, Wold** (LNR), *Neutone* 1086 DB, *Newtuna* c1115 LS, *Niwetuna* c1150 *DuDCCh, Newtona* l12th (1409) Gilb, *Waldneuton* eHy2 (13th) *Alv*, from its situation in a dip in the Wolds. All four names mean 'the new farmstead, village' from OE **nīwe** and OE **tūn**. The forms in *Newentona*, etc. for **Newton on Trent** represent the OE dat.sg. **æt nīwan tūne* 'at the new farmstead or village'.

New York (Wildmore Fen, LSR). *New York* 1824 O; this is a nickname of remoteness, the place being situated near the parish boundary.

Nocton (Kest), *Nochetune* 1086 DB, -*tuna* 1135–54 (p1259) *Kirkst*, 1155 Templar, *Noketun* lHy2 RA x, *Nocton'* 1177 P, probably 'the farmstead where wether-sheep are kept', from OE **hnoc** and OE **tūn**.

Normanby (Burton upon Stather, LWR), *Normannebi* 1067–69 (12th) HC, 1206 Ass, *Normanebi* 1086 DB, c1115 LS, c1128 (12th) ChronPetro, *Nordmanabi* c1115 LS. **Normanby by Stow** (Stow, LWR), *Normanebi* 1086, *Normannæbi* (sic) c1115 LS, *Normannebia iuxta Stou* 1146, 1163 RA i, *Normanebeia* 1160–65 RA iv. **Normanby le Wold** (LNR), *Normanesbi* 1086 DB, *Normannesby* 1208 Cur, *Normanebi* 1086 DB, c1200 RA iv, *Nordmanabi* c1115 LS, *Northmannebi* c1200 RA iv, *Normanby super Waldam* 1294 RSu. **Normanby by Spital** (LWR), *Normanebi* 1086 DB, *Nordmanabi* c1115 LS, *Normanneby* 1200 ChR, -*bi* 1202 Ass, *Normanby* 1246 Ipm, - *next Spyttel* 1545 LP xx. All mean 'the farmstead, village of the Northmen or Norwegians' from late OE **Northmann** and ODan **bý**. The name clearly indicates an isolated settlement of Norwegians. The second p.n. above is described as **by Stow**, the third as "on the Wold" and also *on the Hyll* 1563 *BT*, the fourth as being near **Spital on the Street** and earlier *iuxta Ouneby* (**Owmby**) 1329 *Ass*.

Normanton (Kest), *Normenton* 1086 DB, -*tun* Hy2 Dane, *Normantuna* m12th *AD*, -*tona* 1185 Templar, -*ton'* 1200 P, 'the village of the Norwegians' from late OE **Northman** and OE **tūn**. This is probably an English name given to an isolated settlement of Norwegians, who accompanied the Danes in the settlement of L.

Northorpe (Halton Holegate, LSR), *Northorp'* 1295 *Ass*, 1340 *FF*, *Norththorp* 1422 LNQ vii. **Northorpe** (Thurlby), *Nordthorp'* e13th *Rental*,

Northtorp' l13th *AD*, *Norttthorp* 1327 *SR*. Both mean 'the secondary settlement to the north' from OE, ON **north** and ON **thorp**. The first is named in relation to **Halton Holegate**, the second to **Thurlby**.

Northorpe (LWR), *Ðorp* 1060–66 (m12th) KCD 819 (S 1059), *Torp* 1086 DB, c1115 LS, 1139 RA i, 1198 (1328) Ch, *Thorp* 1146 Dugd i, *Nordtorp* 1190 P, 1196 ChancR, *Nortorp* 1200 Cur, originally a simplex p.n. from ODan **thorp** 'a secondary settlement' to which OE **north** was prefixed to distinguish **Northorpe** from **Southorpe** in the same parish.

North Riding, *Nort Treding*, *Northreding*, *Nortreding* 1086 DB, *Nortriding* c1115. Lindsey is divided into three parts — **North**, **South** and **West Riding**. **Riding** is derived from ON **thrithjung**, late OE **thrithing** 'a third part'. Initial *th-* has become *t-* through Anglo-Norman influence and was later absorbed by the final *-th* of *north* to give *Riding*.

Norton, Bishop (LWR), *Nortune* 1086 DB, *Nordtuna* c1115 LS, *Nortonam*, 1126 RA i, *Nortuna* 1149, 1163 ib, *Nortun'* 1189–99 (1318) Ch. **Norton Disney** (Kest), *Nortune* 1086 DB, *-tun* c1150 Dane, 1196–98, 1200 Cur, *Norton de Iseny* 1299 *HarlCh*. Both are derived from from OE **north** 'north' and OE **tūn** 'a farmstead, a village'. The first is probably **north** in relation to **Glentham**, and is **Bishop** because it was held by the Bishop of Lincoln. The second is probably north in relation to **Stapleford** and was held by the *de Isigny* family from Isigny in Normanby, note Adam *de Ysinni* 1201 Cur.

O

Oasby (Heydour, Kest), *Asedebi* 1086 DB, e13th *AddCh*, 1200–11 RA vii, 1202 Ass, 1242–43 Fees, *Oseby* e14th *AddCh*, perhaps 'Áswith's farmstead, village' from the ODan pers.n. *Ásvithr* and ODan **bȳ**.

Obthorpe (Thurlby, Kest), *Obthorp'* 1075 (c1331) *Spald i*, *Opetorp* 1086 DB, *Obbethorp* l11th (c1331) *Spald i*, 1200 ChR, *Ubetorp* 1204 FF, probably 'Ubbi's secondary settlement (of **Thurlby**)' from the ON pers.n. *Ubbi* and ODan **thorp**.

Oldfleet Drain (Stallingborough, LNR), *holflet* Hy2 (e13th) *Ncot, portu . . . de Houflet* 1155–58 (1334) Ch, *Holflet'* Hy3 (13th-14th) Selby, *portu de Holeflet* 1276 RH, 'the creek, stream flowing in a hollow' from OE **hol** and OE **flēot**.

Old South Eau (Hol), *Suth hee* l12th (m13th) *PipeS*, *Suthee* 1278 *FF*, *Suth'ee* 1294 Cl, *Southee* 1316 Fleet, *le Southee* 1334 Ipm, 'the river to the south' from OE **sūth** and OE **ēa**, of what is not clear.

Orby (LSR), *Heresbi* 1086 DB, *Orreby* c1115 LS, a1184 Semp, *-bia* 1148–56 RA i, *-bi* Hy2, c.1200 Dane, *Orebi* 1166 P, 'Orri's farmstead, village' from the ON byname *Orri* and ODan **bȳ**.

Orford (Stainton le Vale, LNR), *Erforde* 1086 DB, *Iraforda, Ireforde* c1115 LS, *Ireford(')* 1150–60 Dane, c1189 LAAS v, *Yreford(')* 1180 P, a1189 LAAS v, perhaps 'Ēra's ford from the unrecorded OE pers.n. *Ēra* and OE **ford**. The late development to *Orford* 1662 *Terrier* does not seem to have any parallel in English p.ns. It is a deserted village. Recently it has been suggested that the ford carries an ancient line of communication between Louth and Caistor.

Ormsby, North (LNR), *æt Vrmesbyg* 1066–68 (c1200) ASWills, *Ormesbi* 1086 DB, c1115 LS, 1166 RBE, 1199 CartAnt, *-by* a1160 (1409) Gilb, 1210 FF, *Ormesby Monialium* 1293 FF, *Nunormesby* 1386 Peace, *Northormesby* 1355 *FF*. **Ormsby, South** (LSR), *Ormesbi* 1086 DB, c1115 LS, p1169 Dane, Hy2 Dane, *Ormesvi* (sic) c1110 France, *Ormeresbi* c1115 LS, *Hormeresbi* l12th Dane, *Suth Ormesby* 1323 *MM*. Both probably mean 'Orm's farmstead, village' from the ODan pers.n. *Orm* and ODan **bȳ**, but if the two forms

Ormeres-, *Hormeres-* are significant then the first el. of **South Ormsby** is the ODan pers.n. *Ormar*. **North Ormsby** is **Nun** from the Priory of Gilbertine nuns, founded there in the 12th century, and is **North** in contrast to **South** Ormsby.

Osbournby (Kest), *Esbernebi, Osbernedebi* 1086 DB, *Osbernebi* 1086 ib, 1200 Cur, 1202 Ass, 1204 OblR, *Osebernesbi* 1206 Ass, perhaps Ōsbeorn's farmstead, village' from the Anglo-Scandinavian pers.n. *Āsbeorn*, itself from the ODan pers.n. *Æsbiorn*, and ODan **bȳ**. The early forms have medial *-e-* for a Scand. genitive in *-a-* and this speaks in favour of a derivation from ODan **Æsbiornabȳ*, with subsequent anglicisation through association with AScand *Ōsbeorn*.

Osgodby (Kirkby cum Osgodby, LNR), *Osgotesbi, Osgotebi* 1086 DB, c1115 LS, 1139 AC, 1139–42 *DuLaCh, Osgodby* Hy2 (14th) Dugd iii, *Angoteby* 1153–62, 1187 (1409) Gilb, 1210 FF. **Osgodby** (Lenton, Kest), *Osgotebi* 12th HC, 1242–43 Fees, *Angoteby* l12th (l13th) *Stix, -bi* 1207, 1212 P. Both mean 'Osgot's farmstead, village' from the Anglo-Scandinavian pers.n. *Ōsgot, Ōsgod*, a regular anglicised form of ON *Ásgautr*, ODan *Āsgot* and ODan **bȳ**. *Osgot* is recorded independently in DB in L. Forms in *An-* are due to Anglo-Norman influence.

Otby (Walesby, LNR), *Otesbi* 1086 DB, *Otebi* 1086 ib, Hy1 LN, Hy2 Dane, *-by* 1166 RBE, *Ottebi* c1115 LS, 1141–45 RA vi, *-by* 1140–47 Dane, l12 *MiD*, 'Otte's farmstead, village' from the ODan pers.n. *Otte*, an early loan from Old German *Otto*, and ODan **bȳ**.

Owersby (LNR), *Aresbi* 1086 DB, *Auresbeia* 1189 (c1200) CartAnt, *-by* e13 RA iv, *Oresbi* 1086 DB, 1182 P, *Orresbi* 1191 P, *Oursebi* c1115 LS, 1139–41 *DuLaCh*, c1160 RA iv, *Owresbi* 1198 FF, *Ouresby* 1203 Cur. This is a very difficult name, but the most likely suggestion is that it is derived from the ON per.n. *Ávarr* and ODan **bȳ** 'a farmstead, a village'. It is *Longe Ouresbi* 1219 Ass, presumably a reference to a straggling village. In the 19th century it is distinguished as **North** and **South Owersby**.

Owmby (Searby cum Owmby, LNR), *Odenebi* 1086 DB, *Autneby, Authneby* 1100–15 (14th) Whitby, *Oudenbi* 1155–58 RA i, *Outhenebi, Outhenbi* 1155–60 Dane, *Ounebi* c1115 LS. The etymology of **Owmby** is uncertain but it is probably 'Outhen's farmstead, village' from the Anglo-Scand. pers.n. *Outhen*, corresponding to ON *Authun(n)*, and ODan **bȳ** 'a farmstead, a village'.

Owmby by Spital (LWR), *Ounesbi* 1086 DB, *-b'* 1185 Templar, *Ounebi* 1086 DB, c1115 LS, 1166 P, 1196–1203 RA iv, *Ounabi* c1115 LS, *Aueneby* 1210 FF, perhaps identical with **Owmby**, though the forms suggest that we are concerned rather with the variant pers.n. form ON *Aun(n)*, cf. **Aunby**.

Owston Ferry (LWR), *Ostone* 1086 DB, *Ouston* c1180 Bly, 1200 Abbr, *-tona* 1179 P, 1180–90 Dane, *-tun'* 112th *AD*, probably a partial Scandinavianisation of OE **Ēasttūn* 'the farmstead, village to the east (of **Haxey**)' from OE **ēast** and OE **tūn**, with the first el. replaced by the cognate ON **austr**.

Oxcombe (LSR), *Oxetune* (sic), *Oxecumbe* 1086 DB, p1175, a1191 Dane, 1203 Cur, *-cum* c1115 LS, *-cumb* c1200 Dane, 'the valley where oxen are found' from OE **oxa** and OE **cumb**, which usually refers to a bowl- or trough-shaped valley with three fairly steeply rising sides, topographically appropriate for **Oxcombe** which is in a small round-ended valley.

P

Panton (LSR), *Pantone* 1086 DB, *-tuna* c1115 LS, *-tona* 1168, 1175 P, *-tun* 1185–97, lHy2 Dane, probably 'the farmstead, village in a depression or hollow' from OE **panne** 'a pan', in a transferred topographical sense, and OE **tūn**. This is appropriate for the site of the depopulated village.

Partney (LSR), *Peartaneu* 731 Bede, *Peortanea* c890 (10th) OEBede, *Partene, -ai* 1086 DB, *-ay* 1115, c1145 (p1269) *Bard*, *-ey* 1125, m12th (p1269) *ib*, 'Pearta's island of land' from the OE pers.n. *P(e)arta* and OE **ēg** 'an island, dry ground surrounded by marsh'. Bede's form is *-eu* is typically Northumbrian. Cf. **Bardney**.

Pelham's Lands (Hol), *Pelhams Land* 1824 O. No doubt named from the *Pelham* family, which held land here in 1601 ChancP. Charles Anderson *Pelham* was allotted 120 acres in the Holland Fen Enclosure Award. It was formerly extra-parochial but was formed into a parish in 1883.

Pickworth (Kest), *Picheurde, -uorde, -worde* 1086 DB. *-wurtha* 1170, 1175 P, *Pikewurda* 1174 ib, *-word'* l12th Semp, 'Pīca's enclosure' from the OE pers.n. *Pīca* and OE **worth**, identical with **Pickworth** in Rutland.

Pilham (LWR), *Pileham* 1086 DB, 1139 RA i, 1150–60 (14th) *ChorCart*, c1180 Bly, 1195 P, 'Pila's homestead, estate' from the OE pers.n. *Pīla* and OE **hām**.

Pinchbeck (Hol), *Pincebec* 1086 DB, 1188–97 BS, 1194 CurR, *Pyncebek* l12th (m14th) *HC*, *Pincebek'* 1200 (c1331) *Spald i*, *Pyncebeck* 1183 (m14th) *HC*, perhaps 'the minnow stream', from OE **pinc* and ON **bekkr**. OE **pinc* 'minnow' survives as *pink* in dialect in the North and parts of the East Midlands, but *pink* is also recorded in L dialect in the sense 'linnet'.

Pointon (Pointon and Sempringham, Kest), *Pochinton(e)* 1086 DB, *-tun* 1150–60 (1409) Gilb, *Pointun* c1150 *AddCh*, l12th Dane, *-ton'* 1150–60, a1168 Semp, 1173 P, 1196 Cur, 'the farmstead, village associated with or called after Pohha' from the OE pers.n. *Pohha* with the OE medial connective particle *-ing-* and OE **tūn**.

Ponton, Great & Little (Kest), *Pamptune, Pamtone* 1086 DB, *Pantone* 1135–54 (13th) *Stix*, *Panton* 1194 CurP, *Ponton* 1227 Ch, *Magna -, Parva*

Pantone 1086 DB; perhaps identical with **Panton**, but the first el. is uncertain; the second is OE **tūn** 'a farmstead, a village'.

Poolham (Edlington, LSR), *Polum* 1150–60, 1170–75, 1175–81, Hy2 Dane, e13th (l13th) *Stix*, 1212 Fees, 'at the pools' from the dat.pl. **pōlum** of OE **pōl**. The village is extinct but the name is represented by **Poolham Hall**.

Postland (Crowland, Hol), "island called" *le Purceynt* 1415 Pat, *le Purceint*, *le purceynt* 1439 *CrowR*, *the purcent* c1485 LNQ xiii, *Portesand* 1535–43 Leland, *Porsand* 1576 Saxton, from ME **purseint** 'an enclosed space, a circumscribed area'.

Q

Quadring (Hol), *Quedhaveringe* 1086 DB, 1196 ChancR, *-inga* 1167 P, *-havering'* 1200 Cur, *Quadheueringe* 1086 DB, *-haueringe* 1170, 1195 P, from OE *Hæferingas* 'the people, the followers of Hæfer', originally the name of a group of people under their leader *Hæfer*, to which was prefixed OE **cwēad** 'mud, dirt', referring to the fen here. The name belongs to an early period of AS settlement in the area.

Quadring Eaudike (Quadring, Hol), *Quaderyng Eee* 1343 *FF*, *Quadryngedyk* 1403 Pap, from the parish name and OE **ēa** 'a river, a stream' to which was added OE **dīc**, ON **dík** 'a ditch, a draining channel'.

Quarrington (Kest), *Corninctone, -tune, Cornintone* 1086 DB, *Querentone* 1178 (14th) Rams, *Querint'* 1175 (1337) Ch, *Querinton'* 1202 Ass, *Queringtone* a1219 Welles. It is possible that the first el. is OE **cweorning* derived from OE **cweorn** 'a quern, a hand-mill' and the OE place-name forming suffix **-ing**, meaning 'a place with a hand-mill', perhaps any mill. Names derived from **cweorn** often have early forms in *Corn-*. To this was added OE **tūn** 'a farmstead, a village'.

R

Raithby (LSR), *Radebi* 1086 DB, 1170–78 Revesby, Hy2 Dane, *Radabi* 1142–53 ib, *Rathebi* 1170–80, c1200 RA vi, 'Hrathi's farmstead, village' from the ON pers.n. *Hrathi*, ODan *Rathi* and ODan **bȳ**.

Raithby (Raithby cum Maltby, LSR), *Radresbi* 1086 DB, *Raitheb'* lHy2 RA v, *Reitheby* 1200 ChR, 1202 Ass, *Raidehebi* 1212 Fees, *Reidebi* 1218 Ass, 'Hreithi's farmstead, village' from the ON pers.n. *Hreithi* and ODan **bȳ**.

Ranby (LSR), *Randebi* 1086 Db, c1115 LS, 1193, 1200 P, *Randbi* 1155 (p1259) *Kirkst*, 'Randi's farmstead, village' from the ON pers.n. *Randi* and ODan **bȳ**.

Rand (LSR), *Rande* 1086 DB, eHy2, 1165, 1187 Dane, *Randa* c1115 LS, *Rande* 1201 Cur, from OE **rand** 'edge, border, bank', also 'boundary'. 'Bank' would be topographically appropriate here.

Rase, R (LNR), *aqam current' que vocat' Ras'* 1326 *MC*, probably a back-formation from Rasen.

Rasen, Market, Middle & West (LNR), *æt ræsnan* (checked from MS) 973 (13th) ECCE (S 792), *Resne* 1086 DB, *Rase* (sic), *Rasa* 1086 ib, 1090–1100 (1402) YCh vi, c1115 LS, *Rasne* 1135–40 (1464) Pat, 'at the planks' from the dat.pl., **ræsnum**, of OE **ræsn** 'a plank', perhaps with reference to a plank bridge or planks laid across marshy ground. **Market Rasen** is *Parua Rasa* c1115 LS, *Estrase* 1193 P, *-rasne* 1187 (1409) Gilb, *Marketrasyn* 1358 *Cor.* **Middle Rasen** is *Media Rasa* c1115 LS, *Middelrasen'* 1201 FF, *Middel Rasen Drax* 1331 Pat, (from Drax Priory which held land here), *media Rasyn Tupholm* 1291 Tax, (from Tupholme Abbey which also held land in Middle Rasen). **West Rasen** is *Magna Rasna* 1150–54 AddCh, *Mikelrasen* 1367 Ipm, *Westrasen(')* 1175–68 (1464) Pat. **Market, Middle** and **West** are self-explanatory.

Rauceby, North & South (Kest), *Roscebi* 1086 DB, 1197 P, 1202 FF, *Roucebi* 1146 RA i, 1170 P, 1185 Templar, *Rauceby* 1150–60 (1409) Gilb, *Rouscebi* 1193 P, *North Rouceby* 1242–43 Fees, *Suthrouceby* 1241–43 ib, 'Rauth's farmstead, village' from the ON pers.n. *Rauthr* and ODan **bȳ**. The original Scand. gen.sg. survives as [s] today, indicating that the name had been given by Danes.

Ravendale, East & West (LNR), *Ravenedal, -dale* 1086 DB, *Rauendal* 1086 ib, "the other" *Ravenedale* 1086 ib, *Ravendale* 1086 ib, 1202 (1342) Pat, *Est Ravendale* 1238–42 ib, *West Rauendale* 1202 *HarlCh*, 'the valley frequented by ravens', a Scand. compound of ON **hrafn** and ON **dalr**, later differentiated as **East** and **West**.

Raventhorpe (Holme, LWR), *Ragnaldtorp* 1067 (12th) RRAN, *Ragenaltorp* 1086 DB, *Ragheniltorp* c1115 LS, c1128 (12th) ChronPetro, *Ranildethorp'* eHy2 (m14th) *PetML*, *Ragnaldtorp* Hy2 (1314) Ch. 'Ragnald's secondary settlement' from the ODan pers.n. *Ragn(v)aldr*, confused in some forms with the feminine pers.n. *Ragnhildr*, and ODan **thorp**.

Reasby (Stainton by Langworth, LSR), *Reresbi* 1086 DB, c1115 LS, 1147 RA iii, 1185 Templar, *-by* c1115 LS, lHy2 (p1259) *Kirkst*, probably 'Hreitharr's farmstead, village' from the ON pers.n. *Hreitharr* and ODan **bȳ**.

Redbourne (LWR), *Reburne, Radburne* 1086 DB, *Ratburne* 1090 RA i, *Raburna* c1150 (1409) Gilb, 1150–60 Dane, *Redburna* c1115 LS, 1155 (c1200) CartAnt, *Redeburna* 1154 (e14th) Selby, *-burn* Hy2 Dane, 'the reedy stream' from OE **hrēod** and OE **burna**.

Reepham (LWR), *Refam, -an, -aim* 1086 DB, *-ham* c1115 LS, c1128 (12th) ChronPetro, 1189 (1332) Ch, 1196 ChancR, 'the village, the estate of the reeve' from OE **(ge)rēfa** and OE **hām**.

Reston, North & South (LSR), *Ristone* 1086 DB, *-tuna* c1115 LS, 1175–81 Dane, *-tunia* c1180 *MiD*, *-tun* 1160–75 RA vi, *-tona* 1153–69 Dane, *-ton'* 1170 P, *Parva Riston'* 1225 Cur, the same as *North Riston* 1274 Ipm; *Suthriston'* 1271 RRGr, 'the farmstead, village among the shrubs, brushwood' from OE **hrīs** and OE **tūn**. The affixes are self-explanatory.

Revesby (LSR), *Resvesbi* (sic) 1086 DB, *Revesbia* 1135–54, m12th Dugd v, *-bi* 1166 RBE, 1185–95 France, *-by* 1167–68 RBE, *Reuesbi* 1142 NthCh, 1152–55 RA i, *-by* 1163 ib, 'Ref's farmstead, village' from the ON pers.n. *Refr* and ODan **bȳ**.

Riby (LNR), *Ribi* 1086 DB, c1115 LS, *Riby* c1150 (e13) NCot, *Riebi* 1155–58 (1334) Ch, 1159 P, 1198 Cur. This is a hybrid OE and ON p.n., but it is very likely that it was probably originally OE **Rygetūn* 'the farmstead, village where rye is grown' from OE **ryge** and OE **tūn**. If this is so, OE **tūn** was replaced by ODan **bȳ** also 'a farmstead, a village'.

Rigbolt (Gosberton, Hol), *Wrictebaud* 1232 Pat, *Wirchebald* 1237–38 RRG, *Wrichbold* 1240, Hy3 (c1331) *Spald i*, *Wrightebald* 1292 Ch, 'the wright's, the smith's dwelling' from OE **wyrhta** and OE **bold**.

Rigsby (Rigsby with Ailby, LSR), *Righesbi* 1086 DB, Hy2 Dane, *Rigesbi* 1086 DB, c1115 LS, c1150 Dane, *Riggesbi* c1150 ib, *-by* eHy2 (p1259) *Kirkst*. Probably literally 'the farmstead, village of the ridge' from the gen.sg. of ON **hryggr**, which is topographically appropriate, and ON **bȳ**.

Rippingale (Kest), *Repinghale* 1086 DB, c1140 Dane, 1190–1200 AASR xli, l12th Semp, 1200 RA vii, *Repingehale* 1166 RBE, *-hal'* 1182 P, *Ripingahal'* 1185 ib, *-hala* Hy2 RPD, probably 'the nook of land of the Hrepingas' from the gen.pl. *Hrepinga* of the OE group-name *Hrepingas* 'the family, the dependents of *Hrepa*', and OE **halh**. The same group-name occurs as *Hrepingas* s.a. 675 (c1121) ASC E, 675–91 (m12th) BCS 842 (S 1805). The second reference here is from an AS charter believed to have an authentic base. Both forms have been identified with **Rippingale** but this is quite uncertain.

Risby (Walesby, LNR), *Risebi* 1086 DB, 1191 FF, *-b'* 1185 Templar, *Risabi* c1115 LS, *Riseby* 1193 P. **Risby, High** and **Low** (Roxby cum Risby, LWR), *Risebi* 1067–69 (m12th) HC, 1086 DB, c1115 LS, c1128 (12th) ChronPetro, 1192 P, *-by* c1200 BS. Both mean 'the farmstead, village among the shrubs, brushwood' from ON **hrís** and ODan **bȳ**. This name is found as Rejsby and Risby in Denmark and it is possible that it is a p.n. transferred from Denmark. If this were so it was presumably as topographically appropriate for the English names as for the Danish. The affixes, **High** and **Low** are self-explanatory.

Risegate (Gosberton, Hol), *Rysgate* c1209 Cust, *Risgate* c1274 (c1331) *Spald ii*, 1304 *DCAcct*, 1318 Ipm, *Risegate* 1275 RH. Spellings without a medial *-e-* far outnumber those with medial *-e-* and it is likely that **Risegate** takes its name from the family of Robert de *Ry* 1250 FF. The second el. is ON **gata** 'a road, a way'. It was frequently referred to as a manor.

Riseholme (LWR), *Risun* 1086 DB, c1115 LS, 1206 P, *Rison* 1123, 1126 France, *Risum* 1160–70 RA viii, 1166 (13th) *Kirk*, c1200 RA viii, from **hrīsum**, or **hrísum** the dative pl. of OE **hrīs** or ON **hrís** 'at the shrubs'. The modern form is the result of the reinterpretation of the weakly stressed final syllable.

Ropsley (Ropsley & Humby, Kest), *Ropeslai* 1086 DB, *-le* 1106–23 (1333) Ch, 1185 Templar, *-ley* 1150–60 (1409) Gilb, *Roppeslea* 1176 P, *-le* Ass, 'Hropp's wood or glade' from the unrecorded OE pers.n. **Hropp*, a strong form of *Hroppa*, and OE **lēah**.

Rothwell (LNR), *Rodowelle* (sic) 1086 DB, *Rothewelle* 1086 ib, c1155 Dane, *-wella* c1115 LS, c1150, 1160–66 Dane, *Rowella* 1130 P, eHy2 Dane, 'the clearing with a spring' from OE **rōth** and OE **wella**. The early forms in *Rowell*, etc., show Anglo-Norman loss of the medial *-th-*, common in p.ns.

Roughton (LSR), *Rocstune* (sic) 1086 DB. *Ructuna* c1115 LS, 1170–75, *-tun* 1158 *HarlCh*, 1163, lHy2 Dane, 'the farmstead, village on rough ground' from OE **rūh** and OE **tūn**. There is still rough pasturage here today.

Rowston (Kest), *Rouestune* 1086 DB, *-tona* 1182, Hy2, c1200 (1407) Gilb, 1218 Ass, *Rolueston'* 1202–23 RA vii, *Rolveston'* a1221 Welles, 'Rōlf's farmstead, village' a pers.n. hybrid p.n. from the ODan pers.n. *Rōlfr*, ON *Hrólfr* and OE **tūn**. This is almost certainly an earlier Anglo-Saxon settlement taken over and partially re-named by the Danish settlers.

Roxby (LWR) *Roxebi* 1086 DB, *Rochesberia* 1090–1100, 1147–73 (1402) YCh vi, *Rokesbia* 1100–8 ib, *-bi* 1199 FF, *Rochesbi* c1115 LS, 1136–40 (1464) Pat, 1162 P, 'Hrók's farmstead, village' from the ON pers.n. *Hrókr* and ODan **bȳ**.

Roxholm (Kest), *Rochesham* 1086 DB, *Rokesham* 1206 Cur, 1242–43 Fees, *Roxholme* 1615 Admin, 'Hrōc's homestead, estate' from the OE pers.n. *Hrōc* and OE **hām**. For the later development to *-holm*, compare **Bloxholm**. The name survives in **Roxholm Hall**.

Roxton (Immingham, LNR), *Rocaston* 1159–81 (e13th) *NCot*, *Roxtun* a1170 (e13th), 1241 *ib*, *-ton* 1212 Fees, 'Hrōc's farmstead' from the OE pers.n. *Hrōc* and OE **tūn**.

Ruckland (LSR), *Rocheland* 1086 DB, *Rokelunda* 1153–69, 1166–75 Dane, *-lund* eHy3 Ormsby, *Roclund* lHy2 Dane, 1212 Fees, 'the small wood, the grove where rooks are found' from ON **hrókr** and ON **lundr**. The development of **lundr** to *-land* is common.

Ruskington (Kest), *Reschintone, Rischintone* 1086 DB, *-tuna* 1150–60 (1409) Gilb, *-ton'* 1196 ChancR, *Riskinton* 1175 (1337) Ch, 1194 P, 1202 Ass. There are no early spellings for **Ruskington** with a medial *-ing-*, so that the first el. of the name is likely to be OE **riscen** 'rushy, growing with rushes' with OE **tūn** 'a farmstead, village'. Medial *-sk-* is due to Scand. influence.

S

Saleby (Saleby with Thoresthorpe, LSR), *Saleby* 1086 DB, 1153–62 (1409) Gilb, *-bi* 1086 DB, Hy2 Dane, *Salesbi* eHy2, Hy2 ib, perhaps 'Salli's farmstead, village' from the ODan pers.n. *Salli* and ODan **bȳ**.

Salmonby (LSR), *Salmundebi* 1086 DB, 1142–53 Dane, 12th *RevesInv*, *-by* 1198 (1328) Ch, *Salmonebi* c1115 LS, *Salmundbi* 1168 P, c1200 (1409) Gilb, 'Salmund's farmstead, village' from the ODan pers.n. *Salmund* and ODan **bȳ**.

Saltfleet (Skidbrooke, LSR), *Salfluet* 1086 DB, *Saltflet* 1301 Cl, 1361 Pat, 'the salty inlet, creek' from OE **salt** and OE **flēot. Saltfleet Haven** (Skidbrooke, LSR), *portum de Salflet* lHy3 (Hy4) *GCB, - Salfleth* 1277 (Hy4) *ib, - Sauflet* 1278 (Hy4) *ib, Saltfletehaven* 1317 Cl, *Salflethaven* 1322 Pat, from **Saltfleet** and ON **hafn** 'a haven, a harbour'. It is also called *portum de Salfleteby* 1275, 1276 RH, Ed1 (Hy4) *GCB*, from **Saltfleetby** further upstream.

Saltfleetby All Saints, St Clement & St Peter (LSR), *Salflatebi* 1086 DB, c1115 LS, *Salfletebi* c1155 (1409) Gilb, Hy2 Dane, *Salfledebi* c1115 LS, *Saltfletebi* 1185 Templar; *Sauflet Omnium Sanctorum* 1254 ValNor, *Myddle saltfletbye* 1576 Saxton; *Saltfletteby S. Clementis* 1254 RRGr, *Estsaltfletby* 1566 Pat; *Saltfletby Sancti Petri* 1254 ValNor, *Westsaltfletby* 1566 Pat. 'The farmstead, village on or near Saltfleet' from the stream-name which has given its name to **Saltfleet** (in Skidbrooke) and ON **bȳ**. The three affixes are from the dedications of the churches, though each had an alternative, **Middle, East** and **West** respectively.

Sandholme (Frampton, Hol), *Sandome* 1562 Sewer i, *-holme* 1604 *Wills*, 1639 *TP*, 'the sandy piece of raised ground in marsh' from OE **sand**, ON **sandr** and ON **holmr**, the latter a very common word in minor p.ns. and f.ns. in L.

Sandtoft (Belton, LWR), *Santofte* m12th (l13th) *StM, Sandtofte* 1156–57 (14th) YCh i, 1189–99 (1308) Ch, 'the curtilage, messuage on sandy ground', from OE **sand**, ON **sandr** and ODan **toft**.

Santon, High & Low (Appleby, LWR), *Sanctone, Santone* 1086 DB, *-tuna* c1115 LS, *-tun* a1175 Goke, *-ton'* 1196 ChancR, 1197 P, *Upper Santon*,

Neither Santon 1606 *Terrier* 'the farmstead on sandy soil', from OE **sand** and OE **tūn**.

Sapperton (Braceby, Kest), *Sapretone* 1086 DB, *Saperton'* Hy2 Semp, lHy2 *Anc, -tun* e13th (l13th) *Stix, Sapereton'* 1219 Ass, 'the village of the soap-makers' from OE **sāpere** and OE **tūn**. **Sapperton** has been tentatively identified with *Causennis* 4th (8th) AntIt, whose meaning and etymology however are unknown.

Sausthorpe (LSR), *Saltorp* (sic) eHy2, l12th Dane, *Saustorp* 1175 P, 1202 Ass, *Sauztorp* 1190 P, 1193 FF, *Saucetorp* 1195 P, 'Sauth's secondary settlement' from the ON byname *Sauthr* and ODan **thorp**.

Sawcliffe (Roxby cum Risby, LWR), *Saleclif* 1086 DB, 1212 Fees, *Salcliua* l12th (l13th) Blyth, *-clifa* 13th (l13th) ib, *Salecliue* 1230 P, 'the (steep) slope where willows grow' from OE **salh** and OE **clif.**

Saxby (LWR), *Sassebi* (sic) 1086 DB, *Saxsa-, Saxse-* c1115 LS, *Saxebia* c1155 Dane, *-b'* Templar. *-by* 1205 OblR. **Saxby All Saints** (LNR), *Saxebi* 1086 DB, 1166 P, *Saxbi* 1238–43 Fees, *-by* 1332 SR. Both mean 'Saxi's farmstead, village' from the ODan pers.n. *Saxi* and ODan **bȳ**. **All Saints** is from the dedication of the church.

Saxilby (LWR), *Saxlabi* c1115 LS, *Saxlebi* c1115 ib, 1155–60, eHy2 Dane, *Saxelebi* 1143–47, 1160–66 ib, probably 'Saxulf's farmstead, village' from the ON pers.n. *Saxulfr* and ODan **bȳ**.

Scamblesby (LSR), *Scamelesbi* 1086 DB, l12th Dane, *-by* 1163 RA i, *Scamelisbi* 1123–29, 1200 (c1331) *Spald i, Scamlesbi* 1160–70 RA vi, *-by* l12th ib, perhaps 'Skammlaus' farmstead, village' from the ON byname *Skammlaus* 'shameless' and ODan **bȳ**, though the ODan pers.n. *Skammel* might well be an alternative first el.

Scampton (LWR), *Scantone, -tune* 1086 DB, *-tuna* c1115 LS, *Schamtona* 1125, c1145 (p1269) *Bard, Scamtuna* c1155 Dane, l12th ib, *-tun'* m12th *HarlCh*, Hy2 Dane, 'the short village', probably an Anglo-Scandinavian compound of ON **skammr** and OE **tūn**.

Scarle, North (Kest), *Scarle* 1185 Templar, 1234 FF, 1241 Lib, *Scarnell'* 1201 FF, *Northscarle* 1291 Tax. It is possible that **Scarle** means 'the dirty, mucky clearing' from OE **sc(e)arn** and OE **lēah** with initial [sk] due to Scand.

influence. It is **North** to distinguish it from **South Scarle** in Nottinghamshire.

Scawby (LWR), *Scalebi* 1086 DB, *Scallebi* 1086 ib, 1100–8 YCh vi, c1115 LS, 1150–60 Dane, 1163 RA i, 1185 Templar, -*bya* 1146 RA i, 'Skalli's farmstead, village' from the ON byname *Skalli* and ODan **bý**. In the neighbouring parish of Broughton is *Scalehau* a1175 Goke, *Scallehou* 1205 ib, 'Skalli's mound', from the same byname, no doubt named from the same man, and ON **haugr**.

Scopwick (Scopwick & Kirkby Green, Kest), *Scapeuic* 1086 DB, -*wich* 1135–54 (p1259) *Kirkst*, 1175 (1337) Ch, -*wic* c1150 Dane, Hy2 (1407) Gilb, *Scapwic* 1086 DB, 1170 P, 1185 Templar, 'the sheep farm' from OE **scēp** and OE **wīc**, with Scand. *Sk-* for *Sh-*.

Scothern (LWR), *Scotstorne* 1086 DB, c1115 LS, 1207 FF, *Scoztorna* 1166 P, *Scostorne* Hy2 (Ed1) *Barl*, -*thorn* lHy2 *ib*, *Scotorne* (sic) 1086 DB, -*torn'* 1163 RA i, 'the Scot's or Scots' thorn-tree' from OE **Scot(t)** 'a Scot' (as also in **Scotter** and **Scotton**) and OE **thorn**, with the first el. varying in the earliest forms between sg. and pl.

Scotter (LWR), *Scottere* 1061–66 (m12th) KCD 819 (S 1059), *Scotere* 1067 (12th) RRAN, 1086 DB, 1093–98 RRAN, 1189 (1332) Ch, *Scotre* 1086 DB, c1128 (12th) ChronPetro, *Scotra* c1115 LS, 'the tree of the Scots' from OE **Scot(t)** (as in **Scothern** and **Scotton**), gen.pl. **Scot(t)a** and OE **trēow**.

Scotterthorpe (Scotter, LWR), *Scalkestorpe* 1067–69 (m12th) HC, *Scaldestorp* c1128 (12th) ChronPetro, *Scaltorp* 1086 DB, 1212 Fees, -*thorpe* 1189 (1332) Ch, *Scaletorp* c1128 (12th) ChronPetro, 1194 CurR, possibly 'Skalk's secondary settlement', from the ODan pers.n. *Skalk* and ODan **thorp**. The modern form has been influenced by that of the parish, **Scotter**, in which **Scotterthorpe** is situated.

Scottlethorpe (Edenham, Kest), *Scachetorp, Scachertorp* (sic) 1086 DB, *Scotelthorp* c1150 Anc, Hy2 (1227) Ch, e13th (15th) Bridl, 1242–43 Fees, *Scotlatorp'* lHy2 Anc, *Scodlouestorp, Scodlotorp* 1202 Ass; the first el. is quite uncertain, the second being ODan **thorp** 'a secondary settlement (of **Edenham**)'.

Scotton (LWR), *Scottun* 1061–66 (m12th) KCD 819 (S 1059), -*tuna* c1115 LS, *Scotune* 1086 DB, c1128 (12th) ChronPetro, *Scotone* 1086 DB, 1189 (1332)

Ch, 'the farmstead, village of the Scots' from OE **Scot(t)** (as also in **Scothern** and **Scotter**), gen.pl. **Scot(t)a** and OE **tūn.**

Scrafield (LSR), *Scraidefeld* Hy2 Dane, *Screide-* 1183 (l13th) *Stix, Screthefeld* 1189–99 RevesbyS, *Scredefeld* c1200 RA v, *Scredesfeld* 1186–1200 Samson, *Schreithesfeld* c1200 RA v. This is probably a hybrid compound of ON **skreith** 'a land-slide' and OE **feld** 'open country'.

Scrane End (Freiston, Hol), *ueteri* (i.e. "old") *Screinga* a1158, eHy2 Dane, *Screinges* eHy3 (p1259) *Kirkst, Scrainges* 1197 P, *Scrainge* 1202 FF, *Screhinges* 1202 Ass; this seems clearly to be derived from the OE plural suffix **-ingas** denoting a group or association of people, as e.g. in **Healing**. No plausible suggestion can be made, however, for the first part of the name. **End** was added late to the old name.

Scredington (Kest), *Scredinctun* 1086 DB, *-intona* 1189–92 RA vii, *-inton'* 1198 FF, *-ington'* 1189–95 RA iii, *-intune* 1086 DB, *-inton* Hy2 France. This is a difficult name for which no real suggestion can be made.

Scremby (LSR), *Screnbi* (sic) 1086 DB, 1170 P, *Scremby* 1175–78 *Anc, -bi* 1175–84 *AddCh*, lHy2 Dane, perhaps 'Skræma's farmstead, village' from an unrecorded ON pers.n. **Skræma* and ODan **bȳ.**

Scrivelsby (LSR), *Scriwelesbi, Scrivelesbi* 1086 DB, *Scriuelesbi* 1086 DB, 1202, 1206 Ass, *Scriflebi* c1115 LS, *Scrivelby* m12 (l13) KirkstPsalt, probably 'Skrifli's or Skrifill's farmstead, village' from an unrecorded ON byname **Skrifli* or **Skrifill* corresponding to Modern Icelandic *skrifl, skrifli* 'a feeble or wretched person' and ODan **bȳ.**

Scunthorpe (LWR), *Escumetorp* 1086 DB (sic, an Anglo-Norman form), *Scumetorp* 1196 ChancR, *Scummptorp* 1245 FF, *Scumthorp'* 1273–74 RA viii, 1300 Ipm, probably 'Skúma's secondary settlement' from the ON pers.n. *Skúma* and ODan **thorp**. It was named in relation to **Frodingham**, in which parish **Scunthorpe** was earlier situated.

Scupholme (South Somercotes, LSR), *Scupholm* m12th (1649) *Dods 75, Scupeholm* 1179 (13th) *Alv*, lHy2 Dane, l12th (13th) *Alv, Scuppeholm* c1200 RA v, probably from ON **Skupi*, an unrecorded byname belonging to the Germanic root **skūp-, skūf-* 'to bend', and ON **holmr** 'raised land in the marshes'.

Searby (LNR), *Sourebi* 1086 DB, *Sauerbi* 1155–58 RA i, *Seurebi* 1086 DB, c1115 LS, 1197 P, *Safrebi* c1115 LS, *Seuerbi* c1155 Dane, *-by* c1155 (e13th) *NCot*, probably 'Sæfari's farmstead, village' from the ON byname *Sæfari* 'seafarer' and ODan **bȳ**.

Sedgebrook (Kest), *Sechebroc* 1086 DB, 1156–62 (1396) Ch, *Segebroc* 1135 (13th) Dugd iii, 1195, 1202 P, *Seggebroc* 1202 Ass, 'the brook where sedge grows' from OE **secg** and OE **brōc**.

Sempringham (Pointon, Kest), *æt Sempingaham* 852 (12th) ASCharters (S 1440), 1066–68 (c1200) ASWills, *of Sempigaham* s.a. 852 (c1121) ASC E, *Sepingeham* (sic) 1086 DB, *Sempingeham* 1148–68 RA i, 1168 P, *Simplingeham* (sic) 1168 RBE, 1182, 1187 P, *Simpingeham* 1172 ib, *Sempingham* 1135–54 *AddCh*, 1147 RA iii, c1150 Dane, *Simpingham* c1155 ib, *Semplingham* 1199 CurP. Probably 'the homestead, the estate of the Sempingas' from the gen.pl. *Sempinga* of an OE group-name *Sempingas* 'the family, the dependents of Sempa' with OE **hām**. All the earliest forms of this name are without a medial *-r-*; the first so far noted is *Simpringham* 1202 Abbr.

Shepeau Stow (Whaplode, Hol), *Shephe* 1135–54 (p1343) *Crow*, *Shepee* lHy3 (c1331) *Spald ii*, *Sepeshe* 1227 Ch, *Sceppeseye* 1281 QW, *Schephe* 1352 *Cor*, *Shepeshe stowe* 1439 *CrowReg*, 'the river where sheep are found' from OE **scēp** and OE **ēa. Stow** has been added later and in south Lincolnshire has the meaning 'a dam'.

Shillingthorpe (Braceborough, Kest), *Scheldintorp* 1193, 1194 P, *Cheldintorp* 1202 FF, *Skeldingtorp* 1213 Abbr, *Skeldintorp'* 1214 FF, apparently 'Skiǫldung's secondary settlement (of **Braceborough**)' from the unrecorded ON pers.n. **Skiǫldungr*, a derivative of the recorded *Skiǫldr*, formally identical with the name of the legendary Danish dynasty of the *Skiǫldungar*, and ODan **thorp.** The name survive as **Shillingthorpe Hall** (now ruined).

Sibsey (LSR), *Sibolci* (sic) 1086 DB, *Sybecia* 1146–53 Dane, *Sibeceie* a1198 Revesby, *-ey* 1199 (1330) Ch, *Cibesey* a1150 (p1259) *Kirkst*, probably 'Sigebald's island of land' from the OE pers.n. *Sigebald* and OE **ēg**.

Sixhills (LSR) *Sisse* (sic) 1086 DB, *Sixla* c1115 LS, 1187 (1409) Gilb, *-le* 1147–66 (1409) Gilb, 1198 P, *-lea* 1176 ib, *-lei* 1196 Cur, 'the six glades, clearings' from OE **sex** and OE **lēah**. The modern development which has been first noted in *Sixil* c1230 RA v, *Sixhill'* 1258 Cl is presumably due to a reinterpretation of the second el.

Skegness (LSR), *Scegnes* eHy2 (l13th) *Stix*, *Shegenesse* 1166 P, *Schegenes* 1184–90 RA vi, *Sceggenes* 1164–90 ib, *Skegnesse* 1198 (1328) Ch, *Sceggenesse* l12th *Dane*, 'Skeggi's headland' from ODan *Skeggi* and ON **nes**. For a discussion of the change in the coastline here see JEPNS 7, 47–50. **Skegness** has been identified with the p.n. *Tric* 1086 DB, the etymology of which is unknown.

Skeldyke (Kirton, Hol), *Skeldyke* 1329 *Ass*, *-dyk'* 1332 *SR*, *Skeldik* 1358 *Cor*, 'the boundary ditch, drainage channel', a Scand. compound from ODan **skial** and ON **dík**.

Skellingthorpe (Kest), *Sceldinhopa* ?1085–89 (14th) *Westm*, *Scheldinchope* *Schellingop* 1086 DB, *Sceldinghop* 1135–54 (p1269) *Bard*, *Sceldinghop* 1141 RA i, *Eskelinguehop* (a Norman form) eHy2 (p1269) *Bard*, *Cheldintorp* 1198 FF, *Skeldintorp'* 1215 OblR. This is a very difficult name. The second el. is OE **hop**, probably here in the sense 'enclosure in marsh' as has been suggested. The first el. has been interpreted as OE **Scelding** 'the shield-shaped hill', but no certainty is possible. The replacement of **hop** by ODan **thorp** is recorded early.

Skendleby (LSR), *Scheueldebi* (*-u-* = *-n-*) 1086 DB, *Skendilby* 1115 (14th) *Bard*, *Skendelbi* 1124, 1156 (p1269) *ib*, *Schendelbi* 1135–54, c1145, 1178 (p1269) *ib*, *Scendelby* 1147–56 (1331) Ch. The first el. is obscure; the second is ODan **bȳ** 'a farmstead, a village'.

Skendleby Psalter (Skendleby, LSR), *Salterhage* 1135–54, eHy2, l12th (p1269) *Bard*, *-haga* l12th *Dane*, *Skendelby Sawtrye* 1597 *ExchKR*, 'the salters' enclosure' from OE **saltere** and OE **haga**, with the parish name added later. The modern form is presumably due to popular etymology.

Skendleby Thorpe (Skendleby, LSR), *Torp* 1135–54, l12th, e13th (p1269) *Bard*, *Thorp* 1256 *AddCh*, *Skendilby Thorp'* 1430 *FF*, from ON **thorp** 'a secondary settlement' in relation to **Skendleby**.

Skidbrooke (Skidbrooke with Saltfleet Haven, LSR), *Schitebroc* 1086 DB, c1115 LS, l12th RA v, *Scitebroc* 1086 DB, c1115 LS, 1189–95 *Anc*, 'the dirty, muddy brook' from OE **scite** and OE **brōc**. Initial *Sh-* has been Scandinavianised to *Sk-* or the first el. has been replaced by the cognate ON **skítr** 'dung'.

Skillington (Kest), *æt Scillintune* 1066–68 ASWills, *Schellintune* 1086 DB, *Scellitona* 1163 RA i, *Schillintune, -tone* 1086 DB, *Schillingetona* 1146 RA i, *Scillingetun* 1160, Hy2 (m13th) *NCot, Skilintuna* a1183 Dane, *Scilinton'* 1185 Templar. This is a difficult name for which no plausible suggestion can be made. The final element is OE **tūn** 'a farmstead, a village'.

Skinnand (Navenby, Kest), *Schinende* 1086 DB, 1185 Templar, *Schinande* 1185 ib, c1250 (Ed1) *Barl, Skinnand'* 1230 Welles. This is probably the present participle **scīnende** 'shining' of OE **scīnan** 'to shine' denoting 'the shining one' i.e. 'the shining river, stream'. The initial consonant, *Sh-* was subsequently Scandinavianised to *Sk-*.

Skirbeck (Hol), *Scirebec* 1086 DB, 1125–35 (1316–17) YCh iv, 1156–57 (14th) YCh i, *Scirbec* lHy2 Dane, 1200 Cur, *Skirbec* 1210 FF, 'the clear stream' from ON **skírr** and ON **bekkr**, perhaps replacing an OE name with the same meaning, from **scīr** and **bece**. Note the reference to "the water of" *Skirebek* 1372 Ipm. The stream is now dry, but according to Thompson (1856) "the former course of that stream may yet be traced without any difficulty".

Skirbeck Wapentake (Hol), *Scirebech* 1168, 1188 P, 1185 RotDom, *-bec* 1199 P, *Skirebek* 1202 Ass, taking its name from **Skirbeck**, where the wapentake (ON **vápnatak**, late OE **wæpengetæc** 'a sub-division of a shire') meeting-place must have been. The forms are preceded or followed by some form of Latin *wapentacium*.

Skitter Beck (Ulceby, LNR), *Scithere* 1150–60 Dane, *aque de schitere* a1170 (e13th) *NCot, super Schitaram* (sic) p1170 (e13th) *ib, aque de Scitere* p1186 Dane, *aqua de Scytre* Hy2 (e13th) *NCot, Scitter* e13th *HarlCh* from OE **scitere** 'a sewer, a stream used as an open sewer' with initial *Sh-* replaced by Scand. *Sk-. Beck* from ON **bekkr** 'a stream' was added later, presumably when the meaning of Skitter was forgotten. **Skitter** gave name to **Ulceby Skitter**, *Skyter* 1327 SR, *Ulseby Skittere* 1375 Works.

Slackholme (Hogsthorpe, LSR), *Slekholm* c1220 (1351) *Barl, -holme* 1294 *Anc, Slechom'* c1220 (Ed1) *Barl, Sclekeholm'* e13th (Ed1) *ib, Slecholm* 1259 *HarlCh*. The forms are late, but it has been suggested that the first el. is OE **slēc**, ME ***slēk** in a developed sense 'muddy'; the second el. is ON **holmr** 'raised land amidst the marsh'.

Slea, R. (Kest), *super aquae Slafordie* (sic) eHy2 (1634) *Dods 144, aquam Slafordie* Hy2 (1639) LNQ xvii, "the water of" *Lafford* 1337 Ch. The present r.n. is a back-formation from **Sleaford**, where the etymology of the p.n. is discussed.

Sleaford, New & Old, (Kest), *æt Sliowaforda* 852 (12th) ASCharters (S 1440), *of Sliowa forda* 852 (c1121) ASC E, *Eslaforde* 1086 DB, *-ford* 1139, 1146, 1149, 1163 RA i, *Slaford* 1126 ib, c1160 Semp, *Slafordia* 1147–53 RA i, *Slafford'* 1188 P, *Sleforde* c1170 Semp, *Lafford'* 1163 RA i, *Laforda* a1187 Dane. **New Sleaford** is *Noua Sleford* 1272 Ass, *Noua Lafford'* 1296 *ib* and **Old Sleaford** *in veteri Scleford* c1225 (14th) Queen's, *in Veteri Lafford'* 1230 Cur. Forms showing loss of initial *S-* and prosthetic *E-* are due to Anglo-Norman influence. The first el. of **Sleaford** is an OE r.n. **Sliowa*, etymologically identical with the name of the **Schlei** 'muddy waters; a body of water with slimy vegetation', in Schleswig-Holstein. Hence the name means 'the ford over the Sliowa', the second el. being OE **ford**. The post-Conquest forms apparently show the influence of the Danish name of the Schlei, ODan *Slæ*. The modern r.n., the **R. Slea**, is a back-formation from **Sleaford**.

Sloothby (Willoughby with Sloothby, LSR), *Lodeby* (sic), *Slodebi* 1086 DB, *Slothebi* 1199 CurR, 1208 FF, *Slodebi* 1200 Cur, 1200 Abbr, probably 'Slōthi's farmstead, village' from the ON pers.n. *Slōthi* and ODan **bȳ**.

Snarford (LWR), *Snerteforde, Snardesforde* 1086 DB, *Snarteforde* c1115 LS, *-ford* c1180 Bly, 1221 Welles, *Snartford'* 1203 Cur, 1208 FF, 'Snǫrt's ford' from the gen.sg. *Snarta(r)* of the ON pers.n. *Snǫrtr* and OE **ford**. The ford crossed Barlings Eau and it has recently been suggested that Snarford may well have been situated on an ancient line of communication between the Lincoln area and the Wolds.

Snelland (LSR), *Esnelent* (sic, an Anglo-Norman form), *Sneleslunt* 1086 DB, *Snelleslund* c1115 LS, 1160 Dane, c1180, l12th ib, *Snellund* 1198 Cur, either 'Sniall's grove' or 'Snell's grove'. The first el. is a pers.n. either ON *Sniallr* or OE *Snell*, the second el. is ON **lundr**.

Snitterby (LWR), *Snetrebi* 1086 DB, *Snitrebi* c1115 LS, *Sniterby* 1194 CurP, 1196 ChancR, 1212 Fees, probably an Anglo-Danish hybrid 'Snytra's farmstead, village', from the OE pers.n. *Snytra* and ODan **bȳ**.

Somerby (LNR), *Sumerledeby* 1100–15 (14th), 1190–96 (c1240) Whitby, *Sumertebi, Summertebi* 1086 DB, *Sumeretebi* 1219 Ass, *-by* 1254 ValNor, *Sumerdebi* c1115 LS. **Somerby** (Corringham, LWR), *Sumerdebi* 1086 DB, c1115 LS, 1214–21 RA ii, *Summerdebi, Summertebi* 1086 DB, *Sumeretebi* 1188 P. **Somerby, Old** (Kest), *Summerdebi* 1086 DB, *-by* Hy2 (1316) Ch, *Sumerdebi* 1086 DB, 1138 NthCh, 1172 Dane, *Sumertheby* 1129 RRAN. These are identical names, with the same etymology as **Somersby**, 'Sumarlithi's farmstead, village' from the ON byname *Sumarlithi* and ODan bȳ. This pers.n., which means 'the summer traveller', is recorded six times independently in DB in L. **Old Somerby** is in contrast to **New Somerby** which was formed into a township in 1894.

Somercotes, North & South (LSR), *Summercotes* 1086 DB, l12th Dane, *Sumercota* c1115 LS, 1194 P, *Sumercotis* c1115 LS, *Sumerecotes* eHy2, *Nortsumercotes* 1281 RSu, *Suth Sumercotes* 1294 Ass, 'the cottages, huts used in summer' from OE **sumor** and OE **cot**. The affixes are self-explanatory.

Somersby (LSR), *Summerdebi* 1086 DB, *Sumerdebi* c1115 LS, 1206 Cur, *Sumertebi* 1196 ChancR, *Sumeretebi* 1190 P, *Sumerettebi* 1195 ib. This has the same etymology as **Somerby**, 'Sumarlithi's farmstead, village' from the ON byname *Sumarlithi* and ODan bȳ.

Somerton (Boothby Graffoe, Kest), *Summertune* 1086 DB, *Sumerton'* 1177, 1180, 1182 P, 1205 Cur, 'the farmstead used in summer' from OE **sumor** and OE **tūn**. The name survives in **Sumerton Castle**, "castle of" *Somerton* 1309 Cl.

Sotby (LSR), *Sotebi* 1086 DB, c1115 LS, 1150–60 Dane, 1165, 1178 P, *Sottebi* c1155 Dane, 'Sóti's farmstead, village' from the ON pers.n. *Sóti*, ODan *Sōti* and ODan bȳ.

South Forty Foot Drain (Hol), *the South Forty Foot* 1717 *MiscDon 111*, and was earlier *Middilfendik* 1189–99 (c1331) *Spald i*, *MidFendik* (sic) 1199 (c1331) *ib*, *Midfendic qui est divisa inter Kestevene et Hoylande* 1199 (1330) Ch, *Midfendic* 1200 ChR, self-explanatory, from OE **middel**, OE **fenn** and OE dīc or ON **dík** 'a ditch'. It formed the boundary between **Kesteven** and **Holland** as stated in the 1199 reference. It was also called *priourdike alias midfendike* 1500 FenNQ ii and is recorded earlier as *Priurdik* 1189–99 (c1331) *Spald i*, from the **Prior** (of Spalding Priory) and OE dīc or ON **dík**.

South Holland Main Drain (Hol), *Holland Drain* 1824 O, *South Holland Sluice* 1826 *Map*, constructed in 1793, but its course was earlier called *Asegeresdich* lHy2 (m13th) *PipeS*, *-dik* 1263 FF, *Asegerdich* l12th (m13th) *PipeS*, recorded as late as *Asgerdyke Bank* 1797 *StJ*. 'Ásgeirr's dyke' from the ON pers.n. *Ásgeirr* and ON **dík**. For the same name pers.n. cf. **Asgarby**.

Southorpe (Northorpe, LWR), "the other" *Torp* 1086 DB, c1115 LS, c1128 (12th) ChronPetro, 1191 P, 1232 Cur, *Sutthorp* 1189 (1332) Ch. Like **Northorpe** in the same parish, **Southorpe** was originally a simplex p.n. from ODan **thorp** 'a secondary settlement'. OE **sūth** was prefixed later to distinguish it from **Northorpe**.

Southrey (Bardney, LSR), *Sutrei(e)* 1086 DB, *Suderei* c1115 LS, *Sudereie* Hy2 (p1269) *Bard*, *Sudreia* Hy2 (13th) *Kirkst*, *Surrea* 1163 RA i, *Surreie* 1202 Ass, from OE **sūther** or **sūtherra** 'southern' and OE **ēg** 'an island, dry ground surrounded by marsh'. It was named in relation to **Bardney**.

South Riding, *Sudtreding* 1086 DB, *Suttriding* c1115 LS, *Sudtridinga* 1189–99 Cur, *-riding* 1212 Fees. Lindsey is divided into three Parts — **North**, **South** and **West Riding**. **Riding** is derived from ON **thrithjung**, late OE **thrithing** 'a third part'. Initial *th-* has become *t-* through Anglo-Norman influence and was later absorbed by the final *-th* of *south* to give *riding*.

Spalding (Hol), *Spaldingis* c1074 (c1331) *Spald i*, c1115 LS, *Spaldinges* 1135–54 (1330) Ch, 1190 P, *Spalingis* 1100–13 (1330) Ch, *Spallinges* 1194 CurR, *Spallinge* 1086 DB, *Spalding'* l11th (c1331) *Spald i*. **Spalding** is an OE group-name, *Spaldingas* 'the people of the Spalde', who have given their name also to **Spaldingmoor** and **Spaldington** in the East Riding of Yorkshire, to **Spaldwick** in Huntingdonshire and to **Spalford** in Nottinghamshire. *Spalde* is the name of a tribe, recorded in the 7th/8th century tribute list known as the Tribal Hidage. The tribal name belongs to an unrecorded OE **Spald* 'a narrow opening, slit' (in this case denoting a topographical feature).

Spanby (Threekingham, Kest), *Spanesbi* 1086 DB, *Spanebi* 1086 ib, 1138 NthCh, Hy2 (p1269) *Bard*, *Spannebi* 1170 P, 1202 FF, probably 'the farmstead, village where shingle for tiling is obtained' from ON **spánn** and ODan **bȳ**.

Spilsby (LSR), *Spilesbi* 1086 DB, l12th Dane, *-by* 1214–20 RA vi, *Spillesby* c1221 Welles, 1234 FF, 'Spillir's farmstead, village', from the ON byname *Spillir* and ODan **bȳ**. This pers.n. is recorded in DB from L.

Spital in the Street (Hemswell, LWR), *de Hospitali* 1166, 1168 P, *in hospitali* c1190 RA iv, *- Hospitale* l12th RA ii, *apud Hospitale super Stratam* 1281 QW, *Spytelothestrete* 1295 *Ass*, 'the hospital' from ME **spitel**; it is situated on **Ermine Street**.

Spittlegate (Grantham, Kest), *Spitelgate* 1284 *FF*, 1310 *ib*, 1332 *SR*, 1316 FA, 'the road to the hospital' from ME **spitel** and ON **gata**. The dedication of the hospital is apparently uncertain.

Spridlington (LWR), *Sperlintone, Spredelintone* 1086 DB, *-ton'* 1200 Cur, *Spirlintuna* 1146 RA i, *Sperlinctone* 1086 DB, *-tona* 1175–81 Dane, *Sperlingtun'* l12th RA ii, *Spritlingtuna* c1115 LS. Though the forms are difficult, the first el. appears to be an OE pers.n., perhaps an unrecorded OE **Sprēotel* with the OE connective particle **-ing-** and OE **tūn**, hence 'the farmstead, village associated with Sprēotel'. This pers.n. would be a pet form of a nickname based on OE *sprēot* 'a pole, a spike, a spear'.

Springthorpe (LWR), *Springetorp* 1086 DB, 1196 ChancR, 1224 Welles, *Springthorp* 1170–78 Dane, a hybrid p.n., 'the secondary settlement by the spring' from OE **spring** and ODan **thorp**.

Stain (Withern with Stain, LSR), *Stein* 1086 DB, c1115 LS, 1180 P, 1201 Ass, *Stain* l12th *DC*, 'the stone' from ON **steinn**. This was presumably named from a prominent stone.

Stainby (Gunby & Stainby, Kest), *Stiandeby* 1194–1201 YCh v, 1212 Fees, *Stiyandebi* l12th Semp, *Stihandeby* 1201 YCh v, *-bi* 1210 Cur, 'Stígandi's farmstead, village' from the ON pers.n. *Stígandi*, a weak form of *Stígandr*, and ODan **bȳ**.

Stainfield (Haconby, Kest), *Steintone* (sic) 1086 DB, *Stentuith* 1086 ib, *Steinwath* Hy2 (1316) Ch, 1211 Cur, *Steinthweit* Hy2, 1199–1216 *AddCh*, *Stenweit* (sic) 1202 Ass, *Steynthweyt* lHy3 *MiD*, probably 'the clearing on stony ground' from ON **steinn** and ON **thveit**. There is some confusion in the early spellings with other second els., but the evidence suggests that it is **thveit**. This was replaced by **field** by the end of the 17th century.

Stainfield (LSR), *Stainfelde* 1086 DB, *-feld'* 1198–99 (l13th) YCh xi, *Steinfelde* 1086 DB, *-felda* c1115 LS, *-feld'* 1188 P; this was no doubt originally OE **Stānfeld* from OE **stān** 'a stone' and OE **feld** 'open land', denoting stony open country. The first el. was replaced by the cognate ON **steinn**.

Stainsby (Ashby Puerorum, LSR), *Stouenesbi* a1158 Dane, *Stauenesbi* 1175–78 *Anc*, Hy2 RA ii, *-by* c1210 RA vi, *Stafnebi* 1170–78 Revesby, *Stafnesby* 1197 P, 'Stafn's farmstead, village' from the ON byname *Stafn* and ODan **bȳ**.

Stainton by Langworth (LSR), *Staintune* 1086 DB, *-ton'* 1212 Fees, *Steintuna iuxta Langwat* (sic) c1115 LS, *Steintuna* l12th Dane, *-ton'* 1202 Ass. **Stainton le Vale** (LNR), *Stainton* 1086 DB, *Staynton(?)* eHy2, 1240 (13th) *Alv*, *Steintuna* c1115 LS, *Stantune* a1135 (c1240) Whitby. **Stainton, Market** (LSR), *Staintone* 1086 DB, *-ton* 1215 LAHW, *Steintuna* c1115 LS, *-ton* 1206 Cur, *Steynton Market* 1286 Ipm. **Stainton** is a partial Scandinavianisation of OE **Stāntūn* 'the farmstead, village on stony ground' from OE **stān** and **tūn**, with the cognate ON **steinn** 'a stone' replacing OE **stān**. It has recently been pointed out that all three **Staintons** in Lindsey adjoin a Roman road or a prehistoric trackway. It is possible that stone here may refer to Romano-British remains. **Stainton le Vale** is variously described as *Northstaynton* 1274 Ipm (probably in contrast to **Stainton by Langworth** (LSR)), *Wald Staintona* e13th (13th) *Alv*, with reference to its situation on the Wolds, *Waldstaynyon' in the Hole* 1440 Pat 'in the hollow' from OE **hol** and *Staunton in Valle* c1300 RA iii. The present-day affix, **le Vale**, does not become common until the 19th century and is topographically appropriate. The affix in **Market Stainton** is self-explanatory.

Stallingborough (LNR), *Stalingeburg* 1086 DB, 1204 Cur, *Stallingeburc* 1200 ib, *-burg* 1202 FF, *Stallinburg* 1086 DB, c1115 LS, *Stalingburg* 1109–19 (c1300) Selby. 'The fortified place of the Stallingas' from the gen.pl. *Stallinga* of the OE group-name *Stallingas*, 'the family, the people of Stalla' and OE **burh**. **Stalla* is an unrecorded OE (Anglian) pers.n. belonging to OE *(ge)stealla* 'comrade, companion'.

Stamford (Kest), *Stean forda* s.a. 922 (c924) ASC A, *Stanford* s.a 942 (c955) ib, s.a. 963 (c1121) ASC E, *Stanforda* c1000 Ætheweard, s.a. 1016 (m11th) ASC C, *Stanforde* s.a 1070 (c1121) ASC E, *Stanford Burgun Regis* 1086 DB, 'the stony ford (over the **R. Welland**)'.

Stapleford (Kest), *Stapleforde* 1086 DB, *-fort* c1140 Dane, *Stapelford* Hy2 (1291) Ch, *-forda* l12th (1409) Gilb, *-ford'* 1200 Cur, 1202 Ass, 'the ford marked by a post' from OE **stapol** and OE **ford**.

Steeping, Great & Little (LSR), *Stepinge* 1086 DB, 1156 (p1269) *Bard*, 1171 P, *Steping'* 1125, c1145 (p1269) *Bard*, a1172 Dane, *magna Stepinge* 1272 *Ass*, *Estepinges* Hy2 Dane, *paruo Stepinge* Hy2 ib, *Parua Steping'* 1199 P. 'The family, the people of Stēapa', a group-name derived from the OE pers.n. *Stēapa* and the OE suffix **-ingas** 'the people of'; for further details of this formation see **Healing**. The affixes are self-explanatory.

Steeping, R. (LSR), *The River of Steepinge alias the Limbe* 1661 Imb, the name of the lower reaches of the **R. Lymn**, named from **Steeping**. It is also called **Little Lymn**, see **R. Lymn**.

Stenigot (LSR), *Stangehou* 1086 DB, *Staningho* 1185 Templar, *Staningeho* 1202 Ass, *Steninghog'* 1199 (1330) Ch, *Steningot* 1207 P; probably from OE **Stāninge*, dative sg. of OE **Stāning* with OE **hōh** 'a heel, a spur of land' added later, hence 'the spur of land at a place called Stāning'. OE **Stāning* is derived from OE **stān** 'a stone' and the singular OE **-ing** used as a p.n. forming suffix, denoting 'the stony place'. Forms in *Steyn-* reflect substitution of the cognate ON **steinn**. Those in final *-t* are curious and presumably reflect a spontaneous sound change in this particular name.

Stenwith (Woolsthorpe by Belvoir, Kest), *Stanuualt* (sic), *-wald* (sic) 1086 DB, *Steinwath* Hy2 (1329) Dugd v, 1206 Cur, 1212 Fees, 'the stony ford' from ON **steinn** and ON **vath**.

Stewton (LSR), *Stivetone, Stiueton* 1086 DB, *Stiuetuna* c1115 LS, *-tun* 1199 FF, l12th RA v, 1202 Ass, probably 'the farmstead, village marked by a stump' from OE **styfic** and OE **tūn**.

Stickford (LSR), *Stichesforde* 1086 DB, *Sticceforda* 1142 NthCh, *Esticheford* (an Anglo-Norman spelling) Hy2 Dane, *Stikeford* 1185 Templar, 1188 (1328) Ch, 1189–99 (1328) ib. This has clearly to be taken with **Stickney**, *Stichenai* 1086 DB, *Sticcenaia* 1142 NthCh, *Sticheneie* a1148 Dugd v, 1170–78 Revesby, *-eia* 1180–90 NthCh, *Stikenei* 1170–78 Revesby, *-eye* 1198 (1328) Ch. The two villages are situated between two streams, now Catchment Drains, on land which forms an elongated island. It has been suggested that this was called *Sticca* 'the stick'. **Stickford** would then mean 'the ford in the narrow island called *Sticca*' with a second el. OE **ford**, and **Stickney** 'the island called *Sticca'* from OE **ēg**. It has recently been pointed out that the ford here carries a north-south line of communication used both in prehistoric and Roman times.

Stickney (LSR), see Stickford.

Stixwould (LSR), *Stigeswalt, -wald* 1086 DB, *Stichesweld, -wald* c1115 LS, c1140 Dane, *-walda* 1130 P, *Stykeswald* l12th (13th) *Stix, Sticeswald'* 1190–93 Dane, 'Stig's stretch of woodland on higher ground', a hybrid compound from the ODan pers.n. *Stig* and OE **wald**, topographically appropriate.

Stockwith, East (LWR), *Stokhede* 1188 P, *Stochith'* 1226 ClR, *Stockhyd'* 1275 RH, *-yth* 1286 Pat, 'the landing-place made of stocks, tree-trunks' from OE **stocc** and OE **hæth. West Stockwith** is on the opposite bank of the R. Trent.

Stoke Rochford, Stoke, North & South (Kest), *æt Stoce* 1066–68 (c1200) ASWills, *Stoche* 1086 DB, 1172–80 Dane, *Stoches* 1086 DB, 1146 RA i, *Stoke* 1123–35 CartAnt, c1160 Dane, *Stoke Rocheforthe* 1545 AASR xxxix, *Nortstoches, Sudstoches* 1086 DB, from OE **stoc**, a word having a variety of meanings 'a place, a dairy farm, a secondary settlement, an outlying farmstead'. The affixes **North** and **South** are self-explanatory; the *Rochford* family held land here, note *Radulphus Rochefort* 1412 FA.

Stow (LWR), *mynster æt Sancte MARIAN stowe* 1053–55 (l12th) ASCharters (S 1478), *beate Dei genetrici attribui Stou* 1054–57 (12th) Eyns (S 1233), *Into sancte MARIAN stowe* 1066–68 (c1200) ASWills, *ecclesæ sancte Mariæ Stowensi, abbatiæ de La Stou* 1066–87 (12th) Eyns, *Sancta Maria de Stou* 1086 DB, *Stou* 1061 RA i, from OE **stōw** in the sense 'a holy place', dedicated to St Mary.

Stow (Threekingham, Kest), *Stou* 1086 DB, a1189 Semp, *Stoua* 1138 NthCh, *Stowe* c1177 Semp, 1195 P, l12th Semp. **Stowe (Barholm, Kest),** *Estou* (a Norman spelling) 1086 DB, c1128 (12th) ChronPetro, *Stowe* 1189 (1332) Ch, l12th AASR xli. Both names mean 'the place of assembly', from OE **stōw**. The first survives as **Stow Farm**, the second as **Stowe Farm**.

Stragglethorpe (Brant Broughton, Kest), *Stragerthorp'* l12th Semp, 1242–43 Fees, 1275 RH, *Tragertorp* 1212 Fees, *-thorp* 1242–3 ib, *Thragerthorp* 1270–71 RA viii (three Anglo-Norman forms), *Stragelthorpe* 1306 Abbr. The first el. is obscure, the second being ODan **thorp** 'a secondary settlement (of **Brant Broughton**)'.

Stroxton (Little Ponton, Kest), *Strothistune* 1066–68 (c1200) ASWills, *Stroustune* 1086 DB, *Stroweston'* 1185 RotDom, the first el. is uncertain, the second OE **tūn** 'a farmstead, a village'.

Strubby (Langton by Wragby, LSR), *Strubi* 1086 DB, c1115 LS, *Strutebi* c1115 ib, l12th (p1259) *Kirkst*, *Strubbi* 1212 Fees. **Strubby** (Strubby with Woodthorpe, LSR), *Strobi* 1086 DB, *Strubby* 1115 (14th) *Bard*, c1200 RA iii, *Strubi* 1125, 1178 (p1269) *Bard*, lHy2 Dane. Both probably mean 'Strút's farmstead, village' from the ON pers.n. *Strútr* and ODan **bȳ**. The same pers.n. is apparently found in **Trusthorpe**.

Stubton (Kest), *Stobetun, Stubetune* 1086 DB, *-tun'* 1185 Templar, *-ton'* 1206 FF, 1212 Fees, *Stubbeton'* 1202 Ass. It is impossible to be certain whether this is 'Stubba's farmstead, village' from the OE pers.n. *Stubba* and OE **tūn** or 'the farmstead, village among the tree-stumps' from OE **stubb** and OE **tūn**.

Sturgate (Springthorpe, LWR), *Steresgard* 1197 P, *Sterisgard'* 1230–39 RA ii, *Steresgarth* 1319 Pat, 1346 Orig, *Steregard* 1198 ib, *Steregarth* 1276 RH, perhaps 'the enclosure for steer, young bullock(s)' from OE **stēor** and ON **garth**.

Sturton (Scawby, LWR), *Straitone, Stratone* 1086 DB, *Stratton* 1203 Ass, *Strettun* 1212 Fees, *Straton'* 1225 Cur, *Stretun'* 1226 ib. **Sturton, Great** (LSR), *Stratone* 1086 DB, *Stratona* 1147 (p1269) *Bard*, *Strattun* Hy2 Dane, *-ton* 1199 CurR, *Strettuna* c1115 LS, *Stretuna* 1140–50 Dane, *Northstretune* 1140–50 ib, *magna Stretton'* lHy3 *HarlCh*. **Sturton by Stow** (LWR), *Stratone* 1086 DB, *Strettuna* c1115, *-tona* 1155–70 (13th) YCh iii, *Stretona* 1150–60 RA iv, *Straton* 1191 P, *Stratton'* 1202 Ass. Each means 'the farmstead, the village near or on the Roman road' from OE **strǣt** and OE **tūn**. The first is on Till Bridge Lane, the second is near a Roman road leading to Lincoln, the third is on Ermine Street. The affixes are self-explanatory.

Sudbrook (Ancaster, Kest), *Suggebroch* 1168 P, *Soggebroc* 1169 ib, *Suggebroc* Hy2 Dane, 1218 Ass, *Sugebroc* 1214 Cur, *Sudbroc* 1201 Ass, 'the brook where hedge-sparrows are found' from OE **sugge** a bird name, possibly 'a sparrow', cf. dialect **hey-suck** 'hedge-sparrow' and OE **brōc**. Spellings in *Sug-* persist into the 16th century.

Sudbrooke (LWR), *Sutbroc* 1086 DB, c1115 LS, *Sudbroche* c1128 (12th) ChronPetro, *-broc* 1180–90 (13th) *Kirkst*, *Suthbroc* 1166 RBE, *Suthebroc* l12th Dane, 'the brook to the south' from OE **sūth** and OE **brōc**, apparently so named in relation to **Scothern**.

Surfleet (Hol), *Suerefelt* (sic) 1086 DB, *Surflet* 1133 (c1331) *Spald i*, 1171 P, 1173 ChancR, 1200 ChR, 'the sour inlet, creek' from OE **sūr** and OE **flēot** and note "the water of" *Surflete* 1327 Pat.

Susworth (Scotter, LWR), *Silkeswath*, *Sirkeswad*, *Sirkewad* 1202 Ass, *Sikeswad* 1204 P, *Sikewad* 1205 ib; the forms of the first el. are too varied to suggest a convincing etymology; the second is ON **vath** 'a ford'.

Sutterby (LSR), *Sutrebi* 1086 DB, c1115 LS, *Suterbi* 1180 P, lHy2, l12th (p1259) *Kirkst*, *Sutereby* 1202 FF, 'the shoemakers' village' from ON **sútari** and ODan **bȳ**. Cf. **Sutterton**.

Sutterton (Hol), *Suterton* 1177, 1200 P, 1200 Cur, 1202 Ass, 1229 Cur, 'the shoemakers' village' from OE **sūtere** and OE **tūn**. Cf. **Sutterby**.

Sutterton Dowdyke (Sutterton, Hol), *Duuedic* 1086 DB, 1202 FF, 1218 Ass, *Duvedic'* 1206 Cur, *Duuedich'* 1207 FF, 'the ditch frequented by doves' from OE **dūfe** and OE **dīc**. The village-name **Sutterton** was prefixed later.

Sutton (Beckingham, Kest), *Suttona* c1145 (p1269) *Bard*, *-ton'* 1176 P, *Sudton'* 1205 Cur, 'the farmstead, village to the south (of **Beckingham**)', from OE **sūth** and OE **tūn**.

Sutton, Long, Sutton Bridge, Sutton St Edmund and **Sutton St James** (Hol), *Sudtone* 1086 DB, *Sutttona* 1111 (c1331) *Spald i*, c1120 (13th) *Castleacre*, 1126 RRAN, 1177 P, *Suton'* c1120 (13th) *Castleacre*, 'the farmstead, village to the south' from OE **sūth** and OE **tūn**, but it is not clear which place it is south of. It is situated in the south of the county near the boundary with Cambridgeshire. **Long Sutton** is *Langsutton* 1385 Pat, descriptive of a long, straggling village, while **St Edmund** and **St James** are from the dedications of the churches. **Sutton Bridge** was formed as a separate parish after a Local Government Act in 1894, named from the Bridge over the Nene Outfall Cut.

Sutton on Sea or **in the Marsh** (LSR), *Sudtone* 1086 DB, *-ton'* 1200 CurR, *Sudtune* 1086 DB, *Sutune* 1086 DB, *-tuna* 1147 (p1269) *Bard*, *Suttuna* c1115

LS. Like **Sutton** and **Long Sutton,** this is 'the farmstead, village to the south' from OE **sūth** and OE **tūn,** but it is uncertain which place is referred to since **Sutton** lies in the middle of Scandinavian-named villages. The affixes are self-explanatory.

Swaby (LSR), *Suabi* 1086 DB, c1115 LS, p1169 Dane, 1175–84 *AddCh, Swabi* p1169 Dane, *Suauebi* 1160–75 RA vi, l12th Dane, perhaps 'Svavi's farmstead, village' from the ODan pers.n. *Svavi* and ODan **bȳ**. For the pers.n. see **Swarby**.

Swallow (LNR), *Sualun* (sic) 1086 DB, *Sualwa* c1115 LS, *Sualwe* 1196–1203 RA iv, *Swalue* a1155 (e13th) *NCot, Swalwe* 1163 RA i, *Sualewa* 1143–47 Dane. This is likely to be derived from an archaic Old European r.n. based on the Indo-European root **swel-* in the sense 'shine' and so belongs to the context of Old European r.ns., i.e. to an archaic phase of undifferentiated Indo-European. Swallow is therefore a very ancient name, i.e. pre-Celtic in origin. A stream rises here from an underground source and flows, in an easterly direction, from a pond in the Rectory grounds, and disappears again immediately to the north-east. This must be the stream which gave its name to the place.

Swarby (Aswarby, Kest), *Suarrebi* 1086 DB, 1199 P, 1199–1216 Abbr, e13th *AddCh*, 1202 Ass, *-by* 1202 FF, 'Svarri's farmstead, village' from the ON byname *Svarri* and ODan **bȳ**.

Swaton (Kest), *Suavintone, Suauitone, Suavetone* 1086 DB, *Suavetona* 1123, 1126 France, *Suauetona* c1150 (13th) *Castleacre*, 1189–92 RA vii. This is probably an Anglo-Danish pers.n. hybrid 'Sváfi's farmstead, village' from the ON pers.n. *Sváfi* (as also in **Swaby**) and OE **tūn.** The pers.n. is recorded in L in DB as *Suaue* and also in Swaton itself as *Radulfus filius Swaue de Suauetona* Hy2 Dane. This is probably an earlier Anglo-Saxon settlement taken over and partially renamed by the Danes.

Swayfield (Kest), *Suafeld* 1086 DB, *Swafeld* 1198 FF, 1199–1214 Abbr, 1205 Cur, 1206 Ass, *Swauefeld'* 1202 ib, perhaps 'the open country with a track' from OE **swæth** and OE **feld**, though the exact sense of **swæth** here is uncertain.

Swinderby (Kest), *Sunderby, Suindrebi* 1086 DB, *Suinderbi* 1185 Templar, *Sondreby* 1201 France, *Sunderby* a1221 Welles, *Swinderby* c1221 ib, 'the farmstead, village to the south (probably of **Morton**)' from ON **sundri** and ODan **bȳ**.

Swineshead (Hol), *Swineshæfed* s.a. 675, *Swines heafde* s.a 777 (c1121) both ASC E, *Suinesheabde* (sic) 786–96 (12th) BCS 271 (S 1412), *Suineshafd* c1160 (1409) Gilb, *Swineshaued* 1185 RotDom, *Suinesheued* 1163, 1184 P, probably 'the source of the creek' from OE **swīn** and OE **hēafod** and note the reference to the creek in *aqua de Swyn'* 1276 RH and probably also in *Swynesheved Ee* 1361 Works. *Ee* is from OE **ēa** 'a river, a stream'. It is possible that the lost name **Swinefleet**, in **Swineshead**, *Swireflet* (sic) 1202 Ass, *Swynfleet* 1337 Ch, *Swynflete* 1348 Misc, is the early name of the creek itself, for it means 'the creek stream', the second el. being OE **flēot**, as in **Surfleet**.

Swinethorpe (Eagle, Kest), *Suenestorp* 1181 P, *Suinetorp* 1191, 1194 P, *Swainestorp* 1202 FF, *Sweynestorp* 1240 ib, 1242–43 Fees, 'Sveinn's secondary settlement (of **Eagle**)', from the ON pers.n. *Sveinn* and ODan **thorp**. The later development to *Swinesthorp* 1266 Pat is no doubt due to popular etymology.

Swinhope (LNR), *Suinhope* 1086 DB, *Suinopa, Suinahopa* c1115 LS, *Swinope* 1185 RotDom, *Suinehop* 1212 Fees, *Swineop* 1229 FF, 'the secluded valley where swine are found' from OE **swīn** and OE **hop**, topographically appropriate.

Swinstead (Kest), *Suinham* 1086 DB, *Suinhamstede* 1086 ib, 1130–39 (m14th) *Drax*, 1185 Templar, *-sted'* 1203 Cur, *Swinsteda* c1150 *Anc*, 1168 ChancR, 'the homestead where swine, pigs are reared' from OE **swīn** and OE **hāmstede**. There is an alternation in the forms of the second element between OE **hāmstede** and OE **stede**, which is found in other names derived from **hāmstede**.

Swinthorpe (Snelland, LSR), *Sonetorp* (sic) 1086 DB, *Sunetorp* c1115 LS, 1159, eHy2, l12th (p1259) *Kirkst*, l12th Dane, 'Súni's secondary settlement' from the ODan pers.n. *Súni* and ODan **thorp**, in this case presumably of **Snelland**. The later development to Swin- is not paralleled elsewhere.

Syston (Kest), *Sidestan* 1086 DB, 1205 Cur, 1207 FF, *Sithestan* lHy2 (l13th) *Stix*, 1212 Fees, *Sigestan* (sic) 1159 (l13th) *Stix*, 'the large stone' from OE **sīd** and OE **stān**.

T

Tallington (Kest), *Talintone, -tune* 1086 DB, 1106–23 (1333) Ch, 1230 P, *Talingtun* 1212 Fees, *Tallinton* c1221 Welles, probably 'the farmstead, village called after or associated with T(e)alla' from the unrecorded OE pers.n. **T(e)alla* with the OE connective particle **-ing-** and OE **tūn**.

Tathwell (LSR), *æt Tathawyllan* c1002 ASWills, *æt Tathawillan* 1004 KCD 710 (S 906), *Tadewelle* 1086 DB, 1168 P, 1195 FF, *-wella* c1115 LS, 1169 P, *Taddewella* Hy2 (1409) Gilb, *Thathewella* c1150 (1409) ib, *Tathewelle* 1202 Ass, 'the spring where toads are found' from OE **tadde** and OE **wella**. The forms in *-th-* are due to Scand. influence. Below the church is a large pool, the source of a stream. It is not certain that the two earliest forms actually belong to Tathwell.

Tattershall (LSR), *Tatesala* 1086 DB, *Tateshal'* 1162, 1194 P, *-hala* 1140–50 Dane, *-hale* 1170–75 ib, *Tatersalla* c1180 ib, *Tatersale* 1187 ib, c1200 RA ix, 'Tāthere's nook of land' from the OE pers.n. *Tāthere* and OE **halh**.

Tattershall Thorpe (LSR), *Torp* 1086 DB, c1115 LS, lHy2 Dane, *Thorp* 1150–60, Hy2 ib, 'the secondary settlement (of **Tattershall**)' from ODan **thorp**.

Tealby (LNR), *Tavelesbi* 1086 DB, *Tauelesbi* 1086 ib, 1136–40 (1464) Pat, 1195 P, *Tauelebi* 1086 DB, 1209 P, *-by* 1202 Ass, *Teuelesby* a1183 RA iv. This is a very difficult name. It has been suggested that **Tealby** contains the East Germanic tribal-name *Taifali*, OE *Tāflas, Tǣflas*, detachments of whom are recorded in Britain by the early 5th century. It is possible that they retained their separate identity for some time in the post-Roman period. Tealby would then be originally the simplex form of the tribal-name *Tāflas, Tǣflas* and though such simplex tribal-names are rare in English p.ns., a parallel is **Wales** in the West Riding of Yorkshire from OE **Walas** 'Welshmen'. The second el. ODan **bȳ** 'a farmstead, a village' would then have been added to the simplex form after Scandinavian occupation of the area.

Tetford (LSR), *Tesforde* (sic), *Tedforde* 1086 DB, *-forda* c1115 LS, *-ford'* c1150 Anc, *Thetfort* eHy2 (1409) Gilb, *-ford* Hy2 Dane, *Tetford* c1180 RA ix, literally 'the peoples' ford' from OE **thēod** and OE **ford**, probably denoting a public ford and identical with **Thetford** (Kest). It has recently been suggested that the ford carried an ancient north-south road from Horncastle towards Louth over the R. Lymn and it is highly likely this is a Roman road. Interestingly, this name has a Continental parallel in the German p.n. **Dietfurt a. d. Altmuhl** which is formed from the etymologically identical Old High German *Diotfurt*.

Tetley (Crowle, LWR), *Tetteley* 1310 Selby, *Tetelay* 1327 *SR*, *Tetley* 1332 *ib*, 1352 Selby, 'Tetta's or Tette's glade, clearing' from the OE masc. pers.n. *Tetta* or fem. *Tette* and OE **lēah**.

Tetney (LNR), *Tatenaya* 1085 (16th) Dugd iii, *-ai* 1086 DB, c1115 LS, *Tetanai* eHy2 RA iv, *Tetenay* eHy2 *AD*, *-aia* 1212 Fees. 'Tǣte's island of land' from the OE fem. pers.n. *Tǣte* (gen.sg. *Tǣtan*) and OE **ēg**. Tetney is situated on a distinct island of land in a low-lying marshy coastal area, typical of places with names derived from OE **ēg**.

Thealby (Burton upon Stather), *Tedulfbi* 1096 DB, *Tedolfbi* c1115 LS, *Tedelbi* 1202 Ass, *Teuilby* 1287 Ipm, *Theleby* 1289 *FF*, *Theuelby* 1298 Ass, 'Thjóthulf's farmstead, village' from the ON pers.n. *Thjóthulfr* and ODan **bȳ**.

Theddlethorpe All Saints & St. Helen (LSR), *Tedlagestorp, Telagestorp* 1086 DB, *Dedloncstorp* (sic), *Tedolftorp* c1115 LS, *Tedlactorp* 1153–69 Dane, *Thedilthorpe* eHy2 (1409) Gilb, *Tedlauetorp* Hy2, l12th Dane, *Thedelthorp' Omnium Sanctorum* 1254 ValNor, - *Sancte Elene* 1254 ib. The forms are varied and difficult, but the first el. is perhaps an unrecorded OE pers.n. **Thēodlāc*, a name cognate with the Old High German pers.ns. *Theodolaicus* and *Theotleih*. The second el. is ODan **thorp** 'a secondary settlement'. **All Saints** and **St Helen** are from the dedications of the churches.

Thetford (Baston, Kest), *Thefford* 1241–2 RRG, *Theford* 1253 Ch, *Tetford'* 1259 CrowEst, *Thetford* 1281 QW. This is identical with **Tetford** and means literally 'the peoples' ford' from OE **thēod** and OE **ford**, probably denoting a public ford. It is situated where the Roman road **King Street** crosses the **R. Glen**.

Thimbleby (LSR), *Stimblebi* (sic) 1086 DB, *Themelebi* 1100–15 YCh ii, *Timlebi* c1115 LS, *Timelbi* 1162, l12th Dane, *Timelebi* 1175 ChancR, 1199 CurR, *Thimelbi* 1196–98 Dane, probably 'Thymli's farmstead, village' from the ON pers.n. *Thymli* and ODan **bȳ**, as also **Thimbleby** in the North Riding of Yorks.

Thonock (LWR), *Tunec* 1086 DB, -*eic* c1115 LS, *Tunnec* 1226 ClR, *Tunaik* 1232 Cl, *Tunneyc* 1236 FF, *Thunneck* 1276 RH, 'the slender oak-tree' a Scandinavian compound of ON **thunnr** and ON **eik**.

Thoresby, North (LNR), *Toresbi* 1086 DB, c1115 LS, 1202 Ass, *Thorisbeia* 1137–39 YCh iii, *Thoresbi* 1202 FF, *North Thoresby* 1292 RSu. **Thoresby, South** (LSR), *Toresbi* 1086 DB, c1150 Dane, 1206 Ass, -*by* 1204 Cur, *Thoresbi* p1217 *HarlCh*, *South Thoresby* 1426 Cl. Both mean 'Thōrir's farmstead, village' from the ODan pers.n. *Thōrir*, as in **Thoresthorpe**, and ODan **bȳ**. This pers.n. is recorded independently in L in DB. They are named **North** and **South** in contrast to each other.

Thoresthorpe (Saleby with Thoresthorpe, LSR), *Thuorstorp* (sic) 1086 DB, *Thorestorp* Hy2, l12th Dane, l12th RA vi, *Torestorp* 1210–18 RA vi, 'Thōrir's secondary settlement', presumably of **Saleby**, from the ODan pers.n. *Thōrir*, as in **Thoresby**, and ODan **thorp**.

Thoresway (LNR), *Toreswe* (sic, 2x) 1086 DB, *Toresweia* c1115 LS, *Thoresweie* 1187 (1409) Gilb, 1199 FF, -*weye* 1242–43 Fees. This is usually interpreted as an Anglo-Danish hybrid name meaning 'Thori's road' from the ODan pers.n. *Thōrir*, *Thori* and OE **weg** 'a road'. Only three major p.ns. with **weg** in England have a pers.n. as first el. and only one, a field-name in Derbyshire, has a Scandinavian pers.n. If, however, the DB form, repeated twice there, is to be taken at face value, it could stand for a heathen name, ODan **Thoreswǣ* 'the shrine dedicated to Thor'. The second el. (ON **vé** 'a heathen shrine, sanctuary') would then have been replaced at an early date by **weg**, being no longer understood. A direct parallel to **Thorswǣ* is actually provided by the Swedish p.n. Torsvi. If we accept this etymology, the name must belong to the earliest phase of Danish settlement in north L.

Thorganby (LNR), *Turgrimbi*, *Turgrebi* 1086 DB, c1148 YCh vii, 1166 RBE, *Torgrembi*, *Torgrebi* 1086 DB, *Torgrimbi*, *Torgrimebi* c1115 LS, *Thorgrimbi* lHy2 Dane, 'Thorgrim's farmstead, village' from the ODan pers.n. *Thorgrim* and ODan **bȳ**.

Thorley (now **Minting Park**, Minting, LSR), *Turlai* 1086 DB, *Thorleia* l12th *DC*, -*lay* e13th RA iv, *Torle* 1202 Ass, *Myntyng Parke alias Thorley* 1551 Pat. Probably 'the thorn wood' from OE **thorn** and OE **lēah**, with the early loss of -*n*- between two consonants.

Thornton (LSR), *Torintune* 1086 DB, *Torentuna* c1115 LS, 1150–60 Dane, *Thorentun'* 1170–98 Revesby, *Torinton* 1210 (1252) Ch, *Thorntone iuxta horncastre* 1313 YearBk. **Thornton Curtis** (LNR), *Torentune, -tone* 1086 DB, *-tu*na c1115 LS, *-tun'* 1157 P, *Torntune* 1155–60 Dane, *Thorentona* 1148–52 LAAS vii, c1150 *TYR*, *Thorneton(')* 1203 P, *Thornton Curteys* 1430 Pap. **Thornton le Fen** (LSR), *Torntuna* 1163 Dane, *Tornetun* 1212 Fees, *Thorenton'* 1218 Ass. **Thornton le Moor** (LNR), *Torentun, -tune, -tone* 1086 DB, *Torntuna* c1115 LS, *Thorenton'* 1221 Welles, *Thorneton* 1236 Cl, 1263 FF. It is - *in Mora*, 1291 RSu, - *in the More* 1341 NI. All are identical in meaning, 'the farmstead where thorn-trees grow' from OE **thorn** and OE **tūn**. The affixes **by Horncastle, le Fen** and **le Moor** are self-explanatory; that of **Curtis** is unknown.

Thorpe (Trusthorpe, LSR), *Fugelestorp* 1210 Cur, *Fugletorp* 1218–19 Dugd vi, *Fuhelestorp* 1226 FF, *Fuelestorp* 1225 Pat, *Fulestorp* c1200 Dane, apparently 'Fugl's secondary settlement' from the ON pers.n. *Fugl* (or OE *Fugol*) and ODan **thorp**. It is now represented by **Thorpe** in **Trusthorpe**.

Thorpe in the Fallows (LWR), *Torp* 1086 DB, c1115 LS, 1174 (13th) *Kirkst*, c1175 Dane, 1185 Templar, 'the secondary settlement' from ODan **thorp**. It is also recorded as *Turuluestorp* c1115 LS and *Thorelthorp* 1254 ValNor, the first el. being the ODan pers.n. *Thurulf* which must have been lost at an early date. The earliest reference to the affix so far noted is *Thorp en les Falous* 1325 FA, from OE **falh** 'land broken up for cultivation, ploughed land', later 'fallow land'.

Thorpe Latimer (Helpringham, Kest), *Torp* 1199–1214, 1203 Abbr, 1204 Cur, *Thorpe* 1212, 1242–43 Fees. **Thorpe on the Hill** (Kest), *Torp* 1086 DB, 1178, 1202 P, *Thorp* 1254 ValNor, *Thorp' super Collem* 1277 RRGr, *Thorp onthehille* 1351 Cor. **Thorpe St Peter** (LSR), *Torp* 1086 DB, c1115 LS, 1185 P, Hy2 Dane. All mean 'the secondary settlement'. The first is named in relation to **Helpringham**, the second is uncertain, the third perhaps of **Wainfleet**. *Latimer* is from the name of the family which held the manor, cf. Thomas *le Latimer* 1212 Fees. The affix in the second is self-explanatory and the third is from the church dedication.

Thorpe le Vale (Ludford, LSR), *Fruntorp'* 1160–70 RA v, *-thorpa* Hy3 (1409) Gilb, *-thorp* 1274 Ipm, *Frumthorp'* a1175 YCh xi, 1240–50 RA v, *Frimtorp* 1212 Fees, *-thorp* 1240–50 RA v, *Thorp'* 1230–40 RA v, *Thorp' iuxta Lodeford'* 1335 *HarlCh*, *Thorpe in the myrres* 1507 Wills i. The first el. of the earlier name is obscure and had been lost by the late 14th century. It survives as a simplex p.n. from ODan **thorp** 'a secondary settlement', presumably of **Ludford**. The modern form has not ben noted before *Thorpe le Vale* 1842 White.

Thorpe Tilney (Timberland, Kest), *Torp* 1170 P, 1175 (1337) Ch, 1177 P, 1203 Cur, *Thorp'* Hy2, l12th (1407) Gilb, *Thorp' Tilney* 1454 *FF, Tymbreland Thorpe* 1553 Pat, 'the secondary settlement (of **Timberland**)'. The affix **Tilney** is derived from the *de Tilney* family (from Tilney in Norfolk) who held land here. All the early spellings are of surnames, note Ralph *de Tiln'* 1184–90 RA vi, Ralph *de Tilneie* a1199 Dane, Peter *de Tileneia* c1200 (1407) Gilb. The earliest reference to **Tilney** as the name of a place is *Thorp et Tilney* 1539–40 Dugd vi.

Threckingham (Kest), *Trichingeham* 1086 DB, *Trichingham* 1086 ib, 1155–60 Dane, *Tricingeham* p1131 (e13th) LibEl, *Thrikingeham* 1178–84 YCh iii, *Trickingham* 1093–1100 Rams, *Trikingham* 1101–7 (l13th) RamsChron, eHy2 Dane, *-yngham* 1100–23 (14th), 1102 Rams. This is the gen.pl. **-inga** of an OE group-name in **-ingas** 'the family, the dependents of X' with OE **hām** 'a homestead, an estate'. There is, however, no Germanic pers.n. which would fit the forms and a British loan might be considered. *The Book of Llan Dav* has such pers.n. forms as *Trycan, Tric(h)anus* and an OE unrecorded pers.n. **Tric* might be conceivable as a hypocoristic form for such a borrowed name. The similarity of the first part of the name with *Tric* 1086, an earlier name for Skegness, cannot be explained. The present day spelling, **Threckingham** is probably due to popular etymology.

Threo Wapentake (Kest), *Tre(h)os* 1098 DB, *Treho* 1130, 1170, 1182, 1200 P, *Trehou* 1183 ib. The early spellings are usually preceded or followed by some form of Latin *wapentacium*. The name means 'the three mounds', from ON **thrír** and ON **haugr**, but the site of the meeting-place of the wapentake (ON **vápnatak**, late OE **wæpengetæc** 'a subdivision of a shire') is not known. It is now a joint wapentake — **Winninbriggs and Threo Wapentake.**

Thurlby (Kest), *Torulfbi, Turolvebi* 1086 DB, *Torolbi* c1128 (12th) ChronPetro, *Torlebi* 1188 P, *Turlebi* 1189 (1332) Ch, 1195 Dane. **Thurlby** (Bilsby, LSR), *Toruluesbi* 1086 DB, *Turlebi* 1190, 1198 P, e13th RA vi, 1202 Ass, *Thurleby* 1207 FF. **Thurlby** (near Lincoln, Kest), *Turulfbi, Turolfbi, Toruluebi, Toruluesbi* 1086 DB, *Torlebi* 1141 RA i, *Turleby* 1163 ib. All three mean 'Thorulf's farmstead, village' from the ODan pers.n. *Thorulf* and ODan **bȳ**.

Thwaite (Welton le Marsh, LSR), *Thuait* m12th (p1268) *Bard*, *Thueit* l12th (p1269) *ib*, *Lythelthwaitt* (*Lythel-* 'little') 1190 (1301) Dugd vi, 'the clearing, the meadow' from ON **thveit**, a rare word in L. The name survives as **Thwaite Hall**. It was a cell of Thornton Abbey.

Till, R. (LWR), *Tyllebroc* 1226 FF, *Tyl* m13th, Hy3 (Ed1) *Barl*, *Tylle* Hy3 (Ed1) *ib*, 1327 *SR*, *le Westtyl* m13th (Edl) *Barl*. It has been suggested that **Till** is a Celtic r.n., but this has been rejected by Celticists. It may well be an OE r.n. from the OE adj. **til** 'useful, good'.

Timberland (Kest), *Timberlunt*, *Timbrelund* 1086 DB, *Timberlund* 1154, 1158 *HarlCh*, c1155 Dane, 1202 Ass, *Timberland* 1185 Templar, 'the grove where timber is obtained' from OE **timber** and ON **lundr**.

Toft (Toft with Lound & Manthorpe, Kest), *Toftlund* (sic), *Toft* 1086 DB, 1205 Cur, 1205 Abbr, 1210 Cur. **Toft Grange** (Kirkby on Bain, LSR), *grangiam de Toftes* 1198 (1328) Ch, *Thoft* 12th *RevesInv*, *Toft* c1200 NthCh; it was a grange of Revesby Abbey. **Toft next Newton** (LNR), *Tofte* 1086 DB, 1205 Cur, *Toft* c1115 LS, p1169 Dane, "by" *Neuton* 1311 Ipm. Each means 'the curtilage, the messuage, the building site' from ODan **toft**. The last named place is near **Newton by Toft**.

Torksey (LWR), *æt Tureces iege* s.a. 873 (c900) ASC A, *æt Turces ige* s.a. 873 (m12th) *ib* D, s.a. 873 (c1121) *ib* E, *æt Turkes ege* s.a. 873 (c1000) *ib* B, *in Turcesige* c1000 Æthelweard, *Torchesey, -ig, -yg* 1086 DB, *Torchesi* 1110–14 RA i, *-eia* a1139 *ib*, *Torkeseie* 1147 (p1269) *Bard*, probably 'Turc's island of land' from an unrecorded OE pers.n. **Turc*, and OE **ēg**. This pers.n. is an OE loan from British and belongs to British **torco-* 'a boar', cf. the Breton pers.n. *Turch*. Torksey was a mint in the late Anglo-Saxon period and the name occurs on coins as *TOR* 975–78, c997–1003, c1018–30, *TVR* c985–91, *TVRCE* c978–79.

Torrington, East & West (LSR), *Terintone* 1086 DB, *Tiringtuna* c1115 LS, *-tun'* 1165 Dane, Hy2 Dane, *Tirintuna* c1140 *AD*, *Tyrington* eHy2 (m13th) NCot, *Tirryngtona* eHy2 (m13th) *ib*, *Est Tyrington'* 1232 Welles, *Westiringtun* 1195–1200 RA ii. 'The farmstead, village called after, associated with Tira' from the OE pers.n. *Tira*, with the OE medial connective particle **-ing-** and OE **tūn**, identical with **Terrington** in Norfolk.

Tothby (Alford, LSR), *Touedebi* 1086 DB, *Toudebi* 1153–62 (1409) Gilb, *Touthebi* 1198, 1199 P, e13th *HarlCh*, *Toutheby* 1226 FF. The first el. is obscure; the second is ODan **bȳ** 'a farmstead, a village'. The name survives as **Tothby Manor**.

Tothill (LSR), *Totele* 1086 DB, 1158 France, 1202 Ass, 1221 Cur, 1242–43 Fees, 'Tota's wood, glade, clearing' from the OE pers.n. *Tota* and OE **lēah**. Forms representing OE **hyll** 'a hill' do not appear till the 14th century and then only sporadically. Those in *-(e)le* are common and develop normally to *-il(l)*. The current spelling is due to popular etymology. There is no "hill" here and the local late name **Toot Hill**, not noted before the 19th century, is that of a Motte and Bailey.

Tows, Great & Little (Ludford, LSR), *Tows* 1386 Peace, *Towes, Towse* 1535 VE iv, *Towis, Towes* 1535–46 *MinAcct*, obscure.

Toynton, All Saints & St. Peter (LSR), *Totintun* 1086, 1141–54 RA vi, *-ton'* 1142 NthCh, 1148–51 RA vi, 1185 P, *-tune* 1170–80 RA vi, *Totingtun* Hy2 Dane, *Thoynton' Omnium Sanctorum* 1254 ValNor, *Thoynton Sancti Petri* 1254 ib. 'The farmstead, village associated with or called after Tota' from the OE pers.n. *Tota* with the OE medial connective particle -**ing**- and OE **tūn**. The affixes are from the church dedications.

Toynton, High & Low (LSR), *Tedlintune* (sic), *Tedintone* 1086 DB, *Tidington'* 1166 P, *Teinton'* 1199 ib, *Tintun* c1200 RA iv, *-ton'* 1204 P, *Tointon'* 1208 FF, *Magna Tynton'* 1220 Cur, *Tynton Superior* 1254 ValNor, *Ouertincton'* 1272 Ass, *Parua Tintun* 1195–1205 RA vi, *Toynton Inferior* 1254 ValNor. Probably 'the farmstead, village associated with Tēoda', from the OE pers.n. *Tēoda* with the OE medial connective particle -**ing**- 'associated with, called after' and OE **tūn**. The two villages were later distinguished as "big" and "little", then as **High** and **Low**.

Trent, R. (Kest/LWR), forms in L documents include: *be Trentan* s.a. 679 (c1121) ASC E, *andlang Trentan* s.a. 1013 (m11th) ib C, *iuxta fluuium Treanta* 731 Bede, *mid Treontan streame* c890 (10th) OEBede, *in Trente* m12th (c1331) *Spald i, iuxta ripam Trente* 1163 *And*, *ad Trentam* 1139 RA i. This is from PrW **trisantona**, a r.n. of doubtful meaning, but which has been translated as 'strongly flooding' which would be appropriate enough for the **R. Trent**.

Trusthorpe (LSR), *Druistorp, Dreuistorp* (sic) 1086 DB, *Struttorp'* 1196 FF, *Struttorp* 1201 Ass, *Trustorp'* 1189–99 Cur, 1212 Fees, probably 'Strut's secondary settlement' from the ON byname *Strutr* and ODan **thorp**. The same pers.n. appears in **Strubby** but here initial *S*- has been lost through dissimilation. The DB forms are not supported by any later spellings of the name.

Tumby (LSR), *Tunbi* 1086 DB, *Tunnebi* 1209 P, *Tumbi* c1115 LS, 1170–75, c1187, Hy2 Dane, probably from ODan **tūn** in the sense 'an enclosure' or perhaps 'a fence' and ODan **bȳ** 'a farmstead, village'.

Tupholme (LSR), *Tupeholm* c1175 Dane, 1200 Cur, 1208 ib, *Tupholm* 1208 Cur, *Tuppeholm* 1218 FF, 1229 Pat, 'Túpi's raised land in the marsh' from the ON pers.n. *Túpi* and ON **holmr**. Alternatively, the first el. may be ME **tup** 'a ram, a tup'. The name is represented today by **Tupholme Hall Farm**.

Twigmoor (Holme, LWR), *Twiggemore* 1202 Ass, e13th (m14th) *PetML*, *Twigemor'* 1202 Ass, probably from the OE pers.n. *Twicga* and OE **mōr** 'moor, marsh'.

Twyford (Colsterworth, Kest), *Tuiuorde, -forde* 1086 DB, *-fort* 1163 Dane, *-ford'* 1201, 1206 Cur, 'the double ford' from OE prefix **twī**- and OE **ford**.

Tydd Gote (Tydd St Mary, Hol), *Tyddegot* 1361 Pat, *Tiddegote* 1362 *Cor*, *Tydgote* 1365 Pat, 1428 FenNQ v, from the village name **Tydd St Mary** and OE **gotu** 'a sluice'.

Tydd St Mary (Hol), *Tite* 1086 DB, *Tit* 1094 France, *Tid* 1086 DB, 1168, 1191 P, *Tyd* 1205 ChancR, *Tydd'* 1200 CurR, probably from OE **titt** 'a teat' in the transferred topographical sense of a slight hill. **Tydd** is almost certainly named from the saltern or salthill on which it is situated. It is identical in meaning with **Tydd St Giles** nearby in Cambridgeshire and is **St Mary** from the dedication of the church.

Tytton (Wyberton, Hol), *Titton* 1167 P, 1189–99 Cur, *Tyttone* 1183 (m14th) *HC*, *Tittun* c1185 *AddCh*, Hy2 Dane, *-tune* 1197–98 RA vii. 'Titta's farmstead', from the OE pers.n. *Titta* and OE **tūn**. The name survives as **Tytton Hall**.

U

Uffington (Kest), *Offintone* 1086 DB, *-tona* 1114–16 RA i, *-tune* 1086 DB, c1128 (12th) ChronPetro, *-tuna* 1106–23 (1333) Ch, *Offington* 1219 FF, *Uffinton'* 1219 Ass, 1225 Welles, probably 'the farmstead, village called after or associated with Uffa' from the OE pers.n. *Uffa* with the OE connective particle **-ing-** and OE **tūn**.

Ulceby (LNR), *Ulvesbi, Ulvesbi, Vluesbi* 1086 DB, *Ulesbi* c1115 LS, a1147, c1150 Dane, *Ulseby* 1163–76 (e14th) YCh x, 1228 Cur. **Ulceby** (Ulceby with Fordington, LSR), *Vlesbi* 1086 DB, eHy2 (p1259) *Kirkst*, *Ulesbi* 1086 DB, c1115 LS, *Ulsebi* c1115 LS, lHy2 (p1259) *Kirkst*, *-by* 1201 Cur. Both these names mean 'Ulf's farmstead, village' from the ODan pers.n. *Ulf* and ODan **bȳ**. The first el. has the Scand. gen.sg in *-s*, which survives as [s] in the present-day pronunciation. The name must have been given by Scand. speakers.

Ulceby Skitter (Ulceby. LNR), see **Skitter Beck**.

Upperthorpe (Haxey, LWR), *Hubaldestorp* 1086 DB, *le Ouerthorp'* 1331 *AD*, *Westwood Overthorpe* 1559 WillsStow, originally 'Hubald's secondary settlement' from the Continental Germanic pers.n. *Hubald* and ODan **thorp**, the first el. being replaced by OE **uferra** 'upper, higher' from its situation. It was probably named in relation to **Westwoodside**.

Upton (LWR), *Opetune* 1086 DB, *Uppetune, Uptuna* c1115 LS, *Upton* 1185 Templar, 1190 (1301) Dugd vi, 1202 Ass, 'the higher farmstead, village' from OE **upp** and OE **tūn**. It is on the rising ground above the R. Trent.

Usselby (LNR), *Osoluabi, Osoluebi* c1115 LS, *Osolfby* c1221 Welles, *Oselby* Hy2 (p1269) *Bard*, 1275 RH, *Osselby* 1267 AD, *Uselby* 13th ib, 'Ōswulf's farmstead, village', from the OE pers.n. *Ōswulf* and ODan **bȳ**. There is no trace of the OE gen.sg. *-es* in the forms for Usselby. It is possible that the 12th century *-a-* and *-e-* represent a Scand. gen.sg. *-a-* < *-ar-*, suggesting that the p.n. had been given by Scand. speakers.

Utterby (LNR), *Uthterby* 1150–60 (1409) Gilb, *Vthterbi* l12 RA ii. *Utterby* Hy2 (1409) Gilb, c1221 Welles, *Vttrebi* 1195 P, *Vtterby* e13 RA ii, perhaps 'Ūhthere's or Ūhtrēd's farmstead, village' a hybrid compound from an OE pers.n. *Ūhthere* or *Ūhtrēd* and ODan **bȳ**.

V

Vaudey Abbey (Edenham, Kest), *de Valle Dei* 1150–60 (1409) Gilb, 1150–60 Semp, *de Ualle Dei* eHy2 Dane, 1157, 1158 P; the early forms are all in Latin, the earliest vernacular form so far noted is *le Vaude* 1347 Pat, *de Valledey* 1413 Pap. The meaning of **Vaudey** is 'the valley of God' and the modern form is from French. The **abbey** was founded at a place called *Brachecurt* (sic) p1147 Dugd v, *Bracthuait* 1189 ib, perhaps 'the clearing in the thicket' from OE **bræc** and ODan **thveit**.

W

Waddingham (LWR), *Wadingeham* 1086 DB, *Wadingheheim* c1115 LS, 1168, 1191 P, 1202 Ass, *Waddingeham* 1200 FF, *Wadingham* 1086 DB, c1115 LS, 'the homestead, the estate of the Wadingas' from the gen.pl. *Wadinga* of the OE group-name *Wadingas* 'the family, the dependents of *Wada*' and OE **hām**. The form in *-heim* is from the cognate ON **heim**. The same pers.n. is found in **Waddington** and **Waddingworth**.

Waddington (Kest), *Wadintun(e)* 1086 DB, 1212 Fees, *Wadingtuna* 1178 (p1269) *Bard*, *-ton'* 1185 Templar, e13 *HarlCh*, 'the farmstead, village associated with, called after Wada' from the OE pers.n. *Wada* with the OE connective particle **-ing-** and OE **tūn**. The same pers.n. is found in **Waddingham** and **Waddingworth**.

Waddingworth (LSR), *Wadingurde* 1086 DB, *-worde* 1153–62 (1409) Gilb, *-worda* 1170–75 Dane, *-worth'* 1202 Ass, *Wadigworda* c1115 LS, *-wrht* (sic) lHy2 Dane, 'the enclosure associated with, called after Wada' from the OE pers.n. *Wada* (as also in **Waddingham** and **Waddington**) with the OE connective particle **-ing-** and OE **worth**.

Wainfleet All Saints & St Mary (LSR), *Wemflet (-m- = -in-)*, *Wenflet* 1086 DB, *Weinflet* c1115 LS, 1147, 1159 (p1269) *Bard*, *Waineflet* c1180 BuryF, *Wainflet* 1166 P, *North Weynflet* e13th (l14th) *Ped*, *Weynflet Omnium Sanctorum* 1291 Tax, *Sutht Weynflet* (sic) 1293 *Ass*, *Weynfled Beate Marie* 1254 ValNor; 'the creek, the stream which can be crossed by a waggon' from OE **wægn** and OE **flēot**. The affixes are from the church dedications.

Wainfleet Haven (Wainfleet, LSR), *hauene de Waynflet'* 1186–1200 (14th) Samson, *portum de Weynflet* e13th (l14th) *Ped*, from the parish name **Wainfleet** and ON **hafn** 'a haven, a harbour'.

Waithe (LNR), *Wade* 1086 DB, 1194 CurP, *Wada* c1115 LS, 1212 Fees, *Wathe* 1196 ChancR, 1203 Cur; the earliest forms in *-d-* suggest that **Waith** is derived from OE **(ge)wæd** 'a ford'; the ford still survives today. By the later 12th century the *-d-* had been replaced by *-th-*, either by the Scandinavianisation of *-d-* to *-th-*, as in **Louth** (LSR), or by replacement of **(ge)wæd** by the cognate ON **vath**, hence the modern **Waithe**.

Walcot (Alkborough, LWR), *Walcote* 1066–87 (m12th) Dugd i, *Walecote* 1086 DB, c1128 (12th) ChronPetro, m12th (c1331) *Spald i*, *-cota* c1115 LS, *-cot* 1200 ChR. **Walcot** (near Folkingham, Kest), *Walecote hundred* 1086 DB, *Walecot'* 1125 (p1269) *Bard*, *-cote* c1128 ChronPetro, a1184 Semp, lHy2 *Anc*, 1191 P. **Walcott** (near Billinghay, Kest), *Walecote* 1086 DB, Hy2 (1407) Gilb, *-cota* 1135–54 (p1259) *Bard*, *-cot* 1199 CurR, *-cot'* 1200 FF. Each means 'the cottage, hut, shelter of the Welshmen', from the genitive pl. **wala** of OE **walh** and OE **cot**, indicating isolated groups of Welshmen identifiable as such in Anglo-Saxon England.

Walesby (LNR), *Walesby* 1086 DB, c1115 LS, l12th RA iv, *-by* 1187 (1409) Gilb, 1223 Cur, *Walebi* 1196 Cur, 'Val's farmstead, village' from the ON pers.n. *Valr* and ODan **bȳ**. This pers.n. is also the first el. of **Walshcroft Wapentake**, in which **Walesby** is situated, and presumably the same man gave his name both to the district and to the settlement.

Walkerith (LWR), *Walkerez* l13th *HarlCh*, *Walkreth* 1300 Ipm, *Walcreth* 1316 FA, 1329 Pat, 1332 *SR*, 'the landing-place (on the R. Trent) of the fullers, cloth-dressers' from OE **walcere** and OE **hȳth**.

Walmsgate (LSR), *Walmesgar* 1086 DB, c1160 RA vi, *-gare* c1110 France, c1200 RA iv, *-gara* 1150–60 RA vi, *Walmeresgara* c1115 LS, *Walmesgate* 1196 ChancR, 1284 Abbr, but forms in *-gate* do not reappear until the second half of the 16th century, and are presumably due to popular etymology. Probably 'Waldmǣr's gore of land' from the OE pers.n. *Waldmǣr* and OE **gāra**.

Walshcroft Wapentake (LNR), *Wale-*, *Walecros* 1086 DB, *Walescros* 1183, 1202 P, *-croft* c1115 LS, 1166, 1170 P, *Walscroft* 1242–43 Fees, *Walshecroft* 1287 Ipm. The early forms are preceded or followed by some form of Latin *wapentacium*. The name means 'Val's cross' from the ON pers.n. *Valr* and ON **kross**, late OE **cros**, the latter a word borrowed from Old Irish and brought to England by the vikings. This was replaced at an early date by OE **croft**. *Valr* is also the first el. of **Walesby** in the same wapentake, both presumably named from the same man. The site of the cross which must have marked the meeting-place of the wapentake is unknown. **Wapentake** itself is derived from ON **vápnatak**, late OE **wæpengetæc** 'a sub-division of a shire'.

Waltham (LNR), *Waltham* 1086 DB, c1115 LS, 1177, 1201 P, 1202 *HarlCh*, 1217 Pat, 'the wold estate', from OE **wald** and **hām**. It has been plausibly suggested that **Waltham**, found in several counties, was used in an early period of Anglo-Saxon settlement for a royal administrative centre in a forest area.

Walton (Grantham, Kest), *Waltuna* 1146 RA i, *-tona* 1163, 1198 ib, *-ton'* 1198 P, *Waletun'* 1185 Templar, *-ton* 1212 Fees, 1222 FF, 1242–43 Fees, 'the farmstead, village of the Welshmen' from OE **walh** (gen.pl. **wala**) and OE **tūn**. Compare **Walcot**. This must have been an isolated group of Welshmen, identifiable as such, probably as late as the end of the 7th century.

Waring, R. (LSR), *Waryn* 1359 Cor, *Waring* 1535–43 Leland. The forms are too late to suggest a convincing etymology.

Washingborough (Kest), *Washingeburg* 1086 DB, *Guasineb'* (an Anglo-Norman form) 1093–1136 RA vii, *Wasingburg'* 1156–58 HarlCh, *Wassingeb'* 1177 P, *-burc* 1204 ib, *Wassingburc* 1190, 1193 P. Probably 'the fortified place of the Wassingas' from the gen.pl. *Wassinga* of an OE group-name *Wassingas* 'the family, the dependents of Wassa' and OE **burh**. The OE pers.n. **Wassa* is a loan from British.

Waterton (LWR), *Watretone* 1086 DB, *-ton* 1301 FF, *Waterton* 1246 Ipm, 1256 Cl, from OE **wæter** 'water' and OE **tūn** 'a farmstead, a village'; the name survives as **Waterton Hall** which is situated close to the bank of the R. Trent.

Weelsby (LNR), *Wivelesbi* 1086 DB, 1212 Fees, *Wiuelesbi* 1115 YCh iii, *Wyvelesbi* 1266 Misc, *Wyflesby* 1242–43 Fees, 'Vífill's farmstead, village' from the ON pers.n. *Vífill* and ODan **bý**. The same pers.n. occurs in **Wilsthorpe**.

Welbourn (Kest), *Wellebrune* 1086 DB, *-brunna* 1177, 1188 P, *Weleburne* c1080 (13th) Dugd iii, *-burn'* 1185 Templar, *Welleburn* 1156–62 (1396) Ch, 'the stream running from a spring' from OE **wella** and OE **burna**. A stream rises from a spring north of the village and flows to the R. Brant.

Welby (Kest), *Wellebi* 1086 DB, 1202 Ass, 1202 SelectPleas, *-by* 1189 Dugd, a1209 RA ix, 'the farmstead, village by the spring' from OE **wella** and ODan **bý**.

Well (LSR), *Welle* 1086 DB, eHy2, c1175 Dane, 1195 FF, *Wella* 1158 France, *Well'* 1197 P, 'the spring, the well', from OE **wella**, being named from a spring at the west end of the upper lake.

Welland, R. (Kest), forms in L documents include: *Vueolod* c1000 *Æthelweard, Weland'* 1135–54 (p1343) *Crow,* c1155 (c1200) CartAnt, 1179 (15th) *CrowR,* 1199–1216 (1307) Ch, *Wailand* 1199 (1380) Pat, *Weiland* 1199 (1330) Ch, *Weyland* 1200 ChR. The meaning of **Welland** is unknown, but the name may well be pre-Celtic.

Wellingore (Kest), *Wallingoure* 1070–87 RA i, *-oura* 1196 P, *Walingoure* 1096 RA i, *Welingoure* 1086 DB, *-oura* 1177 P, *Wellingoure* 1086 DB, 1146 RA i, 1199 P, *-oura* 1147–53, 1151–61 RA i. The second el. is OE **ofer** 'a promontory, a flat-topped ridge' descriptive of the rounded promontory jutting out from the Cliff escarpment. The first el. is uncertain.

Wellow (Great Grimsby, LNR), *Welhou* 1155–58 (1334) Ch, Hy2 (1460) Pat, *-howe* 1272 FF, *-how* 1288 Ipm, *Wellehou* 1292 ib, probably from OE **wella** 'a spring' and ON **haugr** 'a mound'. It was reported in 1901 that there was a mound here in the Peoples Park with a spring at the foot.

Well Wapentake (LWR), *Wylle* 1075–92 (12th) Eyns, *Guelle* (an Anglo-Norman form) 1091 (12th) ib, *Welle* 1066–87 (12th) ib, 1086, c1115 LS, 1090, 1123–33, 1135–39 RA i. The early forms are usually preceded or followed by some form of Latin *wapentacium.* The name is derived from OE **wella** 'the spring, the well'. The site of the meeting-place of the wapentake (ON **vápnatak,** late OE **wæpengetac** 'a subdivision of a shire') is not known.

Welton (LWR), *Welletonam* 1070–87, 1146 RA i, *-tone* 1086 DB, 1090, 1147–53 RA i, *-tona* 1103-7, 1107–15 ib, 1130 P, *Wellatuna* c1115 LS, *Welleton'* 1188 P. **Welton le Marsh** (LSR), *Waletone, -tune* 1086 DB, *-tuna* c1115 LS, *Welletuna* c1115 ib, *-ton'* 1185 Templar, 1190 P, l12th Dane, *Welton in le Marshe* 1546 LP xxi. **Welton le Wold** (LSR), *Welletune, -tone* 1086 DB, *-tuna* c1115 LS, c1115 Dane, *-tun* c1155 (1409) Gilb, eHy2 (p1259) *Kirkst, -ton'* p1175 Dane, *Welton iuxta Gaiton* 1156–58 *HarlCh,* - "by Louth" 1323 Ipm. Each means 'the farmstead, village with a spring' from OE **wella** and OE **tūn.** The affixes **le Marsh** and **le Wold** are self-explanatory, but have not been noted before the 19th century.

Westborough (Westborough and Dry Dodington, Kest), *Westburg* 1086 DB, 1160–65 RA ix, 1199 P, *-burgh* a1184 (1407) Gilb, 'the fortified place to the west' from OE **west** and OE **burh.** It is not clear to which place it relates.

Westby (Bitchfield, Kest), *Westbi* 1086 DB, 1172 Dane, *-by* 1212 Fees, 1240 FF, 'the farmstead, village to the west (of **Bitchfield**)' from OE **west** or ON **vestr** and ODan **bȳ**.

Westhorpe (Gosberton, Hol), *Westthorpe* 1318 Pat, *Westhorp'* 1394 Peace, *-thorpe* 1447 Cust, 'the dependent outlying settlement to the west (of **Gosberton**)' from OE **west** and ODan **thorp**. It is probably a late example of the use of **thorp** in south L.

Westlaby (Wickenby, LSR), *Westledebi* 1086 DB, *Westletebi* c1115 LS, *Westletheby* 1202 Ass, *Westladebi* a1187 Dane, lHy2 (p1259) *Kirkst*, *-by* lHy2 (p1259) *ib*, 'Vestlithi's farmstead, village' from the ON pers.n. *Vestlithi* and ODan **bȳ**.

Weston (Hol), *Westune* 1086 DB, *-tun'* 1212 Fees, *-ton* 1176, 1184 P, 1201 Cur, from OE **west** 'west' and OE **tūn** 'a farmstead, a village'; it was presumably "west" in relation to **Moulton**.

West Riding, *West Triding*, *West Treding* 1086 DB, *West Triding* c1115 LS, *Westrithing* c1160 Dane, 1183–89 RA iv, *-riding'* c1190 RA ix. **Lindsey** is divided into three parts — **North**, **South** and **West Riding**. **Riding** is derived from ON **thrithjung**, late OE **thrithing** 'a third part'. Initial *th-* has become *t-* through Anglo-Norman influence and was later absorbed by the final *-t* of *west* to give *riding*.

Westville (LSR) was formed into a township by Act of Parliament in 1812, the name surviving as **Westville Farm**. It was named from **West Fen**, *marisco occidentali* 1180–90 NthCh, *Westfen* e13th Revesby, *-fenne* 1206 Ass, eHy3 (m14th) *HC*, self-explanatory.

Westwoodside (Haxey, LWR), *Westude* 1086 DB, *-wud'* m12th *AD*, *-wude* 1219 Ass, m13th *AD*, self-explanatory, from OE **west** and OE **wudu**; it is *west* of **Haxey**.

Whaplode (Hol), *Copelade*, *Copolade* (Anglo-Norman forms) 1086 DB, *Quappelada* 1170, 1177 P, *-lade* 1194 CurR, *Quapelad'* 1202 Ass, *Quappelod* 1247 *Spald i*, *Wappelade* 1220 Cur, probably from an unrecorded OE **cwappa* 'an eel-pout, burbot' (cf. German *Quappe* 'an eel-pout, tadpole') and OE **lād** 'a water-course'.

Whaplode Drove (Whaplode, Hol), *magnam drauuam de Quappel'* l12th, a1235 (m13th) *PipeS, magnam drauam de Quappel'* lHy3 (c1331) *Spald ii, Quappelade droue* 1326 *StJ*, from the village name **Whaplode** and OE **drāf** 'the road along which cattle are driven'. **Drove** is common in the Lincolnshire fenlands.

Wharton (Blyton, LWR), *Warton* 1086 DB, 1220–20 *Foster, -tona* 1138–39, 1139 RA i, *-tun* 1210–30 *Foster*, probably from OE **weard** 'watch, protection' and OE **tūn** 'a farmstead, a village', though the exact significance is uncertain.

Whisby (Doddington, Kest), *Wizebi* (*-z-* = *-ts-*) 1086 DB, *Wiceby* 1200 Cur, *Wiscebi* 1201 Ass, eHy3 *HarlCh*, 1212 Fees, *Wyseby* 1224 Cur, *Wisseby* 1263 FF, 'Hvit's farmstead, village' from the ODan pers.n. *Hvit* and ODan **bȳ**.

Whitton (LWR), *Witenai* 1086, *Witena* c1115, *Witeneia* 1130 P, *Witene* 1178, 1194 ib, *Witen* 1212 Fees, *Whyten* Hy3 YD ix, either 'the white island of land' from OE **hwīt** (presumably a reference to the soil) and OE **ēg** or 'Hwīta's island of land', from the OE pers.n. *Hwīta* and **ēg**.

Wickenby (LSR), *Wighingesbi, Wichingebi* 1086 DB, *Uichenbi, Uichingebi* c1115 LS, *Wikingebi* a1187 Dane, 1199 (p1259) *Kirkst, Wykyngbi* lHy2 (p1259) *ib, Wikingesbi* 1187 Dane, probably 'Víking's farmstead, village' from the ODan pers.n. *Víking* (recorded several times in DB) and ODan **bȳ**. Alternatively the first el. may be the appellative **víkingr** 'a viking', the source of the pers.n., but the former seems more likely.

Wigford (Lincoln), *Wich(e)ford'* c1107 RA i, 1123–48 RA ii, *Wicford(e)* a1169 RA ix, *Wycford'* 1219–26 ib, from OE **wīc**, a word with a variety of meanings, but here probably referring to a Roman settlement on the right hand bank of the R. Witham and OE **ford**. Compare **Wykeham**.

Wigtoft (Holl), *Wigetoft* 1180, 1188 P, *Wichetoft* 1185 RotDom, *Wikethoft* c1186 (13th) *Castleacre, -toft* 1187 P, 1190–91 RBE; the first el. is uncertain but may be ON **vík** 'a small creek, an inlet, a bay', the second el. being ODan **toft** 'a messuage, a curtilage'. **Wigtoft** is situated near Bicker Haven, which in earlier times was an arm of the sea.

Wildmore Fen (LSR), *Wildamora* c1140 Dane, a1150 (p1259) *Kirkst, Wildemore* m12th (l13th) KirkstPsalt, 1163 Dane, lHy2 *Anc*, 1198 (1328) Ch, from ON **wilde** 'wild, uncultivated' and OE **mōr** in this case 'marshland'. **Fen** is self-explanatory.

Wildsworth (LWR), *Winelesworth* (*n* = *u*) R1 (1232) Ch, *Wyuelesworth* 1199 *HarlCh*, *Wiueleswurth*' e13th *AD*, *Wyveleswurth* 1280 Ch, 'Wifel's enclosure' from the OE pers.n. *Wifel* (as also in **Willingham by Stow**) and OE **worth**.

Wilksby (LSR), *Wilgesbi*, *Wilchesbi* 1086 DB, *Wilghebi* c1115 LS, Wilkesbi 1170–78 Revesby, lHy2 Dane, c1200 NthCh, *Wilghesby* 1198 (1328) Ch, probably 'Vilgeirr's or Vilgerth's farmstead, village' from the ON pers.n. *Vilgeirr* or fem. *Vilgerthr* and ODan **bȳ**.

Willingham by Stow (LWR), *Welingeham* (sic) 1086 DB, *Wiflingeheim*, *Wiflingham* c1115 LS, *Wiuelingeham* 1202, 1218 Ass, *Wivelingeham* 1210–12 RBE, *Wiflingeham* 1233 Welles. **Willingham, North** (LNR), *Wiuilingeham* 1086 DB, *Wiuelingeham* 1193 P, *Wyvelingeham* 1226 Cur, *Wiflingeham* c1115 LS, *Wiflingham* 1086 DB, c1115 LS, *Wiuelingham* 1196–1202 RA iv. Each means 'the homestead, estate of the Wifelingas' from *Wifelinga* the gen.pl. of OE *Wifelingas*, a group-name meaning 'Wifel's family, dependents' from the OE pers.n. *Wifel* (as in **Wildsworth**) and OE **hām**. Forms in *-heim* are from the cognate ON **heim**. The affixes are self-explanatory.

Willingham, Cherry (LWR), *Vlingeham*, *Wilingeham* 1086 DB, *Wllingeheim* (sic) c1115 LS, *-ham* 1176 P, 1219 LAHW, *Willingham* 1163 RA i, *Cherwellyngham* 1373 Peace. **Willingham, South** (LSR), *Ylingeham*, *Vlingeham*, *Ulingeham* 1086 DB, *Wllingheham*, *Wllingheheim* c1115 LS, *Willingeham* 1210 FF, *Willingham* 1200 Cur, *Wylingham super le Wold* 1355 ChantCert, *Southewillyngham* 1442 Pat. Both mean 'the homestead, estate of the Willingas' from *Willinga*, the gen.pl. of OE *Willingas*, a group-name meaning 'Willa's family, dependents' and OE **hām**. Forms in *-heim* are from the cognate ON **heim**. The affix of the first name is ME **cheri(e)** 'a cherry-tree', no doubt denoting a place where such trees grew; that of the second is **South**.

Willoughby (Willoughby with Sloothby, LSR), *Wilgebi* 1086 DB, 1175–84 *AddCh*, 1199 CurR, *Wilghebi* 1199 ib, *Wilegby* 1125 (p1269) *Bard*, eHy2 Dane. **Willoughby, Scott** (Aunsby and Dembleby, Kest), *Wilgebi* 1086 DB, *-bia* eHy2 Dane, *Wilgheby* 1223 Cur, *Wilwebi* 1224 Pat, *Scot Wilegeby* 1239 RRG. **Willoughby, Silk** (Kest), *Wilgebi* 1086 DB, c1150 *AddCh*, *-bia* 1163 RA i, *-by* 1210–12 RBE, *Wilchebi* 1163 RA i, *Wilebi* 1185 RotDom, *Willughby alias Silkwillughby* 1495 IBL. **Willoughby, West** (Ancaster, Kest), *Wlheb*' 1185 Templar, *Willigby* l12th (l13th) *Stix*, *Wilgeby* 1219 Ass, *Wilgheby* 1221 Cur. These are all probably partial Scandinavianisations of an OE *Wiligtūn* 'the farmstead, village where willows grow' from OE **wilig** and OE **tūn**, with the second el. replaced by ODan **bȳ** 'a farmstead, village', cf. **Willoughton**. **Scott** is from the *Scot* family. William *Scot* made a grant of land here to Stixwould Priory eHy2 Dane. **Silk** is from **Silkby**, now lost as a p.n. though the hamlet survives about a third of a mile west of the church. It is *Silkeby* 1189 (1341) Semp, l12th (13th) *Stix*, 1231 FF, *-bi* 1212 Fees, 'Silki's farmstead, village' from the ON byname *Silki* and ODan **bȳ**.

Willoughton (LWR), *Wilchetone* 1086 DB, *Wilgatuna* c1115 LS, *Wilieton'* 1178 P, *Wilketon'* 1185 Templar, *Wilweton'* Hy2 (c1331) *Spald i*, *Wilgheton'* 1200 ChR, 'the farmstead, village where willows grow' from OE **wilig** and OE **tūn**. Compare **Willoughby**.

Wilsford (Kest), *Wiuelesforde* 1086 DB, *-ford'* 1177, 1193 P, *Wivelesford* 1200 OblR, 'Wifel's ford' from the OE pers.n. *Wifel* and OE **ford**. The same pers.n. occurs in **Wildsworth**, **North Willingham** and **Willingham by Stow**.

Wilsthorpe (Braceborough, Kest), *Wiuelestorp* 1086 DB, *Wiulestorp* lHy2 NthCh, *Wiuelisthorp'* 1189–1199 (c1331) *Spald i*, *Wivelestorp'* 1200 ChR, 'Vífill's secondary settlement (of **Braceborough**)' from the ON pers.n. *Vífill* and ODan **thorp**. The same pers.n. occurs in **Weelsby**.

Winceby (LSR), *Wizebi* (sic), *Winzebi* 1086 DB, *Wynceby* 1115 (14th) *Bard*, *Wincebi* c1115 LS, 1140–47, 1154–56 RA i, 1168, 1191 P, apparently 'Vind's farmstead, village' from the ON pers.n. *Vindr* and ODan **bȳ**, with a Scandinavian gen.sg. [s], on which see **Laceby**.

Wingland (Tydd St Mary, Hol) was a new parish made up of land enclosed in 1831, 1848 and 1869 and was named after Tyco *Wing*, agent to the Duke of Bedford, patron and promoter of the Nene Outfall undertaking begun in August 1827, see FenNQ iii, 103–6.

Winkhill (Heckington, Kest), *Vincle* 1185 Templar, *Wynkel* 1289 *Ass*, *Wynkhill* 1559 Pat; although there are only a few early forms this is 'the nook, the corner of land' from OE **wincel**.

Winnibriggs Wapentake (Kest), *Winegebrige*, *Winebruge* 1086 DB, 1172, *-brige* 1176, *Wimeresbrigge* (*-m-* *-ni-*) 1184, *Winierbrige* 1185, 1194, *Winieresbrige* 1186, 1191, *Winierebrige* 1188, 1194 all P. The forms are preceded or followed by some form of Latin *wapentacium*. It has been suggested that this is 'Winegār's bridge' from the OE pers.n. *Winegār* and OE **brycg**, but the first el. is uncertain. The site of the meeting-place of the wapentake (ON **vápnatak**, late OE **wæpengetæc** 'a subdivision of a shire') is said, by B. Street *Historical Notes on Grantham*, 1857 p. 36, to have been at "an insignificant bridge over the Mowbeck on the Harlaxton road, called Winnibriggs". **Winnibriggs** has been joined to **Threo** to form **Winnibriggs & Threo Wapentake.**

Winteringham (LWR), *Wintringeham* 1086 DB, c1115 LS, p1131 (e13th) LibEl, 1202 Ass, 1244 Pap, *Wintringham* c1115 LS, *Uuintrigham* eHy2 Dane, *Wintringham* 1202 Ass, 'the homestead, the estate of the Wint(e)ringas' from the gen.pl. *Wint(e)ringa* of the OE group-name *Wint(e)ringas* 'the family, the dependents of *Winter* or *Wintra*' and OE **hām**. For the same pers.n. compare **Winterton.**

Winterton (LWR), *æt Wintringatune* 1066–68 (c1200) ASWills, *Wintrintune, Wintri(n)tone, Wintretune* 1086 DB, *Wintringtuna* c1115 LS, Hy2 (14th) YCh, *-tune* 1155–60 Dane, *-ton'* 1167 P, l12th RA ii, 'the farmstead, the village of the Wint(e)ringas' from the gen.pl. *Wint(e)ringa* of the OE group-name *Wint(e)ringas* 'the family, the dependents of *Winter* or *Wintra*' and OE **tūn**. **Winterton** is close to **Winteringham**; both are presumably named from the same group of settlers.

Winthorpe (LSR), *Wintorp* 1175–81 Dane, 1206 RA vi, *-thorp'* l12th ib ii, *Winetorp* 1191 P, 1196–1203 RA vi, *-thorp'* l12th RA ii, probably a hybrid p.n. 'Wine's secondary settlement (perhaps of **Skegness** or of **Ingoldmells**)' from the OE pers.n. *Wine* and ODan **thorp**.

Wispington (LSR), *Wispinctune* 1086 DB, *Wispingtuna* c1115 LS, *-tona* l12th (p1269) *Bard*, *-tun'* e13th (l13th) *Stix*, *Wispintune* c1150 *DuDCCh*, *-tuna* 1162 Dane. The first el. is apparently OE **wisp* 'a wisp' used of 'a thicket, brushwood' with the medial connective particle **-ing-** 'associated with, called after' and OE **tūn** 'a farmstead, a village'.

Witham, North & South (Kest), *Wime, Wimme* 1086 DB, 1185 Templar, 1202 Ass, *Widme* 1086 DB, 1185 Templar, *Nortwine* 1086 DB, *Nort Widhem* a1160 Dane, *Suthwyme* 1231 FF. Both are named from the **R. Witham** on which they stand. The affixes are self-explanatory.

Witham on the Hill (Kest), *Witham* 1086 DB, 1100–35, Hy2 (15th) Bridl, 1189 (1332) Ch, 1194 (e14th) Bridl. The first el. is quite uncertain. It might be an OE pers.n. *Wit(t)a*, OE **wita** 'a councillor' or OE **wiht** 'a bend'. The second el. is OE **hām** 'a homestead, an estate'. The affix is self-explanatory.

Witham, R., forms in L documents include: *Withma* c1000 Saints, *Wythum* 1100–35 (1308) Ch, 1115 (14th) *Bard*, c1150 *DuDCCh*, c1152 LAAS vi, *Whithum* 1121 (1308) Ch, *Widme* 1147 (p1269) *Bard*, c1150 Dane, 1170–75 ib, 1173 (l13th) *Stix*, l12th (p1259) *Kirkst*, *Wideme* 1161 (l13th) *Stix*, *Withme* l12th (p1259) *Kirkst*, *Witham* 1162 (p1259) *ib*. This is a difficult name of high antiquity. No Celtic source can be suggested nor can it be explained in terms of any Germanic root. The name is probably pre-Celtic.

Withcall (LSR), *Wichale* (sic) 1086 DB, *-hal'* 1180 P, *Widcale* 1086 DB, *-cal'* 1161 (p1259) *Kirkst*, *-cale* 1193 ib, *Uitcala* c1115 LS, *Witkale* 1185 Templar, Hy2 Dane, *Withkale* 1184–92 RA v. This is a Scand. compound of ON **vithr** 'a wood' and ON **kjǫlr** 'a keel', in the sense 'a ridge', which is topographically appropriate. For the second el. cf. **Keal** and **Keelby.**

Withern (Withern with Stain, LSR), *Widerne* 1086 DB, *-erna* c1115 LS, *Wierne* 1115 (14th) *Bard*, 1147 (p1269) *ib*, *Wiern* lHy2 RA vi, 1202 Ass, *Withern'* 1210 Cur; the first el. is OE **widu** 'a wood', which has been replaced by the cognate ON **vithr** 'a wood', the second OE **ærn** 'a house', with loss of the medial consonant(s) due to Anglo-Norman influence.

Woodhall (LSR), *Wudehalle* Hy2 Dane, *-halla* 1196–98, l12th ib, *Wdehale* 1170–75 ib, *-halle* lHy2 ib, 'the hall in the wood' from OE **wudu** 'a wood' and OE **hall** 'a hall', perhaps, as has been suggested, the hall where the forest court met. **Woodhall Spa** (LSR), *Woodhall Spa* 1824 O. In the early 19th century, spring water rich in minerals issued unexpectedly from an abandoned exploratory coal pit and a **Spa** subsequently developed around the spring.

Woodhouse (Belton, LWR), *Wudehuses* m13th *AD*, *Wodhousis* 1327 *SR*, *Wodhous* 1332 *ib*, self-explanatory, but note there is a variation between sg. and pl. in the earliest forms. It was apparently earlier called *Eluestuait*, *Eluestuayth* Hy2 (e14th) Selby, *Elvesweit* 1204 ChR, *Evilthwaye alias Woodhouse* 1540–41 Dugd iii. The alternative name is probably a Scand. compound 'Ælwar's, Elwer's clearing' from the ODan pers.n. *Ælwar, Elwer* and ON **thveit**, the latter rare in L.

Woodthorpe (Strubby with Woodthorpe, LSR), *Endretorp* 1086 DB, *Wdetorp* 1147, 1178 (p1269) *Bard*, lHy2 *Anc*, *Wudetorp* 1182, 1192 P, a hybrid formation, 'the secondary settlement (of **Strubby**) in the wood' from OE **wudu** and ODan **thorp**. The first el. in the DB form is perhaps the same ON pers.n. *Eindrithi*, as in **Enderby**, but this is quite uncertain. Before the middle of the 12th century it had been replaced by OE **wudu** 'a wood'.

Woolsthorpe by Belvoir (Kest), *Vlestane(s)torp* 1086 DB, *Uulstanestorp* 1106–23 (1333) Ch, *Wullethorp* 1191 P, *Wolestorp* 1202 Ass, a hybrid p.n. 'Wulfstān's secondary settlement', derived from the OE pers.n. *Wulfstān* and ODan **thorp**.

Woolsthorpe by Colsterworth (Colsterworth, Kest), *Wolestorp* 1185 Templar, *Wllestorp* 1205 FF, *Wullestorp* 1212 ib, *Wlfthorp* 1212 Fees, *Wulstorp'* 1229 Cur, probably 'Wulflāf's secondary settlement (presumably of **Colsterworth**)', a hybrid p.n. from the OE pers.n. *Wulflāf* and ODan **thorp**. The forms show reduction of the medial syllable due to weak stress.

Wootton (LNR), *Udetune* 1086 DB, *Wodeton'* 1202 Ass, *Withtun* c1155, c1160 Dane, *Wittuna* c1115 LS, 1200 Cur, *Wituna, Uttuna* c1115 LS, *Wotton* 1185 Templar, 'the farmstead, village in the wood' from OE **wudu** and OE **tūn**. Forms in *Wit-* are from early OE **widu** 'a wood' and those in *With-* may represent a replacement of **wudu, widu** by ON **vithr** also 'a wood'.

Worlaby (LNR), *Ulricebi, Vluricebi* 1086 DB, *Wulfrichesbi* c1115 LS, *Wolurikebi* 1202 Ass, *Wulurikesbi* 1209 P, *Wulurikebi* 1209 Ass, *Wulfrikeby* Hy2 (l3th) *Stix*. **Worlaby** (LSR), *Wlvricesbi, Wluricebi* 1086 DB, *Wlfrichesbi, Wlfrichebi* c1115 LS, *Wlfrikebi* 1212 Fees, *Wulurikebi* 1218 Ass, *Wlvrikeby* 1219 FF. Both mean 'Wulfrīc's farmstead, village' from the OE pers.n. *Wulfrīc* and ODan **bȳ**. Only a small number of forms have the OE gen.sg. *-es*, while *-e* is very common and this probably represents the ODan gen.sg. *-a*, indicating that the name was given by Scandinavians.

Wragby (LSR), *Waragebi* 1086 DB, *Wraghebi* c1115 LS, *Wragebi* c1115 ib, c1175 Dane, *Wraggebi* Hy2, l12th ib, 'Wraggi's farmstead, village' from the ON pers.n. *Wraggi* and ODan **bȳ**. *Wraggi* is also the first el. of **Wraggoe Wapentake** and presumably the same man gave his name both to the settlement and the district.

Wraggoe Wapentake (LSR), *Waragehou* 1086 DB, *Wraghehou* c1115 LS, 1168 P, *Wraggeho* 1169, 1180 ib, *Wragho* 1185 ib, *Wraghow* e13th *HarlCh*.

The early forms are preceded or followed by some form of Latin *wapentacium*. The name is derived from the ON pers.n. *Wraggi* and ON **haugr** 'a hill, a mound, a burial-mound'. *Wraggi* is also the first el. of **Wragby** in the same wapentake, both presumably named from the same man. The meeting-place of the wapentake (ON **vápnatak**, late OE **wæpengetæc** 'a sub-division of a shire') is not known, but was perhaps at a mound near **Wragby**.

Wragholme (Grainthorpe, LSR), *Wargholm* eHy3, Hy3 (1409) Gilb, *-holme* 1314 Ch, *Wragholm* 1269 FF, 1287 *Ass*, *Warghholm'* 1312 Ch, probably 'the raised land amidst the marshes frequented by wolves' from ON **vargr** 'a wolf' (the alternative sense 'a felon, an outlaw' is not relevant here) and ON **holmr**.

Wrangle (Hol), *Werangle* (sic) 1086 DB, *Wrengle* Hy2 (Hy3) *Walth*, 1191 Pap, *Wrengel* l12th RA vii, *Wrangel* c1180 BuryF, l12th RA vii, probably from OE **wrengel, wrangel** 'a crooked place', which may perhaps also refer to a winding stream. The DB spelling is due to Anglo-Norman scribes.

Wrawby (LNR), *Waragebi* 1086 DB, *Wragebi* c1115 LS, *-by* 1276 RH, *Wragheby* c1200 HMCRutl, 1289 *Foster*, *Wraweby* 1276 Ipm, 'Wraghi's farmstead. village' from the ODan pers.n. *Wraghi* and ODan **bȳ**.

Wroot (LWR), *Wroth* 1156–57 (14th) YCh i, 1189–99 (1308) Ch, *Wrot* 1193, 1194 P, 1212 Fees, *Wrote* 1291 Tax, probably from OE **wrōt** 'a snout', used topographically of a spur of land.

Wyberton (Hol), *Wibertune, -tone* 1086 DB, *Wiberton'* 1175, 1180, 1190 P, 1194 CurP, 1200 FF, 'Wibert's farmstead, village'. The first el. is either the OE pers.n. *Wīgberht* or Continental Germanic *Wī(g)bert*, the second is OE **tūn**.

Wyche (Hogsthorpe, LSR), *Wych* 1327 *SR*, *le Wych* 1389 Pat, from OE **wice** 'a wych-elm', no doubt a reference to a prominent tree.

Wyham (LNR), *Widun* (sic) 1086 DB, *Wihum* c1115 LS, a1184 (1409) Gilb, *Wihom* 1147–66 (1409) ib, 1185–87 Dane, *Wium* Hy2 ib, 1200 Cur, *Wiham* c1200 RA iv, 'at the heathen shrines' from the dat.pl. **wīhum** of OE **wīh, wīg**. This is the most northerly example of a surviving place-name commemorating Anglo-Saxon paganism.

Wykeham (Spalding, Hol), *Wicham* l12th *HarlCh*, 1200 Cur, 1205 *HarlCh*, 1234 *DC*, *Wykeham* 1239 *HarlCh*, *Wikham* 1280 Cl. **Wykeham, East** (LSR) & **West** (Ludford, LSR), *Wicham* 1086 DB, 1147–66 (1409) Gilb, c1162 Dane, 1196 ChancR, 1198 P, *-heim* c1115 LS, *-haim* lHy2 (p1259) *Kirkst, Parua Wicheheim* c1115 LS, *Parva Wicham* 1212 Fees, *Hestwykam* c1155 (1409) Gilb, *West Wikham* 1187 (1409) ib. Both these p.ns. are derived from OE **wīc-hām** (forms in *-heim* and *-haim* being from ON **heim**, cognate with OE **hām**), which seems to have denoted a small Romano-British settlement. There is a cluster of Roman sites in the vicinity of Spalding and a Roman road, Baston Outgang, stops short of **Wykeham**, but points directly towards it. **East** & **West Wykeham** are both depopulated, though **East Wykeham** is still a parish and the name survives in **Wykeham Hall**. Evidence of Romano-British settlement, and possibly of a cemetery have been found in the neighbouring parish of **Ludford**. There is also another, depopulated, **Wykeham** (in Nettleton, LNR) with the same etymology and there, too, Romano-British remains have been discovered at seven sites at least; its position is shown on the 2½" O.S. map.

Wyville (Wyville & Hungerton, Kest), *Wiwella* 1106–23 (1333) Ch, *Wyuelle* Hy2 (l3th) *Stix, Wiuelle* e13th RA vii, *Wyvelle* 1266 RRGr, 'the spring by the heathen shrine' from OE **wīh** and OE **wella**. Forms in *Wyville* have not been noted before the late 17th century.

Y

Yarborough Wapentake (LNR), *Gereburg* 1086 DB, *-burc* 1162 P, *Ierburc* c1115 LS, *Yerburg* 1203 P, *Yerdeburga* 1202 Ass, *Yerdeburh* 1298 ib, *Jortheburg'* 1246 *NCot*. The forms are preceded or followed by some form of Latin *wapentacium*. The name is derived from OE **eorth-burg** 'an earth-work', identical with **Yarburgh**, some early forms being influenced by the cognate ON **jarth-borg**. The wapentake (ON **vápnatak**, late OE **wæpengetac** 'a sub-division of a shire') is named from **Yarborough Camp** in Croxton parish where the district meeting must have been held.

Yarburgh (LSR), *Gereburg* 1086 DB, Hy2 (1409) Gilb, *Jertheburgha* c1150 (1409) ib, *-burc* c1170 (1409) ib, *Jerdburgha* 1182 (1409) ib, *Jerdeburch* l12th Dane, *Jereburg'* c1200 RA v, *Ierburc* c1115 LS, *Yerburg* 1156–58 *HarlCh*. This is identical with **Yarborough (Wapentake)**, and is derived from OE **eorth-burg** 'an earth-work', some of the early forms being influenced by the cognate ON **jarth-borg**. The site of the 'earth-work' is not known.

Yawthorpe (Corringham, LWR), *Ioletorp, Iolesthorp* 1086 DB, *Ioltorp, Iolthorp* c1115 LS, *Giolthorp* 1198 (1328) Ch, *Yoltorp* 1212, 1242–43 Fees, 'Jóli's dependent outlying settlement' (presumably of **Corringham**), from the ON pers.n. *Jóli* and ODan **thorp**.

PLACE-NAME ELEMENTS
IN LINCOLNSHIRE PLACE-NAMES

á ON, 'a river a stream'

āc OE, 'an oak-tree'

ald OE (Anglian), 'old'

amer OE, a bird, probably 'a bunting'

askr ON, 'an ash-tree'

austarr ON comparative adj., 'more easterly'

austr ON adj., 'east'

æppel OE, 'apple, fruit in general'

ærn OE, 'a house'

æsc OE, 'an ash-tree'

ætheling OE, 'a prince, a nobleman'

bagge ME, 'a bag', in a topographical sense of something shaped like a bag

bæc OE, 'a back', in a topographical sense of something shaped like a back, 'a ridge'

bæce OE, 'a stream in a valley', see **bece**

bær-tūn OE, 'a barley enclosure, a barley farm' later 'an outlying grange'

b(e)aru (b(e)arwe dat.sg.) OE, 'a wood, a grove'

bece OE, 'a stream in a valley' perhaps more specifically 'a small stream flowing in a fairly well marked, but not dramatic, valley'

beinn ON adj., 'straight, direct; helpful'

bekkr ON, 'a stream, a beck'

*bel OE, probably 'a piece of dry ground in fen'

beorg, berg OE, 'a hill, a mound'

*bēos OE, 'coarse grass, bent grass'

berg ON, 'a hill'

bī, bi OE preposition with dat., 'by, near'; in p.ns. '(place) near or in'

birce OE, 'a birch-tree'

birki ON, 'a place growing with birch-trees, a birch wood'

biscop OE, **biskup** ON, 'a bishop'

bōc-land OE, 'land held by royal charter', a technical term in Anglo-Saxon land-tenure

bold OE, 'a dwelling, a house', compare OE **botl**

bōle ODan, 'a dwelling, a homestead'

bóndi ON, 'a peasant landowner'

bōth ODan, 'a booth, a temporary shelter'

botl OE, 'a dwelling, a house', compare OE **bold**

brād OE adj., 'broad, spacious; wide', cf. ON **breithr**

bræc OE, 'a brake, brushwood, a thicket'

brakni ON, 'bracken, fern'

brant OE adj., 'steep', probably also 'deep'

breithr ON adj., 'broad, spacious', cf. OE **brād**

brende ME past participle adj., 'burnt', 'destroyed by fire'

brōc OE, 'a brook, a stream'

brōk ODan, 'a marsh'

brōm OE, 'broom'

brōthor OE, 'a brother', 'a religious brother, a monk'

bruiere OFr, 'a heath, heathland'

brunnr ON, 'a well, a spring'

brycg OE, 'a bridge', cf. ON **bryggja**

bryggja ON, 'a jetty, a quay', was not used of a bridge, but has influenced the spellings of names derived from OE **brycg**

bulut OE, 'ragged robin, cuckoo flower'

burh, burg OE, 'a fortified place'; it may denote a pre-English earth-work or encampment, a Roman station or camp, an Anglo-Saxon fortification, or later a fortified house or manor. Local archaeology and history sometimes show precisely what is meant by **burh**

burna OE, 'a spring, a stream', the common meaning is the latter

butere OE, 'butter', usually referring to a farm where butter is made, but occasionally denotes good pasture

bȳ ODan, 'a farmstead, a village', a common Danish element in L

byht OE, 'a bend, a curve in a river, a bight'

bythme, bytme OE, 'a broad valley'

*cā OE, 'a jackdaw'

cæster OE, 'a Roman town', the meaning in L p.ns.

calc OE, 'chalk, limestone'

cald OE adj., 'cold, exposed'

*cegel OE, 'a pole', probably in p.ns. referring to a boundary mark

ceorl OE, 'one of the lower classes of freeman, a freeman below the class of noble, a peasant', cf. ON **karl**

cēse OE, 'cheese', usually with reference to cheese-making

cherie ME, 'a cherry-tree'

cirice OE, 'a church', cf. ON **kirkja**

ciric-stede OE, 'the site of a church'

clæg OE, 'clay, clayey soil'

*clæte OE, 'burdock, goose-grass', cf. dial. *cleat* 'coltsfoot'

clif OE, this word covers a wide range of meanings — 'cliff, slope, river-bank'

cnēo OE, 'knee', used in a topographical sense of 'bend (in a river)'

cogel ME, 'a round stone, a cobblestone'

*colestere OE, 'a charcoal burner'

cot neut., cote fem., (dat.pl. cotum) OE, 'a cottage, a hut, a shelter'

cran OE, 'a crane' also probably 'a heron' or similar bird

croft OE, 'a small enclosed field'

croh OE, 'saffron'

cros late OE, a borrowing from ON kross itself from Old Irish cros 'a cross'

*crull OE adj., probably 'winding'

*crūw OE, 'a bend'

cū OE, 'a cow'

cumb OE, 'a coomb'. Recent research has shown that the word is mostly used of shorter, broader valleys which are usually bowl- or trough-shaped with three steeply rising sides

*Cumbre (*Cumbra gen.pl.) OE, 'the Cymry, the Welsh'

*cwappa OE, 'an eel-pout'

cwēad OE, 'dirt, mud'

*cweorn OE, 'a quern, a handmill'

*cymbe OE, 'a depression, a hollow'

cyne OE, 'kingly, royal'

cyning OE, 'a king'

dæld (daldar gen.sg.) ON, 'a small valley'

dalr ON, 'a valley', usually denotes a long valley, cf. OE denu

*dembil ON, 'a pool'

denu OE, 'a valley' usually denoting a long, narrow, curving valley

dēop OE adj., 'deep'

dīc OE, 'a ditch', 'an excavated trench', 'an embankment'

dīk ON, 'a ditch', 'an embankment'. It is difficult to separate dīc and dík in L p.ns

djýr ON, 'an animal, a deer'   *dýr*

dræg OE, 'a portage', 'a dray (a cart)'

drāf OE, 'a road along which cattle are driven', common in the fenlands in minor names

drȳge OE adj., 'dry, dried up'

dūfe OE, 'a dove'

dūn OE, 'a hill'. From a detailed survey of this word it has been shown that it usually denotes a low eminence with a flattish summit offering an excellent settlement-site

duru OE, 'a door', hence 'a pass, a gap'

ēa OE, 'a river, a stream', occurs in the fenlands in a spurious Frenchified form **Eau**, but pronounced [i:] as in *bead*

ēast OE adj., 'east'

ēasterra OE comparative adj., 'more eastern'

ēg OE, 'an island', 'dry ground in fen, raised land in a wet area'

eik ON, 'an oak-tree'

-el OFr diminutive suffix, 'little'

elri ON, 'an alder-tree, an alder wood'

ende OE, 'an end, the end of something'

Engle (Engla gen.pl.) OE, 'the Angles', later 'the English'

eorth-burg OE, 'an earth-work', usually a pre-English site, cf. ON **jarth-borg**

eski ON, 'a place growing with ash-trees', also as a prefix 'ashen'

ey ON, 'an island'

eystri ON adj., ' more easterly'

fær OE, 'a going, a passage'

falh OE, 'land broken up for cultivation, ploughed land'

feld OE, 'open country'

fenn OE, 'a fen, a marsh, marshland'

ferja ON, 'a ferry'

fiscere OE, **fiskari** ON, 'a fisherman'

flēax OE, 'flax'

flēot OE, 'an estuary, an inlet'

ford OE, 'a ford'

foss OE, 'a ditch, an artificially made water-channel'

fresc, fersc OE adj., 'fresh'

Frīsa (Fris(n)a gen.sg.) OE, 'a Frisian, a native of Friesland and the Frisian Isles'. It is believed that they mostly represent isolated settlements of small groups of Frisians during the viking period, but some are probably pre-viking

frogga OE, 'a frog'

fugol OE, 'a bird' in a general sense

fūl OE adj., 'foul, dirty, filthy'

fyrhth OE, 'a wood'; it has been suggested that a better translation might be 'land overgrown with brushwood, scrub on the edge of forest'

gara OE, 'a gore, a triangular plot of land, a point of land'

gāt OE, 'a goat', cf. ON **geit**

gata ON, 'a way, a path, a road' later 'a right of passage', especially in L field-names

gaukr ON, 'a cuckoo'

geiri ON, 'a triangular plot of ground'

geit ON, 'a goat', cf. OE **gāt**

glaumr ON, 'joy'

glēam OE, 'joy, revelry'

*****glen** PrW, forming a r.n. 'the clear one'

*****glente** OE, 'a kite'

golde OE, 'a marigold, a marsh marigold'

*****gotu** OE, 'a water-course', but in L 'a sluice'

grǣg OE, 'grey'

grāf OE, 'a grove, a copse'

grange ME, 'a grange', often 'an outlying farm belonging to a religious house'

grēne OE adj., 'green, young'

grēot OE, 'gravel'

grjọt ON, 'gravel, stones' *grjót*

*****hacathorn** OE, 'a thorn' of some kind

hægen OE, 'an enclosure'

hægthorn OE, 'the hawthorn'

hǣl OE, 'omen, good fortune', **hælu** OE, 'health, healing'

hǣth OE, 'a heath, heather'

hafn ON, 'a haven, a harbour'

hafri ON, 'oats'

haga OE, 'a hedge, an enclosure'

hagu-thorn OE, 'the hawthorn'

halc OE, 'a cavity', **halke** ME, a corner, a nook'

halh (hale dat.sg.) OE, 'a nook, a corner of land'

hall OE, 'a hall, a large residence'

hall-stede OE, 'the site of a hall'

hām OE, 'a homestead, a village, an estate'

hamm OE, 'land hemmed in by water or marsh'; 'a river-meadow'

hamor OE, 'a hill'

hām-stede OE, 'a homestead, the site of a dwelling', cf. ON **heim**

hana OE, 'a cock'

hár ON adj., 'high', cf. OE **hēah**

haugr ON, 'a hill, a mound, a burial mound'

hēah OE adj., 'high', cf. ON hár

hēarpere OE, 'a harper'

heim, ON 'a home, a homestead, an estate', cf. OE hām

hemlok(e) ME, 'hemlock'

hēope OE, 'the fruit of the wild rose, a hip', hēopa OE, 'the dog rose', the early forms of the two cannot be distinguished from one another

heorde-wīc OE, 'a herd farm'

here OE, herr ON, 'an army'. According to the Anglo-Saxon Laws a here was a band of robbers numbering not less than 35 men and the invading Danish army in the 9th century is called the here

hice OE, a bird, probably 'a tit-mouse'

hjallr ON, 'a shed for drying fish', 'a ledge'

hlāw OE, 'a mound, a hill; a burial mound'

hlith, OE, hlíth ON 'a slope, a hill-side', used of a concave hill-slope

hlūd OE adj., 'loud, noisy'

hnoc OE, 'a wether sheep'

hōh OE, 'a heel (of land), a hill-spur'

hol OE, 'a hole, a hollow'

holmr ON, 'an isle, a water-meadow', 'higher dry land in marsh'

holt OE, 'a wood, a holt, a thicket'

hop OE, 'a remote enclosed space', 'an enclosure in marsh', 'a secluded valley'

*horc OE, 'a shelter'

horh OE, 'filth, dirt', 'mud'

horn, horna OE, 'a horn', used topographically of a projecting horn-shaped piece of land

hrafn ON, 'a raven'

hrēod OE, 'a reed', probably also 'a reed-bed'

hrīs OE, hrís ON, 'shrubs, brushwood'

hrókr ON, 'a rook'

hrycg OE, hryggr ON, 'a ridge'

hungor OE, 'hunger', usually used in allusion to 'barren ground'

hūs OE, hús ON, 'a house, a dwelling-house' often in the dat.pl. hūsum, húsum

hwīt OE adj., 'white' in various usages

hyll OE, 'a hill'

hyrne OE, 'an angle, a corner (of land)'

hyrst OE, 'a wooded hill'

hȳth OE, 'a landing place on a river-bank'

-ing OE noun suffix, with the meaning 'place'

-ing- OE connective particle, 'associated with, called after'

-ingas nom.pl., -inga- gen.pl., a suffix denoting groups of people — the family, the dependents of a leader, see **Healing**

Íri (**Íra** gen.pl.) ON, 'an Irishman' used also of a viking who had been to Ireland before coming to England or to Irishmen who accompanied the vikings to England

jarth-borg ON, 'an earth-work', cf. OE **eorth-burg**

karl ON 'a freeman of the lower class', corresponding to OE **ceorl**

ketill ON, 'a kettle', used topographically of a kettle-shaped hollow

kirkja ON, 'a church', sometimes replacing **cirice**

kirkju-bȳ ON, 'a village with a church'

kjarr ON, 'brushwood, a marsh overgrown with brushwood'

kjǫlr ON 'a keel; a ridge, a spur'

klakk ODan, 'a lump; a hill'

kross ON, see late OE **cros**

kunung ODan, **konungr** ON, 'a king'

lād OE 'a water-course'

læfer, lēfer OE, 'a rush, a reed, a yellow iris'

lamb OE, 'a lamb'

land OE, 'land; a tract of land'

lang OE adj., **langr** ON adj., 'long; tall, high'

lēac-tūn OE, 'a leek enclosure; a herb garden'

lēah OE, ' wood; glade; clearing'

lece OE, 'a brook'

*lemo- PrW, 'an elm'

lind OE, 'a lime-tree'

*linn PrW, 'a pool, water'

ló ON, 'a glade, a meadow'

loc OE, 'a lock, a bolt; a fold'

loekr ON, 'a brook, a rivulet'

luh OE 'a pool, a lake'

lundr ON, 'a small wood, a grove', also 'a sacred grove'

lyng ON, 'ling, heather'

lȳtel, lytel OE, **lítill** ON, 'little, small'

mægden OE, 'a maiden'

(ge)mǣre OE, 'a boundary'

malm OE, 'sand, sandy or chalky soil'
melr ON, 'a sand-bank, a sand-hill'
mere, mære OE, 'a pool, a pond'
mersc OE, 'a marsh, watery land'
methal ON adj., 'middle', usually replacing OE **middel**
middel OE adj., 'middle'
mikill ON adj., 'big, great'
monke ME, 'a monk' (from OE **munuc**)
mōr OE, **mór** ON, 'marsh; barren upland'
mos OE, 'moss, lichen'
mūl OE, 'a mule'
myln OE 'a mill'

nes ON, 'a headland, a promontory'
netel(e) OE, 'a nettle'
nīwe OE adj., 'new' i.e. newly built, newly acquired, newly cultivated, or newly reclaimed from waste
north OE adj., 'northern, north'
Northman (Northmanna gen.pl.) late OE, from ON **Northmathr**, 'a Northman, a Norwegian'

ofer OE, 'the tip of a promontory, flat-topped ridge'
oxa OE, 'an ox'

panne OE, 'a pan', used topographically of a depression or hollow
*pinc OE, 'a minnow'
pōl OE, 'a pool, a pond', probably also 'a creek'
port OE, 'a market town, a market'
purceint OFr, **purceynt** ME, 'a precinct, an enclosure'

*ræc OE, 'a reach' used of a stretch of water, a road or path through the fens
ræsn OE, 'a plank', used of a plank-bridge
rand OE, 'an edge, a border, a bank', perhaps also 'a boundary'
(ge)rēfa OE, 'a reeve, a bailiff'
riscen OE adj., 'growing with rushes, rushy'
*roth OE, 'a clearing'
rūh OE adj., 'rough'
rӯge OE, 'rye'

salh OE, 'a willow, a sallow'

salt OE, 'salt'

saltere OE, 'a salter, a salt-worker, a salt-merchant'

sand OE, sandr ON, 'sand' usually with reference to sandy soil

*sāpere OE, 'a soap-maker, a soap-dealer'

scearn, scarn OE, 'dung, muck'

scēp OE, 'a sheep'

scīnende OE present participle, 'shining', used as a r.n.

scīr OE, 'a shire, an administrative district, a county'

scīte OE, skítr ON, 'dung, shite'

*scitere OE, 'a sewer, a stream used as an open sewer'

Scot(t) OE, 'a Scot' in p.ns. usually denoting people from Scotland

secg OE, 'sedge, a reed, a rush'

sex OE numeral, 'six'

sīc OE, 'a small stream usually one in flat marshland', sík ON, 'a ditch, a trench'

sīd OE adj., 'large, spacious, extensive, long' in contrast to OE wīd 'broad'

skammr ON, 'short'

skial ODan, 'a boundary'

skírr ON, 'clear, bright, pure'

skreith ON, 'a land-slide'

*slēc OE adj., probably 'muddy'

sliow OE r.n., 'slimy, muddy stream'

spánn ON, 'a chip, a wooden shingle tile'

spitel ME, 'a hospital, a religious house, a house of the Knights Hospitallers'

spring OE, 'a spring, a well'

stān OE, 'a stone' often with reference to the character of the ground, but also to a stone building or to stone paving, etc., cf. ON steinn

stapol OE, 'a post, a pillar (of wood or stone)'

stede OE, 'a place, a site'

steinn ON, 'a stone, a rock', replacing OE stān in some p.ns.

stēor OE, 'a steer, a young bullock'

stoc OE, 'a place, a religious place, a settlement'

stocc OE, 'a tree-trunk, a stump'

stoth (stothvar nom.pl.) ON, 'a landing-place, a jetty'

stōw OE, 'a place, a place of assembly, a holy place'

strǣt OE, 'a Roman road, a paved road, an urban road'

stubb OE, 'a stub, a tree-stump'

*styfic OE, 'a stump'

*sugge OE, a bird', perhaps 'a sparrow'

sumor OE, 'summer', usually with reference to features which were used or could be used only in summer

sundri ON adj., 'southern'

sūr OE adj., 'sour, damp, coarse (of land)'

sūtere OE, **sútari** ON, 'a shoe-maker' perhaps also used as a byname

sūth OE adj., 'south, southern'

sūther OE adj., 'south, southern'

sūtherra OE comparative adj., 'more southerly'

swæth OE, 'a track, a pathway', **swathe** ME, 'a strip of grassland'

swīn OE, 'a swine, a pig'

swīn OE, 'a creek, a channel', sometimes difficult to distinguish from OE **swīn** 'a swine, a pig'

tadde OE, 'a toad'

thēod OE, 'people', used in the sense 'public'

thorn OE, 'a thorn-tree, the hawthorn'

thorp ODan, 'a secondary settlement, a dependent outlying farmstead or hamlet'

thrír ON numeral, 'three'

thrithjung ON, **thrithing** late OE, 'a third part', 'the third part of a shire'. Initial *th-* was absorbed by the final *-t* or *-d* of the preceding word to give **Riding**

thunnr ON, 'thin, slender'

thveit ON, **thwēt** ODan, 'a clearing, a meadow'

thwang OE 'a thong', used in some topographical sense

thyrnir ON, 'a thornbush'

til OE adj., 'useful, good'

timber OE, 'timber, trees' also 'a wooden building'

titt OE, 'a teat' in the transferred topographical sense of a slight hill

toft ODan, late OE, 'a building site, a curtilage, a messuage'

tré ON, 'a tree', cf. OE **trēow**

trēow OE, 'tree', cf. ON **tré**

tūn OE, 'an enclosure, a farmstead, a village, an estate'

tún ON, 'an enclosure, a farmstead', perhaps 'a fence'

*tūn-stall OE, 'the site of a farm, a farmstead'

tup ME, 'a tup, a ram'

twī- OE prefix, 'double, two', common with OE **ford** usually denoting two fords close together

uferra OE adj., 'upper, higher'

upp OE adverb, 'up, higher up, upon'

vangr ON, 'a garden, an in-field'

vargr ON 'a wolf'

vápnatak ON, **wapengetæc** late OE, 'a wapentake, a sub-division of a shire'

vargr ON, 'wolf'

vath ON, 'a ford', cf. OE **wæd**

vé ON, 'a heathen shrine, a sanctuary'

vestir ON adj., 'more westerly'

vestr ON adj., 'west, westerly'

vík ON, 'a small creek, an inlet'

víkingr ON, 'a roving pirate, a viking'

vithr ON, 'a wood'

wæd OE, 'a ford', cf. ON **vath**

wægn OE, 'a wagon, a cart'

wæsse OE, 'riverside land which floods and drains quickly'

wæter OE, 'water'

walcere OE, 'a cloth-dresser, a fuller'

wald OE, 'woodland, a high tract of woodland', 'wold'

walh (gen.pl. **wala**) OE, 'a Welshman'

w(e)ard OE, 'watch, ward, protection'

wella OE, 'a well, a spring, a stream'

west OE adj., 'west, western'

westerra OE comparative adj., 'more westerly'

wīc OE, 'a trading centre, salt-production centre, a dairy-farm'

wīc-hām OE, 'a small Romano-British settlement'

wice OE, 'a wych-elm'

wīd OE adj. 'broad'

wīh, wīg OE, 'an idol, a heathen shrine'

*****wiht** OE, 'a bend'

wilde OE adj., 'wild, uncultivated, desolate'

*****wilig** OE, 'a willow'

*****wincel** OE, 'a nook, a corner'

*****wisp** OE, 'a wisp', perhaps in some sense such as 'thicket, brushwood'

worth OE, 'an enclosure, an enclosed settlement'

*****wrengel, *****wrangel** OE, 'a crooked place or stream'

wrōt OE, 'snout', in some such topographical sense as 'a spur of land, a hill projecting forward like a snout'

wudu, earlier **widu** OE, 'a wood'

wyrhta OE, 'a wright'